THE PRACTICAL ANGLER'S GUIDE TO SUCCESSFUL FISHING

If you want to be happy for one hour,
    Get intoxicated.

If you want to be happy for three days,
    Get married.

If you want to be happy for eight days,
    Kill your pig and eat it.

If you want to be happy forever,
    Learn to fish.

– Old Chinese Proverb

THE PRACTICAL ANGLER'S GUIDE TO SUCCESSFUL FISHING

KENN OBERRECHT

WINCHESTER PRESS

Library of Congress Cataloging in Publication Data

Oberrecht, Kenn.
  The practical angler's guide to successful fishing.

  Bibliography: p.
  Includes index.
  1. Fishing. I. Title.
SH441.023   799.1'2   77-15126
ISBN 0-87691-250-1

Published by Winchester Press
205 East 42nd Street
New York, N.Y. 10017

WINCHESTER is a Trademark of Olin Corporation used by
Winchester Press, Inc. under authority and control of
the Trademark Proprietor.

Printed in the United States of America.

Text and jacket design by Joseph P. Ascherl

DEDICATION

To my wife, Patty,
who has made life for me
as enjoyable as fishing,
and fishing more fun than ever.

ACKNOWLEDGMENTS

A special thanks is due to some folks who have shown particular interest in my angling and writing ventures. They are Bing McClellan, Burke Fishing Lures; Vern Buchman, Berkley & Company; Dick Jennings, Cortland Line Company; Edward A. Eppinger, Lou J. Eppinger Mfg. Company; Dave Brooks, Factory Distributors; Dick Wolff, Garcia Corporation; Glenn Simms, Plano Molding Company; Dwight Rockwell, Jr., Rockwell & Newell; T. Layton "Shep" Shepherd, Sheldon's Inc.; John L. West, Uniroyal; E. C. Wotruba, Sr., Weber Tackle Company; and John Reid and Grace Morganthall, Woodstream Corporation.

And to all the anglers who have willingly shared their knowledge with me so that I am now able to pass it on to others, my sincere gratitude.

Portions of this book have appeared in *Northwest, Popular Mechanics, Sports Afield,* and *Outdoor Life* magazines.

Introduction

In the introduction to a fishing book an author will sometimes pay homage to his mentors, often singling out one particular person—a father, grandfather, uncle, or friend—who did more than anyone else to teach him the art of angling and to instill in him the thrill in, love of, and respect for outdoor experiences. As I look back on a lifetime of fishing in search of the one person who influenced my angling the most, I find no one. Instead, I see legions of anglers with whom I've shared lakes, streams, and campfires since early childhood. Some took me along on their trips; others came at my invitation. And many more are the nameless acquaintances I have made at tackle shops, on boat ramps, around lake shores, in campgrounds, or up the creek a ways.

Mine has not been an orderly education of structured and systematic tutoring. Rather, it has been a piecing together of many bits of intelligence. Much of it, too, has been the result of experimentation, trial and error, success and failure.

To a great extent, then, what I want to pass on to other anglers with this volume are all the best of those tips and tricks that so many fishermen have shared with me as well as some discoveries I have made on my own. I want to offer some helpful hints on how to save time and money, how to enjoy the sport of angling more, and how to become more proficient at it. I want to show how to avoid trouble and danger, how to select and maintain gear and tackle, how to cram more fishing time into your busy life, how to get to the best fishing spots with a minimum expenditure of effort and cash, even how to photograph your fishing activities.

Almost as important as what I tell you is how I tell it. I don't mean, here, the craft of writing, but how the book has been organized. In any general fishing book it is impossible for everything to be of value to all readers. While there are some areas in the book that should be of interest to all anglers, other portions are more specialized. For example, there are tips on fly fishing, spinning, spin casting, bait casting, natural baits, lines, lures, tackle boxes, tools, terminal gear, and many different species of fish. I have roughly grouped like subjects into chapters, but for added convenience I have identified portions within each chapter with subtitles. If a particular subject is of no interest to you, skip over it and go on to the next.

My intention was to organize the book conveniently, so that you might readily identify those areas that are of interest to you. I also wanted the book to be something that a reader could browse through and spend as much or as little time as is available—ten minutes here, a half hour there. To that end I have tried to be brief in my discussion of any topic. No section in any chapter should take more than five minutes to read. Furthermore, you need not start at the beginning or finish at the end. If you want to dig right into the subject of natural and prepared baits, go directly to Chapter Five. If you have been having problems getting good pictures of your fishing trips, start with Chapter Fifteen, and come back to the others at your leisure.

At the back of the book you will find an appendix, divided into five sections. Whenever reference is made in the text to a company or agency of some sort, the address can be found in the appropriate section of the appendix. Additionally, each section has been enlarged to include numerous other sources of information. So I hope this book will become a useful reference volume that you will want to keep handy.

Most of all, I hope you will be able to learn something from this collection of tips that will make fishing even more fun for you than it already is.

KENN OBERRECHT
Coos Bay, Oregon

Contents

The plug fisherman needs a big box in which to house his tackle and to keep it orderly and untangled.

CHAPTER 1

Tackle Totes and Tools

Compleat Boxes for the Compleat Angler

No sport has a literature as vast and enduring as that of fishing, yet little has been written about tackle boxes. When angling writers do mention them, it is usually in passing, or the comments are buried in the depths of a general coverage of tackle. If a discussion of tackle boxes is a break in the tradition, certainly its placement at the front of a book is even more out of the ordinary. Yet my reasons for doing so are simple: For the majority of anglers, tackle boxes are among the most important of all tackle and gear; and the right box or system of boxes will keep tackle organized, readily at hand, and protected from the elements.

When it comes to buying a tackle box, about the soundest advice for the serious fisherman—or the neophyte, badly bitten by the fishing bug—is to decide how big a box you need; then buy one about three times that size. The secret to being completely outfitted (or as completely outfitted as any fisherman ever considers himself) and organized is to have a sufficiently large tackle box.

I can already hear the light-tackle, tuck-it-in-your-hip-pocket purists shouting that the only way to go is with a whippy stick and a handful of hand-tieds. And I grant that is a great way to fish. Few pleasures can equal that of a morning of solitude on a favorite stream, casting dry flies to wary trout. For that kind of sport I go light—usually a 7½-foot rod, single-action reel with 30 yards of DT7F line, and a vest full of essentials. If I'm packing into the high country, where streams are small and brushy, I go even lighter. There the ticket is a 6-foot wand and DT5F line. Leaders taper to spider's web delicacy and flies are tied on #16 or smaller fine-wire hooks. All my supporting tackle will fit into a pocket of my pack.

But if I'm heading for the boondocks for a week of salmon fishing, or if I'm on the road for one of my frequent fishing holidays, or if I'm probing the waters of one of my favorite nearby lakes for largemouth bass, you can bet I'll be lugging a big box with me. More often than not, I will have several boxes along.

When my fishing takes me away from home for more than a day—
as it often does—I go prepared. I carry several backup rods and
reels, extra spools of line, assortments of hooks and split rings, a
tackle-repair kit, sinkers, leaders, and other tackle so necessary to
the sport. To keep this gear organized and protected requires a good
tackle box or system of boxes.

There's more to an adequate box than size, though. It should be
light and tough. All its hinges and hardware should function
smoothly, without buckling. It should be able to stand plenty of
abuse and to resist corrosion. Your best bet is to pick one of the
many aluminum or plastic models that are available today in a wide
array of designs to fit any angler's needs.

It used to be that a big tackle box was that and not much more.
It was usually hip roofed and had six or seven trays. There were
really few differences from make to make. But as sport fishing has
grown, so have the demands of fishermen. And tackle-box manufacturers are producing innovative boxes to meet those demands.

Plano Molding Co., for example, is manufacturing a jet-age box
they call the 747—a jumbo-size, plastic tackle box with two ways to
get at its contents. It opens conventionally from the top, allowing
the three cantilevered trays to swing back, exposing all the tackle.
Or, the fisherman can drop the hinged panel on the front of the box
and pull the trays out like drawers. The smaller model 727 offers the
same features.

Plano's 777 is another big box, but this one is strictly the cabinet
type, with six drawers for holding plenty of tackle. This tackle box
offers the added advantage of interchangeable drawers that enable
the angler to customize the box to fit his needs.

After outgrowing two worm boxes, I finally decided to end the
problem once and for all and put together a super worm box that
would hold all the various soft plastic baits I like to carry, as well
as worm hooks, slip sinkers, jigs, jig heads, and other supporting
tackle. The box I chose for this task was the Plano 777, but I replaced the large bottom drawer with two shallower drawers with
added compartments.

This super worm box has a total of ninety-three compartments—
enough for all my worming gear. My final effort at systemizing this
box was the labeling of each drawer for ready reference.

Such boxes are ideally suited to fishing in the confines of a boat,
where the box can be kept closed yet readily accessible. The

The big Plano 777 drawer box, with its interchangeable drawers, can be customized to fit the angler's needs.

For the fisherman who needs plenty of room, UMCO Corporation offers a series of Possum Belly tackle boxes. Pictured here is the 3500 UPB, the largest tackle box manufactured today.

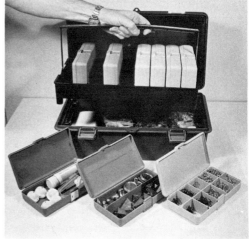

Hefner Plastics is offering a new line of tackle boxes that feature novel lazy Susan rotary trays for tackle storage. These boxes are ideally suited to the tight confines of a boat.

The Vlchek Adventurer 2000 is ten boxes in one. A removable tray holds nine small boxes, and everything is contained in a tough and roomy tackle carrier.

drawer-type box can be stored against a seat or gunwale, yet can be opened without the necessity of moving it, thus reducing unnecessary noises.

Another reason for buying a big box is that a tackle box ought to have sufficient room to carry more than just tackle. Rainwear, first aid kit, tool kit, sunglasses, weighing scales, insect repellent, suntan lotion, and various tackle repair and replacement items are just some of the extra essentials that can be found in many tackle boxes.

UMCO Corporation offers a line of Possum Belly boxes that have been designed to accommodate the angler with a need for extra storage space. The upper section of these boxes is similar to other hip-roofed models with plenty of compartmented tray space for a wide assortment of lures, and sufficient space beneath the trays for reels and other bulky equipment. Single or double "bellies" can be latched onto the main box to add as much as 2,000 cubic inches of space. Insulating liners, which can be used for keeping food, beverages, or bait cold are also available.

Vlchek Plastics manufactures a wide assortment of tough and durable plastic boxes. One of their more innovative designs is their Adventurer 2000, a large box with a removable tray that holds nine smaller boxes. This one is particularly suited to the needs of the multimethod fisherman who wants to keep all his tackle in one box, but still have the ability to go light on the spur of the moment.

Of the nine small boxes in the Adventurer 2000, two have no compartments; two are divided in half by center partitions; and the other four can be used as five-compartment boxes or further divided into ten compartments each by the addition of center partitions. This box is also an excellent choice for the family, since each family member can have his own tackle box and plenty of extra gear can be toted along as well. I use my own Adventurer 2000 to carry extra tackle on extended trips. The labeled boxes hold various essentials, while the main box carries several reels and extra spools of line.

The fisherman who uses only light tackle and spinning-size lures can generally get by with a smaller tackle box, but he must look for one with numerous compartments that will keep small lures in order. The plug plunker will not only require a bigger box, but one with large compartments to house the outsized lures he uses.

If you're strictly a plastic-worm fisherman, or if you use nothing but spinner baits, there are boxes designed to fit those specific needs. But most of us are multimethod fishermen, and this sort of

Woodstream Corporation is manufacturing a coordinated system of Bass Boss boxes. Included is a large drawer box with a clamp-on bottom section for extra storage, as well as boxes for worms, spinner baits, grubs, and plugs.

An organized system of boxes keeps the angler from carrying along unnecessary gear. Here, most of the author's steelhead tackle fits neatly into a small, lightweight box.

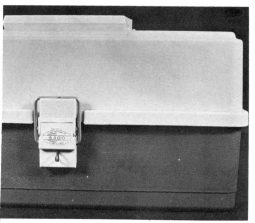

For bait fishing, all the necessary hooks, sinkers, floats, terminal rigging, and accessories can be conveniently stored in a spinning-size tackle box.

A tackle box should have an effective rain lip and a positive-locking latch.

diversity makes it difficult to keep tackle organized and lugable without a well thought-out system.

Tackle-Box Systems

I first began setting up my own tackle-keeping system some years ago when the Army sent me to southern Florida for a ten-month stint. To carry all the tackle I would need, I bought an oversized Woodstream Old Pal tackle box with seven cantilevered trays to hold everything from small spinning lures to big bass plugs. When the box was fully loaded with all these lures, as well as necessary terminal tackle, extra reels, and the like, it was tough enough to lift it out of the trunk of my car, much less carry it any distance. So I bought a smaller spinning-size box for the toting and kept the Old Pal mainly for storage. Since that time my needs have grown as my fishing interests have expanded, but with a system already established, it has been easy to add another box from time to time to fit specific needs.

The true worth of such a system is that I am able to go fully prepared for any situation without being overloaded. For example, if I'm leaving for a weekend of fishing where I might be plug fishing, trolling, using live bait, plastic worms, spinner baits, and jigs—all in the course of a couple of days—I load our pickup truck with a half dozen different boxes of tackle. On the other hand, if I'm heading out for a morning of panfishing with ultralight tackle, everything I need fits in a Plano Pocket Pak that tucks neatly into a pocket of my fishing jacket.

Between these two extremes is the normal run of my fishing outings. For a morning of bass fishing, I will have a plug box, a worm box, and a spinner bait box in the boat with me and will never want for anything more. For a night of catfishing, I need only take along my bait-fishing box. The highly specialized sport of steelheading requires only a small box for all my drift-fishing essentials and a supply of the most productive lures. For stream-trout and smallmouth-bass fishing I keep everything I need in a fishing vest.

At least one company is offering a complete system of tackle boxes. Woodstream Corporation has a series of Bass Boss boxes comprised of five models: a spinner-bait box, a grub box, a worm box, a plug box, and a five-drawer box with a large add-on bottom section for carrying big, bulky items.

The other companies already mentioned offer extensive lines of tackle boxes from which an angler can select those that best fit his needs. If you're looking to set up your own tackle organization and storage system, I suggest you write these companies for their latest catalogs. The addresses can be found in Appendix A in the back of the book.

Tips on Buying and Maintaining Tackle Boxes

There are some particular features that a fisherman should look for when purchasing any tackle box—in addition to sufficient size, light weight, and durability of materials. Of utmost importance is that the box ought to be as rainproof as possible, which means that it should have a good, functional rain lip. In the case of hip-roofed boxes (notorious leakers), seals should be as nearly watertight as possible.

The box should have a positive-locking latch. Some boxes feature spillproof latches that alleviate the problem of dumping the contents of an unlatched box. This is a feature I would like to see on all boxes.

Another feature I wish all my boxes had is a recessed handle. This allows boxes to be stacked one atop the other, either while in transit or while being stored at home. And those boxes that are devised to remain upright, even when they are opened and their heavily loaded trays swing beyond center, possess a distinct advantage.

Most of the plastic boxes made these days are wormproof, so chemical reactions between soft plastic baits and the plastic of the boxes aren't as much of a problem as they once were. But plastic worms, grubs, and twist-tail baits will react with some paints used on fishing lures and must be kept out of contact with these lures. Of course, the best way is to keep all soft plastic baits in a worm box. But if you have an older box that is not wormproof, or if you carry all your gear in one box and don't have enough compartments to keep everything separated,. keep your soft plastic baits in plastic sandwich bags. And be sure to separate them by color, as colors will bleed from one to the other.

Tackle-box maintenance is a fairly simple matter, since there's not much that can go wrong with a well-made box, despite the abuse it gets. It is a good idea to clean your tackle boxes out at least once a season and to discard tackle that you no longer use.

A few drops of oil on hinges, latches, and tray hardware every couple of months will keep moving parts moving. A dry lubricant, such as Du Pont Slip Spray, applied to the drawers of cabinet-type boxes will keep them functioning smoothly.

You can keep your spinners and spoons from getting scratched and rubbed dull by lining the tray compartments with sheet cork. The cork can be cut to size with scissors and simply laid in the trays, or it can be installed permanently with an application of white glue.

When it comes time to shop for a tackle box, whether it's your first, a replacement for one you've outgrown, or an addition to a system of tackle boxes, the best advice I can give you is to shop around. Examine as many boxes as you can. Ask your fellow fishermen for recommendations, and write the manufacturers.

Tips on Fighting Moisture

Rain, spray, mist, fog, and atmospheric dampness all seem to take the shortest possible route to the fisherman's tackle box to wreak havoc on anything corrodible. Moisture, the bane of every fisherman, will rust hooks and hardware in short order.

Of course, the first step in combating the problem is to make sure your tackle box is relatively waterproof and to keep it protected from the elements, but this is not always possible and never a total solution. For example, have you ever returned from a rainy-day fishing jaunt to find a tackle box full of water, even though you kept it closed most of the time? A major source of excessive moisture in tackle boxes can be the rivets affixing the handle to the box lid. Plug these leaky culprits with silicone seal, an excellent moisture-proofing sealant available in most hardware and department stores.

Never return a wet lure to a tackle box; let it completely air dry first. Then, when you return home, open your tackle boxes and set them in a dry place for several hours or overnight so that moisture can evaporate. (This process can be reduced to about five minutes by blowing warm air throughout the tackle box with an electric hair dryer.)

Residual moisture is sometimes tough to eliminate, especially in large tackle boxes, and particularly in the drawer-type boxes. Furthermore, atmospheric moisture is a constant threat, and is doubly

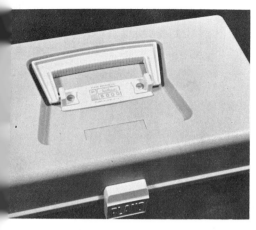

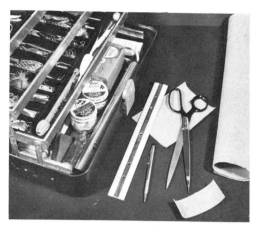

Recessed handles make it easy to stack one box atop another.

To keep your spinners and spoons from being rubbed dull, line your tackle trays with sheet cork.

A few drops of oil on hinges will keep trays functioning smoothly.

Rivets used to fasten the handle to the tackle-box lid will usually leak. Keep your tackle dry by sealing these leaky culprits with silicone seal.

Tackle boxes can be thoroughly dried out in minutes by blowing warm air over the contents with an electric hair dryer.

After returning from a fishing trip, open your tackle boxes and let them stand overnight so moisture can evaporate.

To combat residual moisture, keep a chemical desiccant inside the closed box when you store it away.

troublesome in damp or humid climates. So, to further protect your expensive gear, keep an air-drying agent in your tackle box when you're not using it. Silica gel and other chemical desiccants are available from most chemical suppliers and photographic dealers. Moreover, the military has been using chemical desiccants for years, so a good source of supply is a military surplus store. I bought a half-dozen 1-pound bags at the local surplus store for 25¢ apiece. These will last me for years and might save me many dollars that I would otherwise spend replacing rusty tackle.

Chemical desiccants come in a variety of sizes and shapes to fit any tackle box—from small cartridges to one-pound bags. These air dryers can be used over and over again. Simply place the saturated dryers in a kitchen oven at a low heat for several hours. One cartridge-style dryer even changes color to indicate when it requires recharging.

Boxes for the Traveling Fisherman

Traveling by commercial mass-transit systems—whether plane, train, or bus—creates problems for anyone taking tackle along.

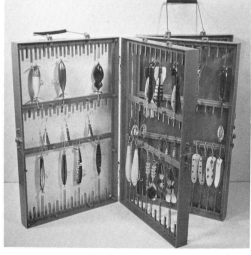

The Jr. Bait File, shown here with optional insert, keeps lures tangle-free.

The ingenious Wille Bait File securely holds lures in place with stainless steel springs. Master hinge system allows the addition of basic and dodger inserts for extra capacity.

Tackle boxes large enough to carry a sufficient amount of gear are usually too large to lug around as carry-on baggage. Those that are small enough to slide beneath a seat are too small to be practical tackle totes. And, of course, lures put in a box packed inside a suitcase are bound to become a tangled mess as baggage handlers toss, tumble, and all but destroy your luggage.

Well, the innovative folks at Wille Products have found a way to accommodate the traveling fisherman and simultaneously outwit the baggage manglers. Their new Bait File and Jr. Bait File tackle boxes are expandable tackle carriers that are perfect for commercial travel.

The basic Bait File is comprised of two tough plastic panels that are 20 inches high, 12 inches wide, and 1½ inches deep, and are joined by a cleverly designed master-hinge system that allows the addition of more panels as needed.

The Bait File opens like a book, to expose storage space for sixty-six lures that are held in place and free from tangles by stainless-steel springs. The unit is flat enough to pack inside a suitcase or to slide beneath an airplane seat.

The basic insert provides storage for thirty-three additional lures. Wille also offers a dodger insert that is identical to the basic insert, but also features twelve pockets for herring dodgers, flashers, and other trolling attractors as well as any tackle that will fit into a flat pocket.

The Jr. Bait File is practically the same as the Bait File, only smaller. This one stands 10 inches high, is 6 inches wide, and will hold twenty-eight lures. Each optional insert will hold fourteen lures.

Although these boxes will also serve any tackle-storage and carrying needs, for commercial travel they are the best I have found.

Coolers Aren't Just for Beer

Lures that are allowed to dry before being returned to a tackle box can cause a lot of clutter in a boat when fish are persnickety and fishermen are forced to try every bait available.

Solve the clutter problem by carrying a small Styrofoam cooler along on fishing trips. Hang baits to dry around the rim of the cooler. At the end of the day, the assortment of baits can be returned to their appropriate slots, free from moisture and tangles.

Fisherman's Gadget Bag

For years, I have enjoyed wading streams or walking the shore-line of a lake with a rod, reel, and only the tackle I can easily carry. Tackle boxes are out of the question for such sojourns, and most bags, pouches, and creels sold for that purpose are inadequate.

Recently, I bought a new gadget bag for my photography equipment and decided to use my old one for a fishing-tackle tote. It will hold plenty of gear, and its compartments keep everything organized. The shoulder pad keeps the strap from slipping, too.

Photographer's gadget bags are available in numerous sizes, shapes, and prices. Some are waterproof, and a few even float. There's one to fit any angler's needs.

Hang lures around the rim of a Styrofoam cooler to let them dry and to keep them from cluttering up your boat.

Photographers' gadget bags make excellent tackle carriers.

Carry a Tackle Pouch When Traveling Light

For those who like to travel light, a zippered tobacco pouch will carry enough tackle for any day's outing. The pouch will fit into a pocket and is just right for the ultralight enthusiast or backpacking fisherman.

When you're traveling light, pack your tackle in a zippered tobacco pouch.

The plastic canisters in which Kodak packs its 35mm film are dandy storage containers for a wide array of tackle and survival gear.

The Many Uses of Film Canisters

Among the handiest throw-away items—that shouldn't be thrown away—to come along in recent years are the plastic film canisters in which Kodak 35mm film comes. Besides being excellent, dustproof, and waterproof film containers, these canisters have numerous uses for the outdoorsman, once the film has been used.

Fishermen will find them handy for storing small spinners, spoons, flies, hooks, swivels, sinkers, and a variety of other tackle. Kitchen matches, shortened with wire snippers, can be kept dry inside these containers, which are also good for survival and first-aid gear. Fly tyers and tackle tinkerers will find unlimited uses for film canisters on the workbench. They're ideal for waterproof storage of fly hooks, spinner blades, and other hardware.

If you're a photographer, be sure to keep a supply of these canisters on hand, or you can ask one of your shutterbug friends to save them for you.

Handy Line Snippers

Fingernail clippers make excellent fishing-line snippers. Find a screw or bolt to fit the chain hole in the clippers, then drill a hole of the same size in the top of your tackle box. Mount the clippers with the screw or bolt, nut, and lock washer and seal with silicone

Attach fingernail clippers to the top of your tackle box where they will be readily at hand for snipping line.

Carry a small pair of scissors in your tackle box to handle all those cutting and trimming jobs.

to prevent water from seeping into your tackle box. Your line snippers will always be handy.

The light-tackle or fly fisherman can keep fingernail clippers handy by hanging them from a lanyard, which can be made from any tough nylon twine, such as duck-decoy anchor rope.

Attach the twine to the clippers with a clinch knot and make a loop in the other end large enough to slip over your head. Or you can simply attach the clippers to a metal D-ring on a fishing vest or creel harness with a short length of twine.

Scissors—Useful Tool for Every Tackle Box

One of the most useful tools a fisherman can carry is a small pair of scissors, yet few anglers tote them along. They are great for trimming long tail feathers and hair when fish are short-striking your flies or poppers. They are much better than a knife for trimming knots or cutting maline cloth on spawn bags. They make short work of opening those tough and troublesome blister packs that so many lures are packed in these days.

Pork rinds and plastic teasers can be cut to any size, quickly and efficiently, with scissors. Live minnows with their tail fins snipped off have to work harder to get anywhere. Consequently, they're a great deal livelier on the hook. Scissors are perfect for clipping off those tail fins.

When you're bait fishing and have caught a fish that swallowed the hook, don't waste time trying to dig the hook out. Cut the line, tie on another hook, and get back to fishing. But before you add the fish to your stringer, clip a portion off of his tail fin with your scissors. Later, when you're cleaning that mess of fish, you'll be able to locate the one with the hook inside, and thereby can clean it with caution and remove your hook, too.

There are numerous uses for these simple, handy tools. Why not add a pair to your tackle box?

The Ultimate Hook Disgorger

There are a number of hook disgorgers on the market today, but by far the best tool for those hard-to-reach hooks are surgical forceps. They will get at deeply imbedded hooks in small-mouthed fish, such as bluegills. They can be used for removing hooks from small trout so the fish can be released with no permanent damage done. And they're long enough for reaching inside the toothy maw of a pike. Since they're made of stainless steel, they won't rust.

Surgical forceps are available from medical supply companies and some drugstores. They can also be mail-ordered from the Orvis Company.

The Folding Fisherman

I have seen fishermen carrying everything from tiny pen knives to big Bowie knives, the former being ideal for cleaning fingernails and the latter for felling small trees. Somewhere between these two extremes is the ideal utility knife.

For more than five years I have been carrying one of the so-called Folding Hunter knives, which, for my purposes, might just as well be called a Folding Fisherman. Of the dozens of knives I have owned since boyhood, this one is by far the best and most useful as an all-purpose knife.

Of course, it is no fillet knife. And there are times when I need something smaller or something larger. But it does about 75 percent of the cutlery jobs in a fishing camp, on lake or stream, in a boat, or around my workshop when I'm tinkering with tackle. It is big and tough enough to take rough treatment, yet folded and at rest in its sheath, I never even notice that it is hanging from my belt. Its stainless steel blade doesn't rust and holds a fine edge.

There are several sizes of such folding knives available from a number of top-flight manufacturers, but be forewarned: None are cheap. Some people contend that a sizable portion of the price paid is for the name etched on the blade. If the knife is manufactured according to strict quality-control methods and is backed by a good guarantee, I don't mind paying a few extra bucks for a name I can depend on. I tend to think one gets what one pays for.

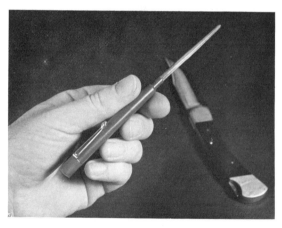

Carry a small sharpening steel that clips into a pocket, and you will be able to sharpen your knives in minutes—anytime, anywhere.

Convenient Pocket Steel

Several Christmases ago, my brother sent me a pocket steel from Solingen, Germany. The business end of this convenient item screws into the handle when not in use, and the whole thing—about the size of a ball-point pen—clips into a shirt pocket. I'm never without it, and my knives are always razor sharp as a result.

When a number of friends expressed their interest in this gadget, I decided to see if I could find pocket steels locally. Sure enough, they're available at most cutlery stores and will range in price from about $3 to $5. I bought a batch of them last year to give as Christmas gifts to my fishing and hunting partners. I don't think I could have pleased them more.

Now is a good time to try one yourself. Next Christmas you can give them as gifts to your outdoor partners.

Other Tools for Your Pockets and Tackle Boxes

Something else I have learned to appreciate is a pair of longnose pliers. I keep a pair in one of my tackle boxes, and if I'm on an extended trip I carry a pair in a sheath on my belt. They have numerous uses in camp and are a must for repairing bent hooks or rod guides. They are also useful for holding rod tip-tops and ferrules over a flame when making emergency rod repairs. When I'm traveling light, I like to carry a tiny pair of hobbyist's pliers instead of the larger ones.

A pocket pipe tool with a pointed shaft is another implement that I have put to many uses while fishing. I have used mine as an ice pick, marlin spike, and punch. It is also good for cleaning the clogged paint out of the hook eyes on new jigs.

X-Acto makes a utility knife for artists, craftsmen, and hobbyists that looks like a fountain pen. It's the perfect knife for gutting and gilling small trout. Its scalpel-sharp blade is replaceable. These knives are available at any hobby shop or artists' supply store.

Lunker Landing Tool

Whether it's the lunker bass of a lifetime that you've finally brought within reach, or a big toothy pike or musky, you can land the fish easily and safely with a pair of Vise-Grip pliers. The jaws of these adjustable pliers will remain open until you squeeze the handles, at which time they will clamp and lock tightly on the lower jaw of the fish, keeping your hand a safe distance from hooks and teeth. It is then a simple matter to hoist your trophy aboard your boat.

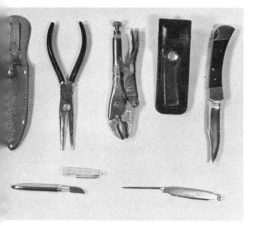 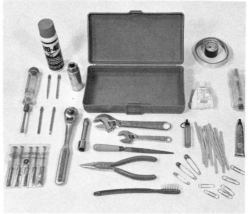

Other tools that most fishermen will find use- | An amazing number of useful tools will fit into
ful are longnose pliers, Vise-Grip pliers, a | a small container that can be tucked into a
Folding Hunter knife, a pocket X-Acto knife, | corner of your tackle box where it will
and a folding pipe tool. | be ready for most emergency repairs.

Fisherman's Tool Kit

When I'm going afloat or am heading out for a fishing trip that will last more than a day, I carry a compact tool kit that will take care of most emergency repair and maintenance jobs. It consists of a small pair of pliers, a screwdriver with interchangeable shafts that store in the handle, a set of jeweler's screwdrivers, a 4-inch adjustable wrench, a 6-inch adjustable wrench, a spark-plug wrench, a small file, a small coil of wire, several paper clips, safety pins, rubber bands, a roll of nylon strapping tape, a roll of plastic electrician's tape, hot-melt patch stick, silicone seal, a small tube of reel oil, gun grease, a small can of WD-40, a toothbrush, and several small swatches of emery cloth.

The purpose and usefulness of most of these tools are readily evident, but others might not normally be found in most fishermen's tackle boxes. A paper clip, for example, can be used to replace a broken or damaged rod guide in an emergency situation, and I once used one to repair the carburetor linkage on my car, thus saving us a long walk after a long day of angling. Nylon strapping tape is tough stuff that can be put to use for any number of repair jobs. It can be used for wrapping rod guides and will hold a reel fast to a rod handle with a damaged reel seat. And once when the latch on my tackle box broke, I was able to tape the box shut when I headed for home.

No, I don't carry safety pins in case I forgot my hooks. But they do have many less dubious uses on any fishing trip. Tears in clothing are quickly closed with safety pins. Unwanted knots in lines and leaders can be worked out with the point of a pin, and clogged fuel jets on camp stoves can be cleaned with the same tool. Emergency patches can be made in tents and rainwear with plastic electrician's tape. And I have mended everything from small punctures in waders to leaky seams in a canoe with silicone seal.

Of course, every fisherman will have his own preferences for the kinds of tools he wants to have along. The important thing is that you carry something to make those emergency repairs and that the kit be compact. Everything I have mentioned fits neatly into a small plastic box for which I find room in one of my tackle boxes.

CHAPTER 2

Rods and Reels

Tips on Rod Care

Fishing rods rank among the most neglected of the angler's tools in terms of care and cleaning. The fisherman who keeps his reels gleaming and functioning like Swiss clockworks will dismantle them and cleanse the springs, gears, bearings, and other parts, coat them with protective lubricants, and put the assemblies back together again with the care of a transplant surgeon. Yet his rods are likely to be showing signs of severe wear and strain, ranging from frayed windings, cracked varnish, and last season's nicks and scratches to yesterday's mud and fish slime.

Of course, today's technology provides us with rods that are able to take much more abuse than the fishing sticks of yesteryear, but there is still a limit to what they can endure. The problem with rods is that they don't complain. An ill-kept or damaged reel will moan and wail about its condition, or just refuse to function. Rods that are not cared for simply deteriorate silently and unobtrusively. A fishing rod that receives the attention it deserves will do its intended job for many memorable years. Because it functions as an extension of the fisherman's arm, a well-kept rod becomes—with years of service —a treasured possession.

Of all the rods I own, my favorite is a 7-foot, medium-action, fast-taper spinning rod that cost me $60 when I was living on army pay back in 1962. That rod has taken more pounds and a wider variety of fish, from bluegills to coho salmon, than any other rod I own, including my salmon/steelhead and heavier salt-water gear. I have had to replace the tip-top twice on that rod and have made a number of other minor repairs. Yet placed side by side with rods I bought last year, this one appears to be a contemporary.

There's one reason for a rod to last and serve its owner—loving care. Stripping rods to bare blanks and rewinding guides, ferrules, and tip-tops is a subject worthy of the coverage it has received in magazines and books. It is also something that can be put off for many years by paying attention to the immediate needs of rod maintenance.

Absolute minimum care includes wiping a rod down with a damp sponge after every outing, and then polishing it with a silicone gun-and-reel cloth. Heavy use in foul weather, of course, demands greater care. When I have been out for an hour or two of easy fishing, I just wipe the rod down before putting it away. If the use has been intensive, however, other measures are necessary. Rods should be thoroughly cleaned, as required, with warm, soapy water. A mild dishwashing soap is best, and a toothbrush is handy for cleaning guides and tip-tops. Remove fish slime and dirt from cork and composition handles with the same suds and brush.

Guides and tip-tops need special attention and should be checked frequently for damage and wear. A tiny burr or groove in a guide or tip-top can fray your line in minutes and reduce its effective strength by 50 percent or more. Accumulation of dirt and silt on guides works as an abrasive and only serves to speed up the grooving process.

It's a good idea to examine guides with a magnifying glass. Early

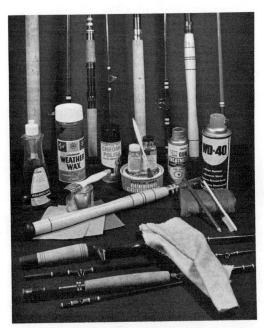

Materials and tools required for keeping rods
in good shape are shown here.

signs of corrosion can be checked with chrome polish or auto-body rubbing compound. Extra-fine (#0000) steel wool is also good for this job. A strand of steel wool drawn through guides and tip-tops will quickly locate tiny burrs and snags that can fray line. Especially tough spots can be worked out with a pencil-type, hard typewriter eraser and then polished with jeweler's rouge or rubbing compound. Any badly worn or damaged guides or tip-tops should be replaced.

Fixed reel seats should be thoroughly cleaned with soap and water along with the rest of the rod. Then, a coating of one of the moisture-displacing lubricants (such as WD-40) will ensure proper functioning. Rod ferrules can be cleaned in the same manner and polished with chrome cleaner. To get to the inside of the female ferrule, use a rifle-cleaning brush of comparable diameter. Follow that with a swab of #0000 steel wool. Lubricate the male ferrule by wiping it with a silicone gun-and-reel cloth, or apply a dry lubricant, such as Du Pont Slip Spray. The fiberglass joints of the so-called ferruleless rods can be cleaned with warm, soapy water. The male piece should then be coated with a thin film of paraffin or beeswax.

Heavy use, over a prolonged period, will eventually cause windings around guides and tip-tops to fray and cause varnish to crack at stress points. The job of rewinding can be postponed for years by periodic applications of rod varnish in such areas of wear.

The wooden handles of trolling and boat rods require special attention. Like gunstocks, these handles will soon take on the appearance and consistency of driftwood if left unattended. Nicks, scratches, gouges, fish slime, sweat, and insect repellent all act against the varnish on these handles. They should be refinished as soon as excessive wear becomes apparent. Remove the butt cap and strip the handle to bare wood with a chemical paint or varnish remover or with sandpaper. If you opt for the latter, start with a medium-grit (#100) sandpaper. Follow that with #220 and #320 paper, polish with #0000 steel wool, and wipe clean. Apply two coats of clear marine varnish or polyurethane, and paint the decorative rings with black enamel, using an artist's spotting brush.

One of the best ways to prolong rod life and appearance is to keep the rod clean and waxed. About every three months I give my rods a coat of car wax. I use a heavy-duty liquid wax for its ease of application and long life. A rod properly cared for can be a lifelong friend. A rod abused and ignored will one day wreak its vengeance; and that's when the biggest fish of all might get away.

How to Detect Burrs in Line Guides

A tiny burr in a rod guide or tip-top can be detected with a small swatch of cotton. Run the cotton through the guide or tip-top both ways, and fibers will catch on any burrs that exist. The burrs can be removed with a small, round file. The guide or tip-top should then be sanded with extra-fine sandpaper or emery cloth and polished with auto-body rubbing compound. (It's also a good idea to carry a swatch of cotton with you when shopping for a new rod to help you avoid buying a rod with defective hardware.)

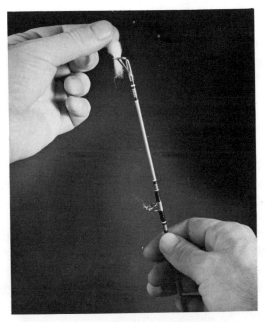

Draw a small swatch of cotton through rod
guides and tip-tops to detect small burrs.

Emergency Rod Repair Kit

The most vulnerable and breakable part of any rod is its tip. While rod tips get broken with great frequency, they seldom succumb to natural causes—like a fish that's too big to handle. Usually, they are the victims of slammed doors, car-trunk lids, and pickup-truck tailgates. The careless fisherman who refuses to prop an idle rod upright will someday painfully learn that rods are as easy to step on as twigs and that they snap in two just as readily.

A day of fishing can be ruined by a broken rod tip unless you carry an emergency rod-repair kit with you. My own kit consists of five different sizes of tip-tops, a stick of hot-melt ferrule cement, and a disposable cigarette lighter. It all tucks into a small change purse that stays in a pocket of my fishing jacket at all times.

In the event that I break a rod tip, I can select a replacement tip-top to fit. Holding the tip-top with a pair of pliers, I heat it with the cigarette lighter and scoop an ample amount of ferrule cement with the hollow end of the heated tip-top. I then reheat it to keep the cement liquid and slip it on the broken rod end, making sure it is properly aligned. Within seconds, the tip-top will cool to form a permanent bond. The entire operation takes about as long as tying on a new lure.

Beware the Adjustable Rod Case

Several times when packing my rods in an adjustable rod case and sliding the inner tube to its proper setting in the outer tube, I have felt resistance and needed to stop. After readjusting the rods I was able to clamp the case closed.

Recently, a fishing partner of mine wasn't quite so fortunate. He did not notice that the tip section of his favorite, custom-built steelhead rod had gotten hung up on one of the guides of another rod in the case. As he pushed the inner section of his new rod case into place, he thought nothing of the resistance—that is, until he heard something snap inside. My rod-repair kit saved the day, but it was still a painful way to learn a lesson.

If you're shopping for an adjustable case, I recommend getting one that features a screw-on cap. Then you can adjust the case to its proper length before putting the rods inside. If you already have one of the other types of cases that closes by joining the inner tube and the outer tube, use it with caution. Don't overload it with too many rods. Always close it slowly, and beware of any resistance. Such precautions could save you a repair job on a favorite rod.

Pick a Pair of Pack Poles

For the backpacking fisherman or the traveler who wants to take his fishing gear along, the compact, multi-sectioned pack rods are ideal. But after trying several, I decided I needed two—one for spinning and one for fly fishing. Critics of sectional rods maintain that the dead space created by ferrules severely impairs the action of any rod. In the case of the two-section rod, such criticism is highly questionable. But a rod with five pairs of ferrules is bound to be less responsive than a one-piece or two-piece rod. This problem has been greatly alleviated by the development of glass ferrules or the so-called ferruleless rods. Some fine pack rods that will satisfy even the most discriminating are being manufactured today.

One type of pack rod that I have not been satisfied with, however, is the combination fly-spinning rod. But since I have never found any combination rod to my liking, I doubt that my objections have anything to do with the number of sections the rod has. Of the combination rods I have tried, all were too soft for good spinning action, and none recovered quickly enough when being used for fly fishing. But the problem was in the action, not the number of sections the rod had.

The pack fly rod I use is a five-piece, 7½-foot lightweight that goes with me on most backpacking trips. Its companion is a four-piece, 6-foot, light-action spinning rod. The fly rod responds most satisfactorily, handling a wide range of wet and dry flies, nymphs, streamers, and small poppers. The spinning rod is tapered adequately to handle light lures, yet it has enough backbone to land lunkers. My wife has a similar pair of rods, and these are what we pack when traveling light. But their greatest value, for our purposes, is as car trunk rods.

Many times I have gone out of town for reasons other than fishing only to come across a fine stretch of cold, clear stream or tule-lined pond just waiting to be fished. Without equipment in instances like these, all I can do is note the location and vow to return. "Why didn't I bring a rod along?" is a question I frequently asked myself.

Usually, I would be out without fishing tackle, because I had no intention of fishing or figured I wouldn't have the time. And then there's the problem of gathering up tackle during the last busy minutes before departure. The fact is that a small amount of fishing tackle can be stored as easily in the trunk of a car as in a closet, basement, or garage. My wife and I keep our spinning and fly pack rods, reels, and fishing vests in a small satchel in the trunk of our compact car, which is the vehicle we drive most often these days.

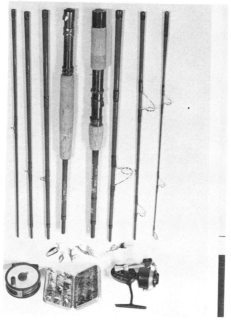

A pair of pack rods—one for fly fishing, one for spinning—will handle most situations the backpacking or traveling angler will face.

Since the kinds of water we usually happen upon in our travels are trout streams or ponds that harbor populations of bass and panfish, we are adequately prepared with the spinning and fly tackle we carry. In our fishing vests we have all our fly fishing accouterments as well as our light and ultralight spinners, spoons, and plugs. We have also packed the satchel with a small box containing a dozen of our most reliable bass plugs and another pocket-size box containing a small assortment of plastic worms, worm hooks, and slip sinkers.

Since we have picked a pair of pack poles for our car trunk, we have not only been able to take advantage of our chance fishing spot discoveries, but we've also learned to anticipate and plan for them. For example, if we're going out of town on business, we study maps before we go and try to find new routes to travel. We also try to take care of business in a minimum of time so that we can test the new waters along the way without having to rush.

Whenever we're just out for an afternoon or evening drive, berry picking, gathering mushrooms, scouting for new hunting areas or photographing wildlife, we have our tackle along just in case we find a stream or pond that looks like it ought to be fished.

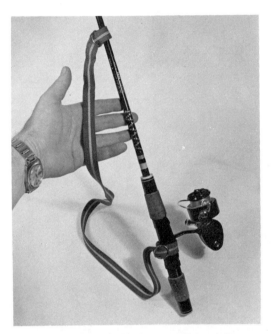

To carry an extra rod with you while wading a stream or walking a lake shore, use a photographer's tripod sling.

Tips on Toting an Extra Rod

Too often during a day of stream wading and fishing for trout or smallmouth bass, I have regretted not having an extra rod along. If I've taken my ultralight spinning outfit, I'll find fish feeding frantically on the surface. If I am fly fishing, I will surely come upon long, deep, dark pools that I would rather probe with small spinners, spoons, or jigs.

I now carry both rods with me and am ready for any fishing situation I might encounter. An extra rod can be carried, fully rigged and ready for fishing, by attaching a tripod sling to it and strapping it across your back. The sling—available at most photographic supply stores—will hold the extra rod safely and securely out of the way while you're fishing. If you have to travel through any thick cover or dense woods, you can slip the rod off your back and hand carry it until you reach the next fishing spot.

You can make your own rod sling with a piece of web belting and two links of plastic chain. Cut the belt to a length to fit your torso—about 40 to 44 inches for a fisherman of medium build. Attach a chain link at each end by riveting or sewing the belting end to itself, putting the link in the loop that has been created. To secure the sling to the rod, pull several inches of the belt through the chain links, and slide the resulting loops around the rod. Cinch one of the loops to the rod handle and another further up the rod, just below one of the guides. Now the rod can be slung and kept out of the way while you fish.

Good Fishing Is a Drag

One of the most misunderstood, misused, and important mechanisms in any casting, spinning, or trolling reel is the drag. These days, most reels are equipped with drags, but few fisherman know how to use the drag correctly and efficiently.

A common mistake made by many fishermen is attempting to set the drag properly and then ignoring it. Drags that aren't checked frequently have a tendency to work loose or freeze tight. A drag that's too loose will seriously impair the hook-setting ability of the rod and reel; a drag that's too tight can cause line to break. Such problems usually become evident when a fish strikes, but by then it can be too late to correct them. Drags should be checked and adjusted before every fishing trip and should be rechecked every hour or two while fishing. It should go without saying that the drag must be reset after changing line from one strength to another.

Drag problems are the greatest at the worst possible time—when a real lunker has been hooked. This isn't just another example of bad luck either, because most fish hooked by the average fisherman will come to net without ever engaging the drag. It's the big fish that will test the limits of the fisherman and his tackle. And when that big one is on, you better have your drag set properly.

A prevalent misconception is that drag is solely a function of the reel. Even though most fishermen know that the drag should be set to slip just below the breaking point of the line, they consider the drag properly set if they can pull line off the reel at that point. This is one reason most drags are set too tight.

To illustrate my own school-of-rotten-luck knowledge of the subject, I lost my first king salmon some years back, because my drag was set way too tight. I was using a new salmon/steelhead rod and heavy-duty spinning reel for the first time. The spool was loaded with fresh 20-pound line, and the drag was set below the breaking point of the monofilament. After several hours of fishing, I had made a cast diagonally upstream near the opposite bank of the river. My lure was nearing the end of the drift when the salmon hit. He was probably a 30- or 40-pound fish, but he might as well have weighed 100 pounds for my ability to hold him. On the strike, I reared the rod back and set the hook solidly. Within a split second, the fish was headed downstream. The line stretched and suddenly went slack when one tine of the treble hook straightened out and another broke off halfway around the gap. With the anti-reverse engaged, I pulled on the line, fully expecting the drag to be frozen tight, but it slipped just as it should have.

My partner walked up, took the end of the line that draped from the rod tip, and told me to hold onto the rod. I held it tightly at the 11-o'clock position while he began pulling away from me. With the rod fully flexed, the drag refused to slip, even when he yanked the line several times nearly pulling the rod out of my hands. "Loosen your drag," he said. I followed his orders, loosening the drag until it slipped with the rod fully flexed. "Now it's right," he said. And evidently it was, because I went on to land seven more king salmon that weekend and dozens more during subsequent trips. And I haven't lost a king salmon since because of an improperly set drag.

There's another drag-related problem that is peculiar to spinning and spin-casting reels. If you hook a fish that is strong enough to run the drag and continue cranking the reel handle as he runs, you're not only wasting energy, but you're also severely twisting the line. This will lead to eventual tangles and snarls, but, more importantly, it will weaken your line. When a fish is running, let him; when he stops or turns, that's the time to regain line.

To properly set the drag on a reel, you need a partner.

Whether you're setting the drag on an ultralight reel, 5-foot rod and 4-pound-test line or on a heavy-duty salmon/steelhead rig, the method is the same. Have someone hold the tag end of the line, then back off at least 15 or 20 feet. If it's a spinning reel you're adjusting, click on the anti-reverse. Hold the rod at the 9-o'clock position, pointing at your companion, and reel in any slack. Now, with the line taut, raise the rod to the 11-o'clock position. If the drag slips before you reach 11 o'clock, tighten it until it doesn't. Continue rearing back on the rod to the 12-o'clock position. Between 11 and 12, with the rod fully arched, the drag should slip. With the reel properly adjusted, return the rod to the 11-o'clock position— again with the line taut and the rod flexed—and have your partner yank the line as a battling fish might. Now the drag should slip at 11 o'clock.

It will seem at first that this setting is far too light, but it is totally adequate. Consider that when you are retrieving a lure, your rod is normally at about the 9-o'clock position. When a fish strikes, you are going to rear back to 12 o'clock, and then go on to land the fish with the rod at about 11 o'clock. On the strike, the drag won't slip until the rod approaches the straight-up position, thus allowing the hook to be firmly set. During the ensuing contest, the drag will slip whenever the fish makes a hard run or turns sharply; and that's the way it's supposed to work.

At the opposite extreme from the fisherman who never checks his drag is the one who is constantly fooling with it. I have seen fishermen who immediately begin fumbling around with the drag as soon as they hook a fish. This can only lead to problems.

While fishing the annual migrations on my favorite salmon stream, I have had the opportunity to observe many fishermen. Often, I have seen anglers hook into big fish that seem determined to strip the reel spool bare in one long, powerful downstream run. That's when most fishermen begin tightening their drags—a natural inclination but the worst possible kind of mistake. The farther the

Set your drag properly every time out and check it regularly, but don't fool with it unnecessarily.

To effectively tighten the drag on an open-face spinning reel without resetting it, apply pressure to the spool lip with your fingertip.

fish runs, the greater the strain on the line. As the spool diameter is decreased by the diminishing amount of line, drag is effectively increased. So if your drag has been set properly in the first place— that is, light enough—the best thing to do when a fish is running is to let him. Keep your rod tip high and let the tension of the rod and the stretch of the line help you to turn and subdue the fish.

Certainly there will be times when some minor adjustments need to be made while fighting a fish, but these will be held to a minimum if the drag is set properly in the first place, and checked regularly in the second.

Finger Drag on Spinning Reels

Open-face spinning reels have a distinct advantage over other kinds of reels when it comes to controlling a fish that is running the drag. Slight pressure applied to the lip of the spool by the forefinger of the casting hand will effectively tighten the drag without permanently resetting it. Of course, you don't want to apply so much pressure that the line will break. Often, just a slight bit of pressure for a second or two is enough to turn a running fish.

This is also a technique to remember when a fish is taking out all of your line, and the bare spool is showing beneath the few feeble feet of line left. In such a situation, apply increasing pressure until you turn the fish. If the line breaks under the pressure, you can find some solace in the fact that you would have lost him anyway when the line ran out—some solace.

Tips on Reel Care

If you dismantle, clean, and lubricate a fishing reel after each outing, you're going to spend more time on maintenance than on angling. If you rarely ever or never perform inspections and maintenance on your reels, they're not going to last long and will probably begin to malfunction at the most inopportune time—when a fish is on. Between these two extremes is the common-sense approach to reel care.

After each outing, I rinse my reels off under a gentle stream of cool tap water, making sure to remove dirt, algae, fish slime, and scales with an old toothbrush. I take a few seconds to inspect such vulnerable areas as bail arms on spinning reels and the level-wind mechanism on casting and trolling reels. Then I shake excess water off the reels and allow them to air dry for several hours or overnight. After they have dried, I wipe them down with a silicone cloth.

Even though my reels get a lot of hard use, I find that I normally need to completely dismantle and clean them only once a year. Since March is the month that I do the least amount of fishing, that's the time I set aside for reel cleaning.

Perhaps the best solvent for cleaning and degreasing reels is carbon tetrachloride, but for two reasons I no longer use it: (1) The fumes from carbon tet are extremely toxic, which means that this solvent should be used outdoors only, and (2) It will dissolve plastic reel parts. Most gun solvents are safe to use, but some will not remove old grease quickly enough for my liking. For this reason, I prefer to use mineral spirits or denatured alcohol, which are available at any home improvement center and most hardware and discount department stores.

Hot soapy water and the old reliable toothbrush also will do an excellent job of cleaning reel parts, after which they can be rinsed in warm water and dried with an electric hair dryer. When the reel parts are clean and dry, I inspect them under a magnifying glass for any signs of wear. Excessively worn parts get replaced. I pay close attention to line guides or rollers on spinning-reel bail arms, as they will wear much the same way as rod guides and tip-tops do and must be replaced when they begin to exhibit signs of grooving. Any drag parts that indicate excessive wear must be replaced, too.

Once the reel has been cleaned, it needs a good lube job that will last. I use gun grease on all gears to minimize friction and protect the gears during the coming year. I then coat all interior parts, including the insides of reel side plates, with outboard motor oil. The viscosity of this oil makes it one of the best heavy-duty lubricants I have ever used. It doesn't break down during the course of a fishing season, and it repels moisture.

About once a month during the fishing season, I inspect and lubricate my reels. It only takes a few minutes to remove the retaining screws on a reel's side plate to get a look at the internal workings under a good light. I look for any tiny metal shavings that indicate something is wearing out, and I visually check gears, bearings, and shafts just to make sure everything is working without undue wear. Then I give a few squirts of sewing machine oil to all moving parts and put the side plate back in place. On spinning reels, I remove the spool to check and lubricate the drag, too. The whole process takes less than five minutes per reel.

With such a thorough annual inspection and cleaning, monthly lubricating, and minor cleaning and inspection after each outing, my reels are kept in top working order at all times. An added bonus of such care is that wear is minimized. Consequently, I rarely ever have to replace parts. It's the corroded spring that will weaken and break, the dirty bail arm line guide that will groove and abrade line, the ill-kept drag that will feed line in a jerky fashion, the gritty gears and bearings that will wear out too soon.

A simple, common-sense maintenance schedule will afford you many trouble-free hours of fishing, and in the long run will save you time and money.

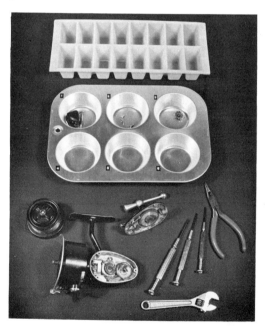

Muffin tins and ice-cube trays make excellent small-parts trays for housing reel parts.

Small-Parts Catch-All Tray

Ever dismantle a fishing reel and have parts left over when you put it back together again? Or, maybe you forgot the order in which the pieces came apart, and, consequently, couldn't remember how it all should be reassembled. A simple solution is to use a small-parts catch-all tray.

Any compartmentalized container will do the trick, such as an ice-cube tray or muffin tin. You can even number the compartments as a way of keeping everything in proper order.

Winterize Your Reels for Cold-Weather Fishing

If you use a reel during cold weather, such as for ice fishing or winter steelhead fishing, it will function much better if you winterize it first. After a thorough cleaning of all parts, lubricate gears with a thin coat of 10-40 multi-grade motor oil instead of using gear grease that becomes gummy at low temperatures. Use light reel oil only on bearings.

Reel drags, bail arms and springs, and level-wind mechanisms will function smoothly if lubricated with a dry lubricant, such as Du Pont Slip Spray. Reels used under severe cold-weather conditions should be checked and relubricated after each fishing trip.

Regal Reel Pouch

Although the distillers probably didn't plan it that way, the purple drawstring bag in which the Seagram's Company packages its Crown Royal Canadian Whisky makes a dandy reel pouch. And surely the inventive outdoorsman can find numerous other uses for these soft, felt bags. In fact, he might even find a way to dispose of the bag's original contents.

Tips on Buying Reels

Money spent on cheap, off-brand reels is often ill-spent. These reels seldom prove to be the bargains they might at first appear to be. Some carry no guarantees, and usually it is impossible to find replacement parts for them.

I bought such a reel some years ago just prior to a salmon-fishing trip. During the first day of using that piece of junk, the weak bail spring ceased to function, and I had to manually close the bail after each cast. By the end of that day, on all but the gentlest of casts, the bail would flop over half way and feather the line. The only way I could get any distance at all was to hold the bail open during the

The soft, felt drawstring bag that Seagram's Crown Royal comes in makes an excellent reel pouch.

cast. The drag refused to be adjusted for smooth operation. Luckily, I hooked no salmon on that trip. By the next weekend, I had purchased a quality reel that I have been using ever since.

The junk reel carried no guarantee and came with no parts list. The reel I bought the following week, however, came guaranteed and with a complete manual, including a list of parts and recommended service centers. Replacement parts are easy to obtain for it, and most major cities have service centers.

Many of the top tackle manufacturers are now offering lines of lower-priced reels that are backed by the same guarantees as their top-of-the-line gear. Instead of trying to save by buying the off-brand reels, pick a less expensive model made by a reputable manufacturer. And look for sales at the end of the fishing season. That's often a good time to pay less for a top-notch reel than you would normally pay for inferior equipment.

It's also a good idea to find one good brand of reels and stay with it. One reason for this is that different size reels made by the same company are generally similar in all other respects, allowing the fisherman to become totally familiar with the design similarities. This not only helps when dismantling reels for cleaning, but it's an aid during the fishing season as well. Drag adjustments are in the same place; bails trip identically; the anti-reverse lever is in the same spot. Having backup reels of the same make and model also makes good sense, since parts are interchangeable, and, in the case of spinning reels, spools can be switched from reel to reel.

When I'm heading out for a day of bass fishing, I always carry several rods with me. The two I use the most are equipped with Mitchell 300 reels. Switching from one to the other is an easy matter that takes no getting used to. Also, extra spools of different weight line can be used on either rig. Similarly, my number one steelhead reel is a fairly new Mitchell 406, and my backup reel is an old Mitchell 406.

Prop Your Rod Properly

The habits you form early in any endeavor usually are the ones that will stay with you. One habit you should get into is propping your rod up against something whenever it's not in use. I'm shocked by the number of fishermen who will lay a rod down where it becomes easy prey for a stray foot that can break a tip or mash a guide. But equally devastating, yet not as readily noticeable, is the damage to reels. A reel on the ground will collect mud, dirt, and sand, all of which are abrasive and will cause excessive friction and wear of moving parts. So develop the good habit of propping your rod and reel up and out of danger whenever it's not in use—even if it is only for a few seconds.

On extended fishing trips, one of the first of our camp chores is to construct a simple rod rack. This consists of saplings at each end, lashed together in an X, with a crossbeam against which rods can be propped. The crossbeam should be located about 3 feet off the ground so that the stiff portion of a rod is propped against it.

If you are propping a rod up indoors, make sure it is not leaning against a wall where the tip could take a set. This is particularly important if the rod is made of bamboo, but even glass rods will take at least a temporary set if propped against a wall for a prolonged period.

In a boat, a rod should never be propped against a gunwhale so that its tip extends outside the craft where it could be damaged when running ashore or docking. Instead, keep rods in racks or laid across seats or thwarts near the bulkheads.

Revive Your Silicone Cloths

A silicone-impregnated cloth is one of the best cleaning accessories available for the sportsman who wants to keep his gear clean and corrosion free. But after extensive use, the cloth will seem to lose some of its effectiveness. When this happens, simply rinse the cloth in lukewarm water, gently squeeze excess water out, and let it air dry. This will fully revive the silicone and the cloth will work like new. If the cloth is extremely soiled, you can wash it in mild dishwashing soap and lukewarm water. To revive the silicone, rinse it thoroughly and allow it to air dry.

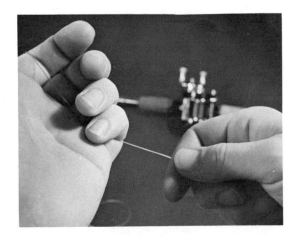

CHAPTER 3

Lines, Leaders, and Terminal Tackle

Living With Monofilament Line

The invention of nylon has led to many product breakthroughs. For the fisherman, nylon monofilament line is probably the most significant. It is the ideal line for use on spinning reels. It is now used widely on casting and trolling reels, and it has revolutionized fly-fishing leaders. Nylon monos have been around since the 1940s, but have been greatly refined and improved in recent years. Today's premium monofilament lines are extremely tough and durable. They are more resistant to abrasion than their predecessors were and than their braided contemporaries are.

While some scientists feel that there are few improvements left to be made in monofilament lines, there are still some inherent characteristics in these lines that fishermen must learn to live with. Even the so-called limp monos are stiff in comparison to braided lines, but this isn't a totally negative characteristic. A certain amount of stiffness is required for the line to spring off a spinning-reel spool as it should. But excessively stiff lines will leave the reel in springlike coils. This increases drag through the rod guides, which will impair casting and can lead to tangles and snarls.

The larger the diameter of a monofilament line, the stiffer it will be. Consequently, heavier monos—above 20-pound test—don't work well on spinning reels. Most premium monos are smaller in diameter than cheaper lines of the same pound-test rating. So better lines will be limper and generally easier to cast.

Nylon monofilaments also stretch much more than other lines. For example, before reaching the breaking point, monofilament lines stretch as much as 15 to 30 percent when dry and 20 to 35 percent when wet, whereas Dacron line has a maximum stretch of about 10 percent. The disadvantage for the fisherman is that it is more difficult to set a hook with nylon monofilament. And the greater the distance between the hook and the reel, the more stretch there will be to overcome. In other words, a fish that strikes a lure shortly after it touches the water on a long cast will be far more difficult to hook than one that strikes near the boat. For this reason, it is a good idea to set a hook more than once when fishing for all but the soft-mouthed species.

Once the fish is hooked, however, line stretch works to the fisherman's advantage in subduing the fish. Usually, when a fish turns sharply, instead of snapping under the impact, mono will stretch and eventually serve to tire the fish. Because of the elasticity of monofilament and the amount of line often paid out behind a boat when trolling, braided Dacron is usually a much better choice for trolling reels.

Although widely used on bait-casting reels, round monofilament spinning line is not a good choice for revolving spool reels. Braided lines and flat or oval monofilaments, made specifically for conventional casting reels, will lay more evenly and snugly on the spool without digging into underlying layers. This facilitates casting and helps to prevent backlashes.

I can't think of a single advantage of twisted line, and while any line can become twisted, monofilament seems to have a penchant for it. An improperly rigged plastic worm will twist line, as will a faulty swivel or cranking the handle of a spinning reel against a fish that's running the drag. Mono also has the habit of taking a set. And the longer it goes unused, the greater the chances of it taking a set, which will cause it to come off the reel in kinky coils.

Moderately twisted or kinked line can be straightened merely by trolling it behind a boat with nothing attached to it. If you fish once a week or more, get into the habit of straightening your line in this manner on the way back to the dock after each outing. If you fish less than once a week, the chances of your line taking a set are greater and increase with the amount of time that lapses between trips. So troll your line behind the boat on the way to your first fishing spot of the day to get the kinks out.

If you're fishing from shore or wading a stream, straighten your line the night before your trip. Simply tie it to a tree or other stationary object, walk off 50 yards or more, close the bail on the reel, and stretch the line several feet. This will straighten out all the twists and kinks.

What Color Line?

Extensive studies conducted to determine the best colors for fishing lines have proved one thing to me: Studies are inconclusive, and we can only speculate on which colors are best. It is reasonable to assume that the less visible a line is to a fish, the more likely the fish will be to take a bait without being spooked. But usually, a fishing line that is difficult for a fish to see is also difficult for the fisherman to see. Some manufacturers have been striving to develop the epitome of fishing lines—one that is invisible to the fish and highly visible to the fisherman. Some manufacturers have even boasted that their lines have these qualities.

Above-water and sub-surface visibility tests have shown that some lines are less visible than others, under certain circumstances, and that fluorescent-pigmented lines are not only highly visible above water but beneath as well. These same tests have shown that opaque lines are more visible under water than are clear monofilaments. But all these tests are based on what the human eye sees. Until we know exactly what and how fish see, we can only speculate about what color our fishing lines should be.

Nevertheless, I think there are some reasonable assumptions to be made that can guide the fisherman who wants to buy the right line. I am skeptical about the highly visible, fluorescent-pigmented monofilament lines. If they are as visible to fish as they are to humans, I feel that their disadvantages far outweigh their advantages. I like to be able to see my line, as it gives me much more control. And when fishing with bait or soft plastic lures, often the only way to detect a gentle pickup is to watch for a tick in the line. Certainly such line movement is much easier to see if the line is brightly visible. But if you're an alert fisherman with normal vision, you should be able to see any line tick where it touches the water, regardless of its color or fluorescence.

Tests have also indicated that clear, colorless monofilaments are less visible in gin-clear waters than other lines are. The blue-green clear monos are least visible in waters of the same tint, and clear-amber monos are least likely to be seen in amber-colored waters. If you do most of your fishing in crystal-clear mountain streams, clear and colorless mono should be your choice. If the waters you fish are blue-green or amber tinted, then buy appropriately colored line.

If you fish a variety of waters, you can either carry a variety of lines, take your chances with the one that matches up with the kind of water you fish most, or settle for a color that is reasonably invisible under various situations. That color is neutral gray. (Tests at Cortland Line Company have shown that neutral gray is least visible in typical fishing habitats.)

My choice for braided-Dacron line is the multi-colored camouflage line which changes color every few feet and, thus, becomes extremely difficult to see under water.

What Pound Test?

Since larger lines are more visible than small ones, the lightest line you can get by with is the best one to use. However, your line weight should be matched to the kind of fishing you do and the sort of tackle you use. I know of fishermen who carry a half-dozen or more different-weight lines with them every time out, but I fear they spend a needless amount of time changing lines instead of fishing. There are times when a fisherman must switch from one line to another in order to catch wary, line-shy fish, but changing lines should be kept within reasonable limits for the sake of simplicity and sanity.

Normally I carry no more than three different-weight lines with me at any time, and usually less than that, because I pay attention to the seasons and am aware of the kind of conditions I am likely to face. In the spring, the waters I fish are generally high and roily, and I can get by with as heavy a line as I want. In the fall, lakes and streams are low and clear, so I go prepared to use light lines. Throughout the summer and early winter, water conditions can change rapidly, and that's when I will carry several weights of line— usually only three, though. When I'm traveling to unfamiliar fishing spots, I go well prepared with a wide variety of line to fit any kind of situation I might face.

For ultralight spinning, I have used 2-, 4-, and 6-pound lines. I have never had a fish in open water break even the 2-pound-test line, but I have had them break off in rocky streams or snag-strewn lakes and ponds. I have lost far too many spoons and spinners to snags on 2-pound-test line to warrant its further use. On the other hand, I have found top-quality, small-diameter, 6-pound-test line to have very little wind resistance, yet enough strength and abrasion resistance to work out most snags and land most fish. Consequently, about 90 percent of my ultralight fishing is with 6-pound-test line. I use 4-pound-test line only for the tiniest of lures.

The line I use for most of my fishing is a premium 15-pound-test line. This is my bassing line, my steelhead line, and the one I use for my medium-weight spin fishing most of the time. When I'm fishing with plastic worms or bait in clear water and not finding takers, I will usually switch to 10-pound-test line. Generally, that will do the trick. If it doesn't, I change baits, tactics, or location instead of line. Only when I'm losing too many lures or fish to snags will I change to a heavier line.

Most of the time, 15-pound-test line is the ideal line for winter steelheading. If the water happens to be unusually clear or the fish unusually spooky, I'll drop down to 10-pound-test. I do the same with coho salmon, but for chinook salmon I use 20-pound-test almost exclusively. The heaviest line I use in fresh water is 30-pound-test. That's the weight I prefer for trolling and for bait fishing for big river catfish and sturgeon. Most of the line I use is monofilament. But I do use braided line on my casting and trolling reels. I have a Mitchell 302 salt-water spinning reel loaded with braided 30-pound-test line that I use for catfish and sturgeon fishing.

The line sizes I would recommend for the all-around fisherman who wants to be adequately prepared for any kind of fresh water fishing would be 4#, 6#, 10#, 15#, 20#, and 30#. But if you pay attention to seasons and become familiar with the situations you are likely to encounter, only two or three different lines need to be on hand on most fishing trips.

How Much Line?

The right amount of line for any reel is a full spool. For the spinning reel, that means a spool that is loaded to within $1/16$ to $1/8$ of an inch of the spool's lip or rim. For the casting reel, it means as much line as it takes to fill up the spool all the way. But many fresh-water fishermen use too much line. If the only fishing you do is for bass and panfish, you don't need 200 yards of line on your reel. This is because bass characteristically fight in short and powerful runs, dives, and jumps. The same holds true for most stream trout fishing.

Salmon and steelhead are runners. When you're fishing for these species, you had better have the largest capacity spool your reel will take. Big catfish and sturgeon can make long and powerful runs, too, which call for plenty of line. But if you never fish for the long runners that are capable of stripping a reel to a bare spool, use a small-capacity spool or put an arbor on your spool to decrease its capacity. As the level of line on your reel gets so low that it impairs your casting, you should change it. If you're using a large-capacity spool needlessly, you are only wasting that extra line when you replace it.

How About Multifilament Line?

Early in 1976, the Cortland Line Company introduced a new braided multifilament line called Polyspin. Although it is billed as a braided spinning line, I think it is far superior as a casting and trolling line. It has some advantages as a spinning line, too, but only under particular conditions.

Being a braided line, it is completely limp and will not take a set. This has its advantages and its disadvantages. My tests with a Mitchell 300 reel and a 7-foot, medium-action spinning rod proved the limpness of the line to be a deterrent to casting, because the line simply did not spring from the reel spool as monofilament does. Furthermore, the textured surface of the line created more drag than the smooth surface of a monofilament as it passed through the rod guides. Other disadvantages are those that are usually associated with braided lines. Its opacity makes it more visible in the water, and braided lines will fray more readily than monofilaments will.

One of its greatest advantages was quite evident the first time I hooked into a bass with this line. I had made a fairly long cast to a sunken log with a heavy spinner bait. Before I had cranked the reel handle a third time, a hefty bass smashed the lure, and I reared back to set the hook. My rod bent nearly double, and I thought I had tied into the log. But that was not the case. I discovered that Polyspin does not stretch nearly as much as monofilament, making it much easier to set a hook with it.

If you've ever used monofilament line during the winter—for ice fishing or steelheading—you'll appreciate another characteristic of the multifilament line. It seems to be as limp at 20° as it is at 80°. But perhaps the greatest asset of multifilament is its superior knot strength. It has proved to be as good as any premium monofilament in this regard, which makes it far superior to braided Dacron. Consequently, I find it an ideal line for casting and trolling reels.

Multifilament is also a good choice on spinning reels for winter fishing and performs better than monofilament when a 30-pound-test line is needed on a fixed-spool reel.

Spool to Reel—The Right Way?

Filling a spinning reel with line should be quite a simple matter. But for most of us, it turns into an infuriating affair as we crank on coil after coil of twisted monofilament. I know there is supposed to be a right way and a wrong way, but I have discovered a number of ways—all of them wrong. Trying to do it precisely the way everyone says I should, I still manage to get twists in my line more often than not. Even when I stop frequently to correct my error, I end up loading the reel with uneven tension on the line, which is nearly as bad as twisting it.

Filling a casting or trolling reel is far more trouble-free. By poking a pencil or similar object through the line spool and having someone hold it for me, I can crank the line onto the reel the same way it comes off the line spool.

I have given up trying to load my spinning reels the right way; instead, I do it the easy way. With the line spool revolving on a pencil or dowel rod—as when loading a casting reel—I load my spinning reel, twists and all. Then I immediately take the rod and reel outside. I untwist the line and make sure it is loaded evenly, with precisely the right tension. For this purpose, I have a large barrel swivel tied to a loop of heavy twine. I wrap this around the bumper of my car, a tree branch, or fence post. To that I clip a large snap swivel that has been tied to the tag end of my new line. Then I open the bail on the reel and walk off the entire length of the line, holding my rod tip high to keep the line off the ground.

During the few seconds it takes to walk the 100 to 200 or so yards to empty the reel, the line untwists itself completely. As I walk back toward the starting point, cranking the line back onto my reel, I keep the rod tip high and hold the rod well forward of the reel. I run the line between my thumb and forefinger and am thus able to keep an even tension on it at all times.

A Convenient Way to Store Line

A coat hanger can be turned into an excellent storage device for fishing line. Use a pair of wire cutters to snip the rung in the center, and bend the two rung pieces outward so that they point straight down. With pliers, bend the tips of the rung pieces to the rear to form a hook with a gap of about a ½-inch. Now, cut a piece of ¼-inch dowel rod long enough to reach from hook to hook with about ¼-inch extra at each end. Drill a hole in each end of the dowel slightly larger than the diameter of the hanger wire.

Gather up your spools of line and run the dowel through the center holes of the spools. Insert the hooks of the hanger into the end holes on the dowel rod and your line is ready to be conveniently stored in closet, workshop, basement, or garage. Line can be loaded on reel spools right from this line hanger, since the spools will revolve freely on the dowel rod.

Line Is Cheap—Change it Often

Today, fishing lines are far tougher and longer lasting than their predecessors were. Virtually all fresh-water lines are now made from synthetics that won't rot the way old fabric lines did. But there are limits to what any line can endure. When these limits are approached, the fisherman has no choice but to replace the line.

Fundamentally, fishing line is the most important part of any angler's gear. Regardless of tackle and techniques, the line always stands between the fish and the fisherman. Yet line is the cheapest part of any fishing trip. Perhaps the inclination many of us have to associate the importance of things with their expense explains why so many anglers tend to ignore their line until it is well beyond the replacement point.

As a matter of habit, all lines should be checked frequently for fraying. They should also be checked after every snag and after every fish that's lost or landed. When a fisherman works a snag loose, the line near the lure will often stretch and rub against whatever it is snagged on, causing the line to fray severely. Even a small fish can scrape a line against underwater debris and fray the line. A large fish can fray the line that much more easily and can cause additional abrasion with any abrupt move he makes, bringing the line in contact with his rough scales or abrasive gill covers.

Any frayed section of line should be cut off at once. It doesn't take long for a serious fisherman to trim his line back so far that the line level on the reel has been significantly reduced and will impair casting. That's the time to replace the line. Any line that has become severely twisted or kinked and refuses to be straightened should, of course, be changed. Even the casual fisherman who only gets out occasionally should replace his monofilament line at least annually, especially if he uses a cheaper grade of line that takes a set more readily than a premium line.

My fishing lines get a lot of use. As a result, my reels usually get reloaded several times a season. On a week-long fishing trip, however, I might replace line three or four times. One weekend, during the peak of a king salmon run on Alaska's Gulkana River, I put new line on my reel five times. That may seem extreme to some, but during that weekend I hooked 32 king salmon. Although I lost several fish to straightened hooks, two to hooks that broke off halfway around the gap, and one to a poorly tied knot that slipped loose, not once did my line break. Other fishermen on the same gravel bar, who paid little or no attention to their lines, weren't quite as fortunate. I saw at least two dozen break-offs that weekend, yet I didn't notice any of the other anglers, except my partner, replacing worn and frayed line. Line is cheap. Change it as often as necessary.

Checking for Frayed Line

The mistake that many fishermen make when checking for fraying is that they run the line between the thumb and forefinger of the hand they favor. These digits are usually calloused and won't detect slight fraying. If you're right-handed, run the line over the sensitive skin at the second joint of the left little finger. If you're a southpaw, vice versa. This method will detect the slightest fraying.

Line showing even the least amount of abrasion should be discarded. Snip off the end of the line about a foot above the detected fraying. The few seconds it takes to check and remedy such problems can save a large fish, expensive lure, or both.

The Two Best Knots for Monofilament

There have been countless magazine articles written about hundreds of different knots that the fisherman "must know how to tie." Many fishing books have whole chapters devoted to dozens of different kinds of knots. In fact, there is at least one book that I know of entirely devoted to fishing knots. Knowing a hundred different

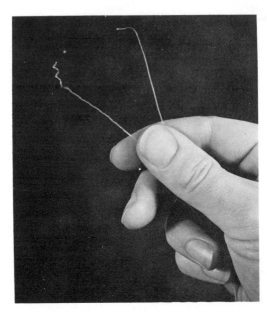

The twisted line on the left indicates that the
knot came untied under pressure. The line
on right broke inside the knot.

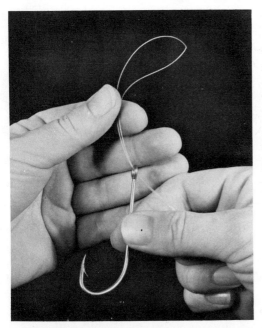

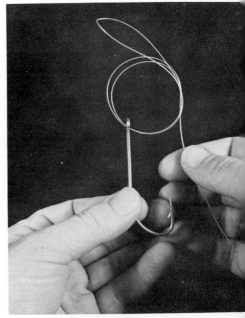

To tie the palomar knot, first double several
inches of the line back against itself to
form a loop; then slip the loop through the eye
of the hook.

Now make a simple overhand knot in the dou-
bled line.

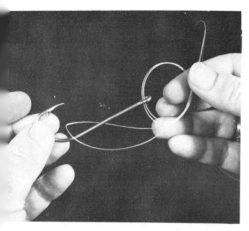 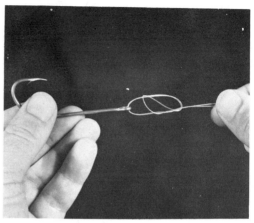

Slip the hook through the loop, and bring the loop up beyond the hook eye.

Slowly pull the knot tight with the double line clasped between thumb and forefinger.

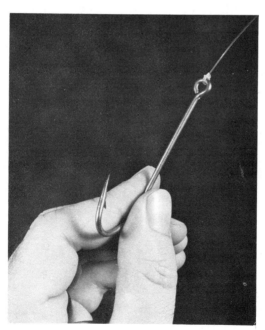

Trim the tag end of line next to the knot, and you have one of the strongest knots there is for monofilament line.

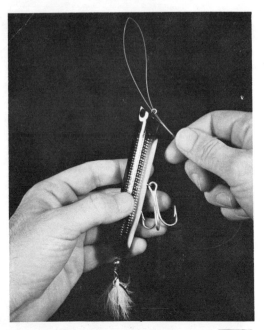

To tie the double-improved clinch knot, double several inches of line back against itself, and slip the loop through the eye of your lure.

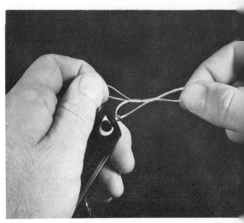

Push the end loop through the loop created in front of the eye.

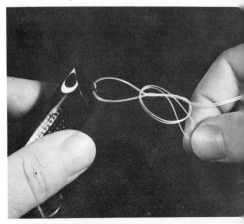

Now pass the end loop back through the large loop near the five twists you made earlier.

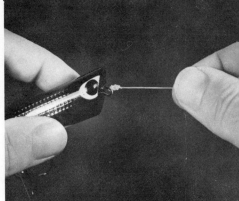

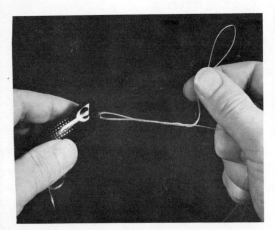

Now make at least five turns around the line, and grasp the end loop between thumb and forefinger.

Finally, pull the knot tight with a slow and steady pull on the line, and trim excess near the knot.

knots might be important for Boy Scouts and sailors, but for fishermen it's an unnecessary complication of the sport. The fisherman who knows how to tie a few good knots well will get along just fine.

Recently, I conducted a series of tests to determine the best knot for general use of monofilament line. I discovered that some writers' and line manufacturers' claims about knots having 100 percent knot strength, or knot strength greater than that of the line itself, are false. When I applied evenly increasing pressure to the knotted lines I was testing, my results coincided with other test reports I have read. But when the knot was subjected to a sharp tug, such as might be expected in most fishing situations, the line broke at the knot every time.

The improved clinch knot is probably the most popular knot that fishermen use on monofilament line, and it is claimed to be one of the strongest. When tested against the double-improved clinch knot, however, it failed every time. In my tests, the simple palomar knot shook out on top and the double-improved clinch knot proved second best—these are the two knots that I use almost exclusively. The palomar is the knot I use when tying on swivels, hooks, and lures that are small enough to fit through the loop of the knot. I use the double-improved clinch knot on most lures and when tying some bottom-fishing rigs.

For those who might not be familiar with these two knots, the photographs opposite and on the previous pages will show you, step by step, how to tie them.

The Versatile Blood Knot

Whether you are a fly fisherman, spin fisherman, bait caster, troller, or bottom fisherman, one knot you should know how to tie is the blood knot. Whenever you need to tie two lines that are of comparable diameter together, this is the knot to use. It is strong, compact, and streamlined enough to slide through rod guides.

Blood knots are ideal for adding more line to a reel spool or for tying a shock leader to the terminal end of your fishing line. Fly fishermen find them especially useful when tying tapered leaders and when tying backing or leader butt to a fly line. A properly tied blood knot gives the appearance of painstaking perfection, yet it is remarkably easy to tie by following a few simple steps, as shown in the photographs on the following pages.

Use a blood knot whenever you need to tie two lines of comparable diameter to one another. If diameters vary greatly, double the thinner line before tying.

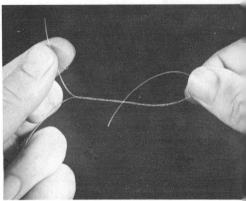

Then, using your left thumb and forefinger, wrap the tag end in your left hand around the line in your left hand five times.

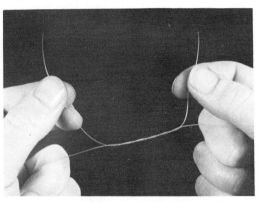

Holding one line in each hand, and allowing several inches of each strand for the tying, wrap the tag end of the left line around the right line five times.

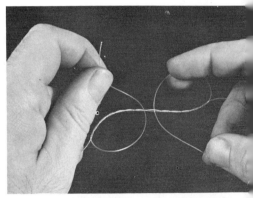

Slip that tag end between the two lines at the same spot you inserted the other tag end, but from the opposite direction. Identical loops will be formed by each tag end.

Now move that tag end back to where you began the wrapping and slip it between the two strands of line.

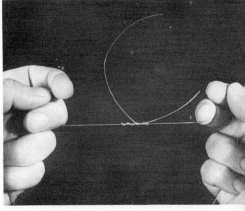

Slowly pull the two main strands of line away from each other and the knot will begin to form. On heavier lines, hold one tag end between your teeth and the other between the thumb and forefinger.

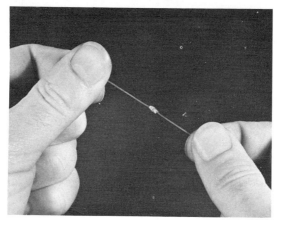

After the knot has been pulled tight, trim off
the tag ends at the knot with scissors or
nail clippers.

Handy Line Keepers

Keep half-a-handful of fat rubber bands in your tackle box to use
as line keepers on your reels and extra spools of line. On line spools
and open-face spinning reels, just slip the rubber band around the
spool. On closed-face spinning and spin-cast reels, lay a couple of
inches of line back against the reel spool cover and slip a rubber

Use fat rubber bands to secure line on reels
and spools.

band around the cover. On bait-casting and trolling reels, lay an inch or two of line across the side plate and hold it in place with a rubber band stretched around the plate.

The Right Way to Thread a Fly Rod

How many times have you hurriedly threaded your fly rod, only to have the knot affixing the leader to the fly line catch in the last eye or tip-top, pulling the leader from your hand and stripping the line back to the starting point? Solve this problem by doubling the leader back against the fly line and threading the line, knot first.

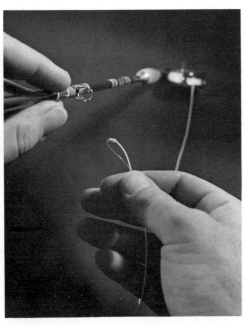 

Double the leader back against the fly line and thread it knot first.

A small piece of inner tube makes a dandy leader straightener.

Free Leader Straighteners

One of the best materials for straightening curled monofilament leaders is a small swatch of rubber. A worn-out inner tube—discarded by a local gas station—will provide enough rubber (or

synthetic rubber) to keep you and all your fishing partners sup
with leader straighteners for a lifetime.

Easy Leaders for Toothy Critters

For leaders to be used to fish for those toothy critters, heavy
monofilament line, from 40- to 100-pound-test, is just as good as
wire—and some say better. You can often get good buys on this
material by purchasing mill ends that come in odd lengths. An
added advantage to using heavy mono for leaders is that it requires
no special tools. You can either carry a supply of line in your tackle
box or make up a batch of leaders in advance. All you need is the
line and a supply of swivels.

For leaders to be used on plugs, tie a barrel swivel to one end and
a snap to the other end. Leaders that will be used on spoons, spinners, and spinner baits should have a barrel swivel at one end and
a snap swivel at the other end.

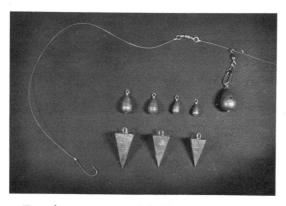

To make a convenient fish-finder rig, tie a barrel swivel into your line 18 to 20 inches
above the hook, with a free-sliding snap swivel
above the barrel swivel. When you need to
change weights, it's a snap.

Versatile Fish-Finder Rigs

Many of us who enjoy bait fishing recognize the value of fish-
finder rigs that allow the bait to drift freely in the current and per-
mit a fish to take the bait without being spooked when it feels the

weight of a sinker. The most popular sinkers used in such a rig for fishing on rocky bottoms are the egg-type slip sinker and the dipsey. For sand or mud bottoms, pyramid sinkers are best.

One problem with most fish-finder rigs, though, is that the fisherman must experiment with different weight sinkers to accommodate the currents. Usually this means changing weights several times. In an area where currents might vary at different times of the day— such as below hydroelectric dams—or on a river where the fisherman moves from spot to spot, weights must be changed frequently.

Changing sinkers on a fish-finder rig is a snap if you make your rig as follows. Run the terminal end of your fishing line through the eye of a snap swivel, then tie it to one end of a barrel swivel. To the other end of the barrel swivel, tie an 18- to 20-inch leader and hook. If you are fishing a rocky bottom, attach a dipsey sinker to the snap swivel. If you are fishing over sand or mud, use a pyramid sinker. Carry an assortment of sinkers in various weights, and change them as required to match the currents.

Use Locking Snap Swivels for Lunkers

The big chinook and I had been locked in battle for about half an hour, and, so far, all had gone well. The 8-foot rod was toughing it out under a strain it was built to take. The reel functioned as a duti-

When you're after the big ones, use snap swivels that lock shut and can't be pulled open by lunkers.

ful servant—giving line at the fish's command and taking it back again at mine. The 20-pound-test line was fresh and unfrayed when I made the cast. A large snap swivel was carefully tied with a strong palomar knot; snapped to it was a bright new #5 Mepps spinner. As I stood knee-deep in the clear, rushing river, I wondered what could possibly go wrong. I learned almost instantly as the rod tip sprang skyward and I recoiled several steps shoreward. When I reeled in I found the swivel still tied in place, but it had snapped open under the prolonged pressure and freed my fish.

It is always painful to lose a lunker, but every loss is a learning experience. This particular time I learned to use interlocking snap swivels when going after the big ones. I use the locking swivels now for all but the tiniest of lures and haven't lost a fish since to an open swivel.

Sinkers for Every Fishing Situation

Although you can tie anything to your line that will sink quickly—rocks, nuts, bolts, or scraps of metal—the well-equipped fisherman will have an assortment of styles and sizes of sinkers to fit every fishing situation he is likely to encounter. Among these might be sinkers for trolling, float fishing, bottom fishing, worm fishing, or drift fishing.

Heavy ball sinkers weighing several pounds are used in conjunction with downriggers for big-fish and big-water trolling in many parts of the country, but most fresh-water trolling is done with smaller weights that are streamlined to alleviate resistance and to get the lure down deep. Probably the best sinker for such purposes is the keel sinker that is molded around a chain swivel. Both the keel and the swivel help to prevent line twist, which can be disastrous in trolling, ruining a spool of line in minutes.

Sinkers used while float fishing depend largely on the type of rig being employed and include split-shot, clinch-on or wrap-on, and dipsey. When using small ball-type or stick floats, split-shot or small clinch-on sinkers are usually the best choice. Dipsey sinkers are best for use with large sliding floats. The dipsey is also the best choice for bottom fishing in rocky areas and deep water. The sliding-egg sinker is good for shallow water and makes an effective fish-finding rig when a small split-shot is pinched onto the line between the hook and the sinker to keep the sinker from sliding down to the

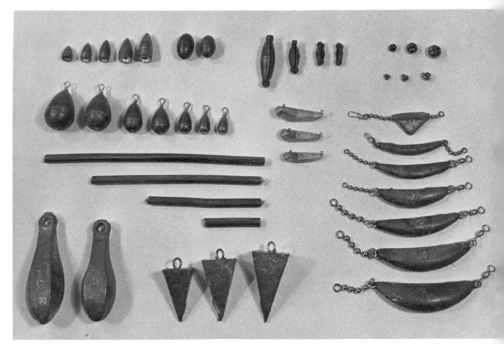

Pictured here are some of the most popular sinker designs. Along the top are sliding worm sinkers, egg sinkers, twist-on sinkers, and split-shot. Centered are dipsey, walking, and pencil sinkers. At the bottom are bank and pyramid sinkers, and at the right are keel-weighted trolling sinkers.

hook. The bullet-shaped worm sinker is similar to the egg sinker, but it is designed specifically for use with plastic worms and similar soft, artificial baits.

Another bottom-fishing sinker, designed for working live bait, is the walking sinker. The bait hook is tied to a leader—usually 10-pound-test and about 36 inches long—with a barrel swivel at the other end. The fishing line is slipped through the eye of the walking sinker and tied to the barrel swivel. The sinker is then slowly walked across the bottom, trailing the bait—such as a live night crawler or minnow—behind it. The design of the sinker makes it relatively snag-free and allows the fish to pick up the bait without feeling the weight of the sinker.

Drift fishing has been advanced to a science in the Northwest steelhead streams, but it is an effective technique in any free-flowing stream for nearly all species of stream-dwelling fish (see "Introduction To Drift Fishing," Chapter Eight). Egg-type and dipsey sinkers are good for drift fishing, as they won't snag up as readily as clinch-on and wrap-on sinkers. On small streams with ultralight tackle, split-shot sinkers often work well for drifting a bait. On the big steelhead streams, pencil sinkers are used most often for drift fishing.

Another sinker setup that's good for drift fishing is a dropper line on which large split-shot sinkers can be attached. The number of sinkers will vary according to currents. And if they snag up in the rocks, they will slide off the dropper to free the rest of the terminal tackle.

Hooks for Keeping Live Bait Alive

In the mid-sixties, I was occupied as a fishing bum in southern Florida. Here much of my light tackle work was with live shrimp that I preferred to hook through the head. An old-timer on Key Largo taught me a trick for keeping these critters alive longer by using extra-fine wire hooks.

Since then I have used these hooks for other live-bait fishing and have found them superior on all counts. I prefer the Aberdeen-style hook, because the rounded gap allows a hooked minnow, crawfish, or helgrammite more freedom of movement. In addition to being

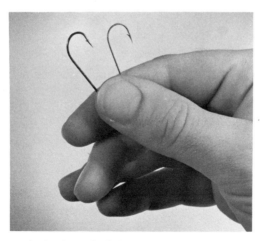

The hook on the left is a standard Carlisle
type. The extra-fine wire Aberdeen on
the right is far superior for live-bait fishing.

less damaging to live bait, the extra-fine wire Aberdeens are lighter in weight than other hooks of the same size and allow baits to be presented more delicately and naturally. I stock these hooks in sizes from #8 through #2/0 and rarely use anything else for live bait.

Set a Sharp Hook

It has been said before, but it bears repeating: Sharp hooks catch more fish, and you must take time to sharpen your hooks when they need it. If you are a fisherman who doesn't bother to keep your hooks sharp, you might find some comfort in the fact that you are part of a vast majority.

I make a habit of observing and questioning other fishermen, both as a way of learning new tricks and tips that take fish and as a way of recording the most frequent mistakes that fishermen make. One June day I was on a large gravel bar with thirty-two other fishermen. Fishing had been slow, so I decided to take advantage of the slack time by conducting one of my informal surveys.

"Pardon me," I said to the fellow a few feet downstream from me, "that last snag really dulled one of my hooks. Could I borrow your hook hone?"

"Uh, uh," he said, patting his pockets as if that would cause a hone to appear. "I don't seem to have one with me."

"Thanks just the same," I said, and continued down the gravel bar with the same question.

"A what?" one fisherman asked incredulously.

"Ask Marv," said another, but Marv didn't have one either.

Finally, I asked my partner if he had a hook hone with him. "Whatsa matter? Lose yours?" he asked.

"No. Just checking," I said. He shook his head, grinned, and held up a tiny file for my inspection.

If you are one of the few fishermen who carry some sort of a hook sharpening instrument, be it a small hone or a file, be sure that you are sharpening your hooks properly and frequently enough. You should check your hooks after every snag and after every fish landed or lost. And don't be misled by the erroneous advice to "keep your hooks needle sharp." Rather, they should be razor sharp.

If you hone a hook down to a fine needle point, it will dull too easily. Such points on hooks made of brittle steel will break off too readily; on soft hooks they tend to curl over. To properly sharpen a hook, hone it down to a sharp wedge in the shape of a triangle. Sharpen the left side, then the right. Then sharpen the front of the hook to form a three-sided wedge. Always sharpen by running the point toward the hone or file, never away from it.

Remember that 10 percent of the fishermen in this country catch 90 percent of the fish. Carrying a hook hone or a file and knowing how to use it is one step toward becoming part of the fish-catching minority.

Making Hooks Barbless

Any hook can be made barbless in seconds. Simply mash the barb against the shank with a pair of pliers. Barbless hooks are best when you want to turn fish loose unharmed. So next time you limit out and want to keep on fishing, make your hooks barbless and release your fish undamaged.

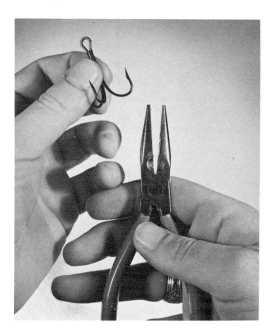

You can make any hook barbless by mashing the barb flat with pliers.

Salmon-Egg Hooks Aren't Just for Salmon Eggs

The single salmon-egg hook is a small, short-shank hook that is used for impaling single salmon eggs. The design of the hook permits it to be totally concealed in a tiny salmon egg, usually no more than a quarter of an inch in diameter. This hook, popular for trout and grayling, is an excellent choice for any bait fisherman who wants to conceal his hook in the bait. It is a top choice for use with a single red worm, tiny dough ball, or single kernel of corn for trout, panfish, and carp.

Salmon Hooks Aren't Just for Salmon

The short-shank salmon/steelhead hook used widely throughout the Northwest is also an ideal hook for the bait fisherman in other parts of the country. The short shank and wide gap of this style of hook enables the fisherman to totally conceal it in the bait he is using. The heavy gauge of the hook makes it one of the strongest hooks available.

This hook is an excellent choice for any live- or prepared-bait fish-

The snelled, single salmon-egg hook (top) is excellent for use with other baits such as whole kernel corn and small doughballs. The salmon/steelhead hook is remarkably strong and ideally suited to all types of bait fishing where hook strength and concealment are of paramount importance.

ing. But perhaps its greatest value away from the salmon and steelhead streams is as a catfish hook. Chicken entrails, dead fish, and stink baits can totally conceal the hook, and the hook is strong enough to hold the biggest of catfish.

Notes on Floats

There's only one rule regarding the selection of the right fishing float or bobber: Use the smallest one you can get by with. Just as some fish will spook when they feel the weight of a sinker, some will shy away from a bait that resists when the buoyancy of the float is too large. Slender, streamlined floats create the least resistance to a tugging fish.

For much of my bait fishing, I use stick-type floats that closely resemble the old quill floats but are made of plastic or balsa wood. Instead of changing to a bulkier, more buoyant float when using a bait that's too heavy for the stick bobber, I prefer to add another identical float—even two such floats offer little resistance to wary fish. I once coaxed a 5½-pound bass out of the shoreline weedbeds on an Ohio farm pond by drifting a live night crawler on a harness that was held off the bottom with two stick floats. The fish picked up the bait gently and moved off about 20 feet or so before I set the hook. A bulkier, more resistant float might well have sent him back to his weedy lair.

When I'm night fishing with bait, I use the same kind of floats, only they are painted fluorescent orange or chartreuse. These floats really stand out in the dim light of a lantern, even when cast beyond the apparent ring of gaslight. For deep-water fishing, I use a sliding float with a plastic bead and a piece of rubber band tied above it. The rubber band can be slid to any position on the fishing line, thus enabling me to fish at any depth I choose. The deeper I am fishing, though, the more weight I need to get a bait down fast. Rather than change to a sliding float of greater diameter, I use a longer float to sufficiently increase buoyancy. Slimmer floats slip more easily beneath the surface when a fish takes the bait.

There are times when the ball-type plastic float is the better choice. When using large, live fish for bait—such as big suckers for northern pike or big chub minnows for those lunker bass—it is essential that a float be bulky and buoyant enough to stay afloat when being tugged by the bait fish. Along with my ultralight spinning tackle, I carry several tiny, plastic ball floats, simply because they're more compact and less likely to get broken in the pocket of my fishing vest.

Just as anything that sinks can be used as a sinker, anything that floats can be used as a float. I suppose most of us, at one time or another, have had to tie a stick on a line to serve as a float. But it's far better to go prepared with the right kind of floats.

CHAPTER 4

Artificial Baits

Money-Saving Tips for Fly Tyers

My wife was with me recently when I was buying some fly-tying materials at a local sport shop. She stopped me when I reached for a spool of red wool yarn. "I have plenty of that left over from the afghan I just finished," she said. My wife has been doing various kinds of needlework about as long as I have been tying flies and has tossed out more scraps of yarn than I have used. Now she saves them for me, and I doubt that I will ever need to buy yarn again.

Before we discard the Christmas tree each year, I pick the pieces of tinsel from the branches and save them for fly tying. The new plastic tinsel is just right for this purpose. I have also found various kinds of feathers and synthetic furs in the hobby and craft departments of discount and department stores. For some reason, these materials are often more expensive in tackle shops.

Other sources of inexpensive materials are Goodwill stores, garage sales, flea markets, and auctions. Look for flowers and centerpieces made with feathers, old, feather-decorated ladies' hats, fur pieces, and ruffs. Buy your muskrat and other skins from a local trapper and save even more by eliminating all the middlemen.

Storing Fly-Tying Materials

If you read outdoor magazines, you will see recommendations from time to time about storing feathers, fur, and other fly-tying materials in air-tight containers along with mothballs or crystals to ward off vermin that would otherwise dine on such tidbits.

Since I find the smell of mothballs to be extremely offensive and have reasoned that some fish might react likewise, I prefer to use one of nature's own moth repellants—cedar. Cedar strips are available at most lumber companies and home-improvement centers and can be used to line cabinets and boxes where fly-tying materials are stored. The fragrant aroma of cedar keeps moths away, imparting no obnoxious odor to flies or tying materials.

New Life for Dry Flies

An old method for refurbishing flies is to hold them over the steam emitted from the spout of a kettle of boiling water. However, some flies won't fully respond to this treatment. Flies that have picked up fish slime, algae, and minute particles of other debris won't float properly and must be cleaned. Wash them gently in warm water and mild dishwashing soap. Then rinse them thoroughly in clear water. The clean, wet flies can be fluff-dried with an electric hair dryer. Hold the flies fast by imbedding their hook points in the edge of a Styrofoam cooler.

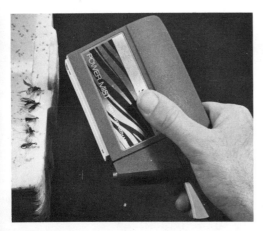

After washing soiled flies in mild dishwashing soap, rinse them thoroughly and fluff dry them with an electric hair dryer.

Kodak Photo Flo 200 makes an excellent dressing for wet flies, nymphs, and streamers.

Float 'em High; Sink 'em Deep

Unweighted nymphs, wet flies, and streamers are often reluctant to sink until they have become thoroughly saturated. Even then, some of them sink too slowly for my liking. Of course, the opposite seems to be true with dry flies; they always want to sink after a few casts. With the latter, the problem is easily solved by an application of one of the silicone dry-fly dressings, available in spray cans or applicator bottles from most tackle shops.

Wet flies will sink like trolling weights if they are first dipped into one of the photographic wetting agents, such as Kodak Photo-Flo 200. Pick up a small bottle at your local photo shop, and fill an empty dry-fly dressing bottle with the wetting solution. Label the bottle for wet flies, and find room for it in your fishing vest. You'll be pleased with the results.

The Versatile Indiana Spinner

The first fish I ever caught on an artificial bait was a fat and scrappy rock bass that fell for a small fly that was clipped behind an Indiana Spinner. I was just a young boy then, and my fishing budget

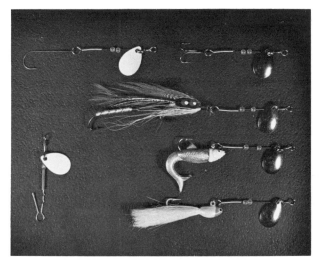

The Indiana Spinner is one of the most versatile of lures. It can be used with single or treble hook, fly, jig, or bait.

was a tight one. Even a couple of years later, my entire collection of artificial baits consisted of a ¼-ounce River-Runt Spook, a yellow Jitterbug of the same weight, a dozen assorted wet flies and streamers, and as many Indiana Spinners in various sizes and finishes.

I suppose what first drew me to the little Indiana Spinner, and caused me to stay with it, was its cost and its versatility. This little spinner can be used by itself, with only a single or treble hook attached. It is also a great attractor for use with a live worm or minnow. With small wet flies or streamers attached to them, they are deadly fare for panfish and trout. A small jig adds some casting weight to the spinner and makes it a great crappie and yellow perch lure. Used in combination with a larger streamer or small, plastic twist-tail bait, it becomes a top-notch smallmouth-bass lure.

I have probably caught more rock bass and smallmouths with the Indiana Spinner than any other kind of fish, but I have also taken plenty of bluegills, crappies, yellow perch, white bass, largemouth bass, several species of trout, grayling, and walleye. I have even caught pike on the Indiana Spinner/streamer combination, and have accidentally picked up channel catfish with the spinner and minnow.

Most often now I use the Indiana Spinner for my boondocks backpacking trips, simply because it is so easy to carry. A handful of these spinners will fit in the corner of one pocket of my fishing vest or will tuck away in my backpack, where they seem to take up no space at all. Used in conjunction with flies, streamers, jigs, and hooks, the Indiana Spinner is the most versatile lure I know.

Try "Ski-Fishing" a Weedless Spoon

On our annual trips to Wisconsin for the great walleye and white-bass fishing there, my partners, Ron and John, and I stayed at a duck-hunting lodge. At dawn each morning—before heading for the lake to troll for the walleyes and white bass—and every evening after we returned, we would fish the duck marshes for largemouth bass and northern pike. It was on the duck marshes that I learned from Ron one of the best techniques I have ever used for fishing in shallow, weedy waters.

Our tackle consisted of bass-weight spinning rods and reels and 10- or 15-pound-test line, to which was tied a snap swivel with a Johnson's Silver Minnow weedless spoon attached to it. The spoon was dressed with a strip of white pork rind. Of course, this is a fish-getting combination in many parts of the country, but our technique made this kind of spoon fishing even more exciting than using surface plugs for bass and pike. As we skulled our skiffs through the intertwining waterways of the marshes, working the weedbeds and floating bogs, we would search for small pockets or indentations that were almost certain to hold a hungry bass or pike. Then we would cast to the bog, trying to overshoot the edge of the water by a few inches. With our arms extended and the rods above our heads pointing straight up, we would gently coax our lures toward the water with gentle jerks. Rather than making a fish-frightening splash, the spoons would quietly plurp into the water.

This, in itself, is enough to improve any fisherman's catch; but it is only part of the technique. As soon as the spoon would touch the surface of the water, we would begin cranking the reel handle as fast as possible, keeping the rod top pointed up and the rod high. The rod would then be lowered gradually to an 11-o'clock position and the retrieve would be slowed to just the proper speed to keep the spoon skimming across the surface.

The spoon would leave a small V-shaped wake behind it as it skied toward the boat. But the most thrilling part of this kind of fishing is when a second wake appears behind the first. Those scant seconds between the time the wake of a following fish first appears and the time when the trailing wake catches up to the leading wake in a furious explosion of water and weeds are among the most exciting moments in fishing.

New Life for Old Spinners and Spoons

Beat-up, tarnished old spinners and spoons might take fish from time to time, but they aren't the fish attractors that bright new ones are. You'll catch more fish by keeping all your spinners and spoons looking and working like new ones. It's important to keep hooks sharp and to replace any that have become rusted or damaged beyond repair. It is also advisable to keep these lures looking good. It only takes a few minutes to perform first-echelon maintenance on the spinners and spoons you have used during a day of fishing. After they have air-dried, wipe the blades clean with a silicone cloth, being careful not to touch the blades with your fingers when you return the cleaned lures to your tackle box. Fingerprints will only speed up the tarnishing process.

Spinner blades and spoons that have become dull or tarnished from use can be returned to their original luster with chrome polish. Wet your thumb and forefinger with chrome polish, and clean the spinners and spoons with your fingers. After tarnish or rust has been worked out in this fashion, allow the lures to dry completely. Then remove the dried polish with a soft cloth. Severely rusted or tarnished lures might require several applications of chrome polish before their original sheen is returned.

On fishing trips you needn't carry chrome polish with you. As spoons and spinners begin to dull, brighten them up by cleaning them with toothpaste and polishing them with a soft cloth or with your handkerchief.

Tackle Tinkerer's Trays

If you're a fly tyer, lure maker, or tackle tinkerer, you can keep assorted hooks, swivels, spinner blades, split rings, screw eyes, and other hardware organized in plastic ice-cube trays. The compartments of the trays can be labeled according to the sizes of the components stored in them to further organize these materials.

Plastic ice-cube trays are far cheaper than storage cabinets and are readily available at most discount department stores. They can be stacked, one atop the other, and stored on shelves above your workbench. The contents can then be labeled on the fronts of the trays for ready reference.

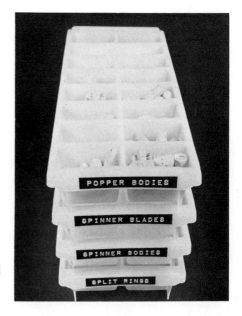

Plastic ice-cube trays are ideal for storing tackle-making supplies. Label the trays, and stack them one atop the other in your workshop.

Try Jig-Bait Fishing

There are times when jigs are among the best fish producers there are. They are especially productive during extremely hot or cold weather when fish are deep. But deep water is often dark water, where fish must rely on senses other than sight to find food. A jig bounced across the bottom will transmit vibrations that will attract fish, but something that will appeal to the fish's keen sense of smell will greatly improve the fisherman's odds. Add a piece of nightcrawler to the jig hook, or cut a fillet from a large minnow and hook that onto the jig. The tail of a shrimp or crawfish can also be effective.

Bits of bait can be added to any kind of jig to improve its fish-getting qualities in deep or murky waters. But another jig-bait technique emphasizes the bait and utilizes the jig to present it enticingly. For this, I use an undressed jig head and a whole nightcrawler or whole minnow. Minnows should be fresh but need not be alive. Large minnows on large jig heads are excellent bass baits; small minnows used on small jig heads are top producers of crappies and perch.

Add Glitter to Your Jigs and Fish to Your Stringer

A bit of flashy tinsel on a bucktail, feather, or nylon jig sometimes makes the difference between catching fish and merely exercising your casting arm. So it's a good idea to add a few strands of tinsel to several of your jigs. Often a jig consisting entirely of tinsel and lead will outshine all others. You can purchase tinsel from any sporting-goods store that sells fly-tying materials, or you can pick the tinsel off your Christmas tree and save it for dressing your jigs.

If you tie your own flies, you already know how to attach the tinsel. If you don't, it's no mystery; there are no fancy tools or techniques involved. You will need a fly-tying vise, thread, bobbin, a jar of head cement, a supply of tinsel, and a few jigs and jig heads.

After clamping a jig in the vise, tie the thread behind the head and make several wraps around the shank. If you are just adding tinsel to an already dressed jig, put two or three strands on each side, and wrap the ends with thread until they are secure. Tie the thread off with several half hitches, and dab a couple of drops of head cement onto the thread with a toothpick.

If you're dressing a jig head entirely with tinsel, the technique is the same. You simply keep adding tinsel, several strands at a time, until you have a full body built up behind the head. After you have tied off and cemented the thread, trim the tinsel with a pair of scis-

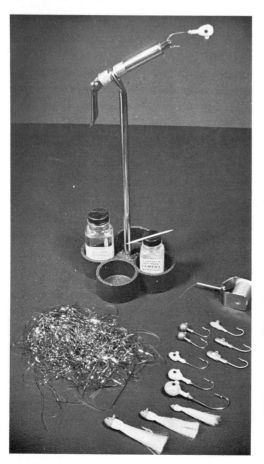

All the tools and materials required to add glitter to your jigs: a fly-tying vise, head cement, toothpick, thread and bobbin, tinsel, jig heads, and jigs.

Two examples of finished products: on the left is a jig with several strands of tinsel added to dressing; on the right is a jig tied entirely of tinsel.

sors to make it even. Sometimes that added glitter is all that's required to coax a persnickety fish into striking.

Mister Line Twister

It's a gratifying feeling to toss a lure into the sauerkraut and stick-ups and be reasonably sure that it won't get snagged. That's one of the beauties of fishing with weedless worm rigs. But if there is one thing more infuriating than snags, it has to be twisted monofilament line. An improperly rigged worm will spin like a whirligig, turning your line into a mass of snarling, monofilament vipers.

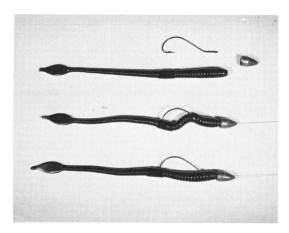

Rigging a worm.

The worm pictured above center is one such culprit. The one at the bottom of the photo is rigged properly, with no hump in the worm's body.

Some fishermen claim a spinning worm will catch bass when other rigs fail. If you want your worm to spin, and you don't want to put up with twisted line, tie a small barrel swivel into your line about 18 inches above the hook.

Slow That Worm Down and Catch More Bass

There are times when plastic worms will get few pickups. Often this is not a matter of the wrong color or the wrong size, but rather a worm that is being worked too fast. By slowing that worm down, you can often entice wary or lazy bass into striking. As you jig the worm along the bottom, hesitate longer between jerks of your rod. Although bass normally take a plastic worm as it flutters toward the bottom, there are times when they will watch the worm settle on the bottom and then take it only after careful observation.

Another way to slow that worm down is to move it only an inch or two at a time across the bottom. Just as there are times when a bass will only take a surface lure that barely twitches on the surface, there are similar times when a barely twitching worm will take the most fish.

Tips on Shallow-Water Worming

Working shallow and relatively clear water with plastic worms is a far more delicate art than the usual kind of worm plunking. Under such conditions, bass will spook more easily and will more readily shy away from a plastic worm that isn't presented properly.

Basically, shallow-water worming calls for a more cautious approach, accurate and quiet presentation of the bait, and lighter tackle than normally associated with worming. In this kind of fishing, you will be casting toward visible cover—shoreline deadfalls, partially submerged trees and branches, weedbeds, and lily pads. Any approach made by boat should always be quiet, but in this case, it is of extreme importance. Quietly skull the craft or allow it to drift toward the fishing grounds with the aid of the wind. Use a trolling motor sparingly and only when necessary to correct position or to set up a good drift.

A low visibility, 10-pound-test line is a good choice. Use small worms—4- to 6-inches long—and the lightest sinker you can get by with. Make your casts carefully and conscientiously. If you can lay the worm on shore or atop a bed of lily pads and then coax it gently into the water, all the better.

There have been times when I have had to go to even lighter line for this kind of sport. A lighter-action rod is a must then, too; a heavy-action worm rod would snap the line when I rear back to set a hook. For this delicate kind of worming, I use a light-action rod and 6-pound-test line. Instead of the usual worm-type sliding sinker, I use a split-shot sinker clamped over the knot at the hook. This is enough weight to sink the worm head first, but not enough to spook a bass. With such light tackle, some fish are lost to snags. But I would rather lose a few and catch a few than not even be able to coax one fish into taking my bait.

Trailers for Your Worms

When you're getting a lot of pickups on plastic worms but aren't connecting, chances are that finicky fish are just taking the tail of the worm instead of sucking down the whole thing. Generally, you have two ways of solving this problem. First, you can open the bail or release the spool of your reel and let the fish take the worm. This will usually work if fish are running with the worms, but it won't work if they are just picking them up by their tails and then dropping them. This technique often results in hooks being imbedded deeper in the fishes' gullets, which makes harmless release unlikely.

The other choice you have is to use a rigged worm. These are generally available with a three-hook arrangement, with hooks located at the head, center, and tail of the worm. Such rigs are usually too stiff and lifeless for my liking. And they get snagged up too easily.

I prefer to keep several worms that have been rigged with trailers in my tackle box. Instead of sewing the trailing hook into the body of the worm, which impedes the action and liveliness of the worm, I make a two-hook rig with a 2/0- or 4/0-worm hook up front, trailed by a #1 hook. The trailer hook is attached to the leading hook with a short strand of clear, 6-pound-test monofilament line. Such rigs greatly improve the catch on those days when the bass are tail-nibbling.

Recycling Damaged Plastic Worms

In my worm box, I carry a disposable cigarette lighter that I use to make minor repairs on plastic worms that have become damaged. By holding a partially torn worm just above the flame of the lighter, I am usually able to mend the tear.

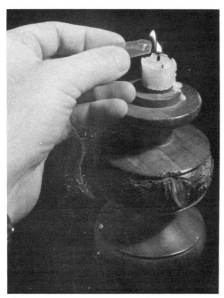

To repair a tear in a plastic worm, hold it over the flame of a candle until the plastic melts and fuses.

Most often, I just lay the damaged worms aside for later repair. After quite a few wounded worms have accumulated, I go to my workshop where I use a candle to make repairs. Those with holes and tears too big to mend, or those that are broken in two, get trimmed down to grub size. The tail sections of large worms are usually best for this purpose. After I trim them to lengths of 1 to 3 inches with a pair of scissors, I hold the head of the new grub above the flame of the candle and rotate it. As the plastic melts, the head becomes rounded off, similar to a store-bought grub.

These grubs are great for use on jig heads or as additions to spinner baits. Damaged 10- and 12-inch worms can often be recycled into usable 6- or 8-inch worms.

Match Your Lures With the Forage Fish

To be sure, countless hundreds of lures look nothing like anything that exists in nature, let alone in the confines of a fish's habitat; yet these lures catch fish. When I am fishing unfamiliar waters, and often on waters familiar to me, I try to match my lures with the forage fish found in those waters.

Lures on left are good choices where bluegills, perch, and other panfish are primary forage fish. Lures in center are best where shad comprise the predators' diet. Lures at right will produce where slender-bodied minnows and fry of trout grayling and similar fish are preyed upon.

Basically, forage fish are of two designs—long and slender or short and squat. In waters where bass feed largely on bluegills, I select chunky lures that most closely resemble bluegills in shape and color. If there are perch living in these waters, lures resembling small perch will also be good producers.

If I am fishing an impoundment where shad comprise the bulk of the predator's diet, I will select from the many shad-type lures in my tackle box until I am able to learn what the local preferences are. In waters where there are minnows and fry of slender-bodied fish for the predators to feed on, I will use similar lures—such as the slender Rapalas and Rebels. These baits are also good choices in northern waters where predators might take them for the fry of trout and grayling.

Split Rings Can Improve a Lure's Action

Swimming-type plugs should never be used with snap swivels, because the swivel can interfere with the lure's built-in action. Many fishermen tie their lines directly to their lures instead. But a bulky knot can also impede the action of a swimming type lure, and a tight knot can seriously interfere with a lure's side-to-side swimming motion.

If you find that a plug simply isn't acting as it should, try attaching a split ring to the line eye and tying your line to the split ring. This should solve the problem.

Use Lure Snaps for Quick Changes

One advantage to a snap swivel is that it prevents line twist when using spinners and spoons. Another advantage is that it permits quick change of lures without the necessity of retying. Since snap swivels should only be used with spinners, spoons, spinner baits, and similar lures whose action won't be impaired by their use, most fishermen find that fishing with plugs doesn't allow for quick lure change. Rather than put up with tying new knots, they will stick to one lure even when they know they ought to change.

If you think for a minute that tournament fishermen restrict themselves to one lure or that they put up with all that knot tying, you're wrong. They, and other serious fishermen, use lure snaps. These small wire snaps allow lures to be changed quickly, but they

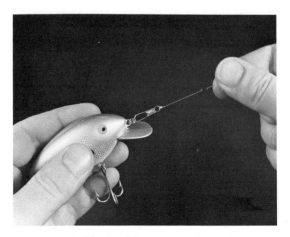

Lure snaps enable the fisherman to change
lures quickly, yet they do not impair the
action of the lures.

don't seriously interfere with the action of the lures the way snap
swivels do.

Use Swivels or Snaps on Jigs

If, when you are fishing with a jig, you tie your line directly to
the jig with one of the traditional knots—such as the improved
clinch knot or palomar knot—you are not getting the best possible
action out of the jig. You should use a snap swivel or lure snap
that will allow the jig to flutter up and down as it should.

Carry Replacement Hardware

You should carry an assortment of hooks and split rings in your
tackle box for replacing damaged hardware on your lures. If you
don't carry a tool kit in your tackle box, you will need to include a
small jeweler's screwdriver and a small pair of hobbyist's longnose
pliers for replacing hardware on some lures.

Some plugs have their hooks held on with hardware attached by
tiny screws. On many lures, though, hooks are attached with split
rings. Although hooks on split rings can be replaced without tools
(use your thumb nail), an inexpensive pair of split-ring pliers simplifies the job. Hooks held on with screw eyes can be removed by first

unscrewing the screw eye, then bending out the eye until enough clearance exists for exchanging the damaged hook for a good one.

Make 'em Weedless

There are times when the best fishing is in weedbeds, lily pads, and flooded timber. In these settings, only the weedless lure will offer trouble-free fishing. But sometimes the fish just don't want anything to do with the old weedless standbys. That is when many fishermen turn to other favorite lures, usually spending a lot of time yanking out snags, losing baits, and uttering indelicate incantations to the muse of water weeds and deadfalls.

To avoid such hangups, carry some weedless hardware along with you and convert your favorite plugs, spoons, and spinners on the spot in seconds. All you need is a bunch of #1- and #3-split rings that will fit most lures, an assortment of weedless hooks, and a pair of small longnose pliers (split-ring pliers optional). Lures that already have split rings holding the hooks can be simply converted by separating the coils of the rings with a thumbnail or split-ring pliers and replacing the non-weedless hooks with weedless ones. Those that have small screw eyes holding the original hooks can be converted in one of two ways. One method requires the removal of the original hooks by prying open the eyes of the screw eyes with the

Many lures can be made weedless if you carry weedless hooks, split rings, and pliers with you.

pliers. After attaching the weedless hooks, use the pliers to squeeze the eyes shut again. A second method gives you the ability to convert such lures frequently: remove the original hooks from the screw eyes and attach split rings and weedless hooks.

If you go prepared to make it weedless, practically any lure in your tackle box—spoon, spinner, popper, deep or shallow runner —can become a real fish getter in the weeds.

Three Ways to Fool Short-Strikers

There were three of us fishing the same pool. We were drifting spawn-bag baits for big chinook salmon, but we had a fish giving us problems. All three of us had had our spawn bags squashed by what we figured was a rainbow trout. Trout usually followed the salmon upstream and fed on the salmon eggs, and we had caught several good rainbows while using spawn bags.

But all this critter would do was grab the spawn bag and squash it, which, of course, ruined the bait. I was getting tired of feeding this fish and growing even more weary of tying new spawn bags. Finally, I attached a split ring to the shank of the treble hook on the Mepps lure I was using and added a trailer hook to that. I then hooked on a fresh spawn bag to the main hook and imbedded the trailer hook in the bottom of the bag.

As my next drift approached the spot where the nuisance fish had been doing his number, I felt one quick tug and reared back to set the hook. I was solidly into what felt like a pretty decent rainbow but which turned out to be a 4-pound jack chinook. We had no more trouble that day with squashed spawn bags. And we had the short-striker for dinner that evening.

Another time I was fishing off a dock, beneath which was a school of Dolly Varden. I was using a small Dardevle spoon, and the water was clear enough for me to watch the fish strike. The biggest fish in the bunch followed the lure several times, but each time a smaller fish got to it first. Twice the big Dolly followed the hooked fish as it fought. I was determined to catch the big one, so I tied on a second Dardevle. After three casts, I again coaxed the big char from beneath the dock. Two smaller Dollies approached and one of them took the leading spoon. The big Dolly Varden then shot forward and grabbed the trailing spoon. What a fight that was! (I have used a similar technique by double rigging jigs when fishing for crappies and perch and have had much success with it.)

One of the most disturbing kinds of short-strikers, though, are trout and panfish that grab the tail feathers or hair on poppers and dry flies. The easiest way to fool these critters is to trim back the tail material. When they come up to nibble next time, they'll be nibbling on a hook instead. Just remember to set it quickly.

No Lure Too Big or Too Small

Many years ago, I was fishing for bass on a small Ohio lake when I noticed something that looked like a fish with a tail at each end swimming on the surface. I moved the boat near enough to retrieve the strange-looking creature with my dip net. What it turned out to be was a small bass that had tried to swallow a bluegill nearly the same size. He managed to get the bluegill down, head first, about half way, but the bluegill was too big for the bass to swallow. It was also impossible for the bass to spit the bluegill out, because the spines in the dorsal fin were caught in the corner of the bass' mouth. I worked the spines loose with the edge of a knife blade and returned both fish to the water, where they made speedy retreats from one another.

I decided on the spot that there must be no such thing as a lure that is too large, and I have proved that time and again. I have caught small bass, walleye, and pike that were no larger than the lures I was using. On one occasion, I was casting a large surface plug in a Florida canal when a big shellcracker (redear sunfish) smashed the plug. When I landed the fish, I noticed that it couldn't have possibly gotten the big plug in its tiny mouth.

At the other extreme are the big fish that take tiny baits. More than one trout or grayling fisherman, using a small spinner or spoon on ultralight gear, has been surprised when a 30- or 40-pound chinook decided to take the lure. I know of another similarly surprised angler who was fishing for shad with 4-pound-test line and a little shad dart and managed to hook into a 25-pound striped bass.

Recently I was bass fishing at one of my favorite lakes and had tried everything in my tackle boxes without raising a bass. It was an unusually hot day for our coastal country, and I figured that if I was going to take any fish home with me, I would have to go for panfish instead. So I switched to my ultralight tackle and tied on a #0

Mepps spinner. I found a likely looking cove and shot a cast for the shoreline weeds. A half-dozen turns of the reel handle and I was fast into a cartwheeling largemouth. That little Mepps took two more bass from the same cove.

I remain convinced that there's no lure too big or too small. So if one isn't working, try the other; you might be pleasantly surprised.

CHAPTER 5

Natural and Prepared Baits

Tips on Seining Bait

When I was a young boy in Ohio, I earned money to buy my fishing tackle by seining bait for a local bait and tackle shop. Most summer mornings, from about age ten until I was old enough to drive, I would gather up my fishing tackle, minnow seine, and bait bucket, climb on my bicycle, and head for a nearby creek or river before daybreak.

During those outings I learned a few things about seining bait that have helped me immensely in later years. For instance, after using several different widths of seines, I gained a preference for a 6-footer. Although a 4-foot-wide, one-man seine is certainly easy for anyone to handle, there are times when additional width is essential. I used an 8-foot, two-man seine one summer but found it too cumbersome to handle by myself. For much of my seining the 6-foot seine was too wide, but it was no problem to roll a foot or so of the net around each pole and reduce it to a comfortable width.

I have used a number of materials for seine poles and have found rake handles or shovel handles (the kind used on long-handled shovels) to be the best. These are generally made of ash, which is a hard and durable wood, and are readily available at any hardware or discount department store. Handle length is a matter of personal preference, but I have found poles that extend a foot or two above the top of the seine to be perfect for seining most baits.

Before attaching the seine to the poles, the poles will need two coats of polyurethane varnish to help preserve them, and they will need to be revarnished at the end of each season. It is important that holes be drilled in the poles near the bottom and toward the top so that the seine can be securely tied in these spots to keep it from sliding on the poles. Then, with small lengths of twine, the seine should be secured about every 6 inches along the poles to prevent it from bowing in a current. I secure the bottom of the seine 1 inch from the bottom of the poles. If it is attached any higher on the poles, too much bait will escape under the net.

Most seines are made of nylon now, which is an extremely tough and long-lasting material that will not wet rot as the old, fabric seines would. But seines should still be rinsed off with fresh water after each use and allowed to dry before storage, mainly to protect the poles. Nylon nets should not be stored in direct sunlight, as this cause them to deteriorate. It is also a good idea to check a seine for small holes after each use; these are easy to mend. An unchecked hole soon grows larger and will eventually ruin the seine.

The helgrammite, which is the larval stage of the dobsonfly, was always my favorite stream-dwelling bait, mainly because it is one of the best natural baits there is for smallmouth bass. They commanded high prices at the bait shop, but are relatively easy to capture if you know the technique.

Helgrammites are found beneath rocks in shallow riffles of free-flowing streams. The easiest way to catch them is with a partner who stands downstream with a seine spread in front of him and the seine poles planted firmly in the bottom so that the weighted end of the seine hugs the floor of the stream. You simply start at the head of the riffle and move slowly toward your partner, turning rocks over so that the current will carry dislodged helgrammites into the seine. In this sort of operation, a rake or fork spade comes in handy for overturning all but the largest of rocks. If the riffles are long, just work a 20- or 30-foot section at a time, and check your seine after each section is worked.

If you are seining by yourself, start at the head of the riffle and work your way downstream. When you begin, open the seine to its full width and extend the poles well out in front of you. Then walk toward the seine, turning rocks over with your feet. As you near the seine, walk the poles downstream in front of you, being careful not to lift the seine off the bottom any farther than necessary. Check your seine frequently, and work the riffles slowly and completely. I have often caught several dozen helgrammites from one stretch of riffles within less than an hour of careful seining.

In most parts of the country, crawfish constitute a substantial portion of many fishes' diets. Consequently, they're a favorite natural bait. Yet most recommendations I have heard or read about for catching crawfish are the least productive. Many fishermen gather them in a fashion similar to the one I described for catching helgrammites. While crawfish can be caught this way, there are methods that are far more effective.

As crawfish grow they shed their shells and, for a brief time, will be as soft as plastic worms. The soft craw is one of the best natural baits to be found anywhere. Medium-size soft craws—about 2 inches in length—are great smallmouth-bass baits, and the largest ones are among the best baits I have ever used for big channel cats. I have found, though, that the soft craws occur in greater abundance away from the mainstream and riffles, in quiet sloughs and backwaters. There I use the seine poles to poke and prod mud bottoms and undercut banks. Sheltered marinas are often good spots, too; here seine poles should be poked around the shore ends of docks, piers, and pilings.

If I want to gather the greatest number of crawfish in the shortest possible time, I seine them at night when they are out of their lairs and are actively feeding. I locate small pools and sloughs during the day so that I can work them over safely at night with some knowledge of their size, shape, and depth. When seining at night, I always have a partner with me for safety's sake.

I always use the soft craws first, since they're best. Next in line are the peelers or paperback craws. These are crawfish whose shells have become pliable before shedding. You can peel the shells off of these crawfish and find beneath a soft craw to present to your favorite quarry.

Of the hard craws I catch, I keep all up to about 2½ inches to use as live bait. I remove the pincers from the largest of these, because I have found fish will take them more readily, and they're easier to handle. I return to the water most of the really big hard craws, unless I want to keep some for their tails. These tails can be pinched off and kept frozen for later use as catfish and panfish bait. I leave the shells on the tails until I'm ready to use them, but I peel them before I offer them to the fish.

Although minnows can be found in just about any part of free-flowing streams, I prefer to seine them in the small, quiet backwaters and in small creeks that tend to pothole during the summer months. Here, again, careful seining is necessary to keep from frightening and scattering the schools. If you take your time making an approach, you will be able to catch all the minnows you can use with one or two scoops of the seine.

If I'm seining by myself, I use my seine at its full width, approaching the pool slowly without stirring the water up too much. I inch my way toward the minnows, herding them into a compact school near the head of the pool or a bank where their escape route has been cut off by my approach.

If the pool is a fairly broad one that might allow the minnows to escape ahead of the seine, I use an old trick I learned from a professional bait dealer when I was a boy. Before wading into the pool, I gather up a half-dozen or so small pebbles that I keep in my right hand. When I have made a cautious approach and have the minnows gathered in a school, I stand perfectly still and work a pebble into the crook of my forefinger. Then I use my thumb to flip the pebble —as a kid would shoot a marble—so that it plunks into the water beyond the already nervous school of minnows. (I'm careful to make no move that will spook the minnows.) When that pebble splashes into the water, more often than not the school will turn and flee right toward the seine. One quick scoop can net dozens of squiggling bait fish.

The Best Way to Transport Helgrammites and Crawfish

Since helgrammites and crawfish come out of the water, many fishermen reason that they should be kept in water if they are to stay alive. While you're on a stream where you can keep the perforated section of a bait bucket in the water, this is a fine way to keep such bait alive. But if you are transporting helgrammites or crawfish or are storing them overnight or longer, there's a better way.

These live baits need not be submerged in water to survive, but they must be kept damp and cool. They can be kept alive for several days in a fiber Bait Canteen to which has been added sphagnum moss and corrugated cardboard in alternating layers. First, soak the moss and pieces of cardboard boxes in water until thoroughly saturated. Then squeeze out excess moisture. Line the bottom of the bait container with an inch or so of damp moss, and put about a dozen helgrammites or crawfish in the moss. Cover it with a sheet of damp cardboard and add another layer of moss, more bait, and more cardboard until the container is full. Leave about an inch of air space at the top. For best results, store the Bait Canteen in a refrigerator. While traveling to your fishing spot and while fishing, drape wet burlap over it to keep it cool by evaporation.

If you are transporting a large quantity of helgrammites or crawfish in hot weather, use a large Styrofoam cooler or Styrofoam bait container. Before putting the moss, cardboard, and bait inside, line the bottom of the cooler with small plastic bags of ice cubes. The ice will keep the bait cool for hours, and the plastic bags will prevent the bottom layer of bait from being inundated with ice water.

Stop Helgrammite Snags

Although the helgrammite is one of the best natural baits for smallmouth bass and large stream trout, many fishermen find them a nuisance to use, since they seem to snag up on just about every drift. The helgrammite uses its tail to cling to rocks. Snipping off the very tip of the tail with a pair of scissors or nail clippers will markedly reduce the number of snags without harming the bait.

Dead Minnows for Live Channel Cats

When you're fishing with live minnows, don't discard the ones that die. They make excellent bait for catfish. Channel cats are particularly fond of dead minnows. I use three different techniques for hooking dead minnows when fishing for catfish. If the minnows are small, crappie-size baits, I load a long-shank hook with them. I run the hook through the heads, just behind the eyes, and fill the hook with them, sometimes using as many as a half-dozen minnows. There are times when such a gob of dead minnows is dynamite on channel cats.

I hook the large minnows individually in two different ways. First, I select a hook size and design to fit the size of the dead minnow. If it is a particularly large bait, I will use a long-shank Carlisle-type hook. For smaller baits I use short-shank hooks. Normally, I use a two-hook rig. One hook will be baited with a curled minnow. I simply insert the point of the hook into the minnow's mouth, and run the bait up on the hook until the hook is completely concealed —the hook gap curls the aft end of the minnow. If you have ever noticed, some fish curl up in this fashion when they die, so this is a perfectly natural presentation of a dead minnow.

The second hook gets a straight minnow, but with a finishing touch that really entices hungry cats. I insert the hook into the mouth of the minnow, as above, but I bring it out of the anus and continue sliding the bait up until the hook shank is concealed. I then turn the hook and embed the point in the body near the tail. Before I cast it out, I squash the minnow with a rock or my boot. There are times when catfish just can't resist mangled minnows.

Sometimes minnows that have been allowed to "ripen" during the heat of the day will be great producers. Other times, only the freshest of dead minnows will do the trick. It only takes a little experimentation to find the right combination.

Ice Fishing with Minnows

Live minnows are one of the best baits to use when ice fishing for such species as yellow perch and walleyes. But a minnow bucket full of minnows can become a bucket full of dead minnows if allowed to freeze. And if you've ever kicked over a bucket of minnows, you already know that it is impossible to gather them up off the ice before they freeze solid.

Keep your minnows in a large Styrofoam cooler that is about half full of water and put one or two large rocks in the bottom. The Styrofoam will insulate the water and keep it from freezing—provided you keep the lid on the cooler—and the rocks in the bottom will keep it from tipping over and spreading your bait all over the ice.

Tips on Transporting Live Minnows

You can keep minnows alive on long trips if you keep the water cool and aerated. If you don't have the equipment for doing this, use the largest Styrofoam cooler you can make room for (or several, if space permits), and don't crowd the minnows. Fill the cooler(s) half full of water and put in several dozen minnows. Drop about a dozen ice cubes into the water, and check your bait about every hour, adding more ice cubes as necessary. The ice cubes will keep the water reasonably cool, and as they melt they will help aerate the water. The water sloshing about in the partially filled cooler will also help to aerate it.

Fishing with Cut Bait

While cut bait is used extensively by salt-water fishermen everywhere, I rarely ever see fresh-water fishermen making use of it. Yet such baits are top producers of catfish. Some of the best bait fishes for this purpose are big chub minnows, small suckers, and carp. In states where it is legal, bluegills and other sunfish are also excellent bait fish.

Sometimes catfish will take both chunk and strip baits with equal relish; other times they will show a preference for one over the other. The best way to determine such preferences is to use a rig with two dropper hooks—one baited with a chunk of fish, the other with a strip.

To make chunk baits, simply steak the bait fish. Begin by cutting off the head, and then make cross-section cuts the full length of the fish. If the bait fish is small, whole steaks can be used. Steaks from larger bait fish can be further divided into several baits each. To make strip baits, just cut fillets from each side of the bait fish. Use whole fillets from small bait fish and cut larger fillets into strips. Whether you are using chunk or strip baits, be sure to leave the skin on; it will help to keep the bait on the hook.

The size of your baits should be determined, somewhat, by the size of the fish you're after. If you are fishing for those giant flathead or channel catfish in one of our major rivers or impoundments, you will want to use big baits and heavy tackle. A whole fillet or steak from a foot-long sucker isn't too large for this kind of fishing.

If you expect to catch catfish that will normally run from 2 to 5 pounds, and an occasional fish of 8 or 10 pounds, your chunk baits should approximate 1-inch cubes and can be just slightly larger. Your strip baits should be about ½-inch thick, no wider than 1 inch, and cut to lengths from 2 to 4 inches.

An added bonus to cut-bait fishing is the fun you can have catching your bait fish on ultralight tackle.

Add a Worm

There's an old trick that smallmouth-bass fishermen use when the fish aren't eagerly taking live minnows. Before hooking the minnow through the lips, they will put a small red worm on the hook. This combination is then allowed to drift with the current into a likely looking pool where, more often than not, it will entice a picky smallmouth that wasn't interested in the minnow alone. The same technique also works with catfish. You can add a nightcrawler to a hook with a chunk bait or strip bait. You can do the same with whole dead minnows.

One of my favorite ways to rig a dead minnow and nightcrawler is on a long-shank hook. I insert the hook in the minnow's mouth and slide the fish up the hook shank, bringing the hook point out the anus. With the minnow straightened out and the hook gap now almost fully exposed, I thread on a fat, squirming nightcrawler. I like to keep this trick up my sleeve for those times when nothing else works; it has taken some dandy catfish for me.

The Right Way to Keep Worms

It's easy to keep a constant supply of nightcrawlers, red worms, or angleworms on hand if you have several well-built worm boxes in which to house them. Such boxes can be constructed from ½-inch plywood and can be made in dimensions to fit your own needs. Or, if you haven't the time or inclination to make your own, there are a number of excellent worm boxes that are available commercially, are relatively inexpensive, and are most efficient. Whether you make your own or buy them, there will be times when you want to empty them—either in search of worms or in order to clean the boxes out—so remember that several smaller boxes are easier to manage than one giant box.

Some fishermen will bury their worm boxes in a yard or garden, reasoning that during hot weather the soil will keep the worms cool. However, if you live in a part of the country where summer temperatures are consistently in the 80s and 90s, this isn't the best means of cooling your worms. In the heat of a summer day, try digging worms out of the top 2 or 3 feet of soil. That's when worms bore deep into the ground to keep cool; worms confined to a hot worm box just perish.

Worms will be healthiest when kept within a temperature range from 50 to 70 degrees. An old refrigerator is ideal for keeping worms cool and healthy, but is not the only way. You can store worm boxes in a cool basement. If you have no basement, keep them in a garage or on a porch or patio out of the direct sunlight. Remember to provide adequate ventilation and cooling through evaporation.

To assure proper circulation, any worm box should have plenty of holes in the sides. If you build your own boxes, you will want to line them with fine-mesh fiberglass screen to prevent the worms from escaping through the ventilation holes. One commercial worm box that I like is made of Styrofoam and resembles a cooler with vents in the sides.

Fill your boxes within 4 to 6 inches of the top with damp worm bedding. On top of that spread a layer of damp sphagnum moss about 2-inches deep. Then lay several sheets of damp corrugated cardboard or newspapers over the moss. The moss will not only retain moisture, but it will also scour the worms and toughen them. The cardboard or newspaper facilitates the cooling of the box as water evaporates from it.

Worm boxes do not require constant attention, but they should be checked regularly—during hot weather at least once a day. The bedding should be kept damp, not wet. The cardboard or newspapers that lay atop the bedding should be dampened as they begin to dry. When it's hot, I do this by tossing in a handful of ice cubes. This helps keep the box cool and replaces evaporated moisture as the ice melts.

A heat wave can be disastrous for your worm supply, so some special attention is necessary when the temperature soars. If you keep your worms on a porch or patio, you can combat the extreme heat by draping several layers of sopping-wet burlap over the boxes during the heat of the day. In a basement or garage, use a small electric fan to circulate the air around and through your worm boxes and to speed up the cooling evaporation of moisture. Set the fan several feet away from and slightly above the boxes for optimum circulation. Check the bedding, moss, and cardboard or newspapers frequently and moisten them as often as necessary—usually daily.

Make Your Own Worm Bedding

It's easy to make your own high-quality worm bedding. Begin by filling a tub or sink with cold water and adding newspaper that has been shredded in small pieces. When the shredded paper has become totally saturated, remove handfuls and wring out all excess moisture. I like to add equal quantities of sphagnum moss that has been moistened in the same manner. Once the newspaper and moss have been mixed together, I add a cup of coffee grounds and a cup of corn meal to as much bedding as it takes to fill a five-gallon bucket and mix it thoroughly.

The healthier your worms are the more active they will be—and that's when they'll eat plenty. You should examine the bedding about once a week, and as the visible corn meal disappears, feed them more. They will also eat fine cracker meal and powdered milk. I make new bedding and change all the boxes two or three times a year, depending on the level of activity and the population of worms held in the boxes. And whenever I discover the bedding contaminated with insects of any kind, I replace it immediately.

The Correct Way to Hook a Worm

Angling books and magazine articles, since time immemorial, have misled countless thousands of fishermen on the seemingly simple task of hooking a worm. In fact, one of the newest fishing books that I recently added to my own library shows the reader seven ways to hook a worm—all of them wrong. The first angling scribe to hook a worm incorrectly and tell others about it might have known a lot about fishing, but he sure didn't know anything about worms.

Whether you're hooking up a bunch of worms on one hook, delicately impaling a single worm on a hook, or running three hooks of a harness through a nightcrawler, there's one rule to remember: NEVER hook a worm through the collar—that light-colored band that appears about a third of the way down from the worm's head. Beneath that collar is the worm's nerve center, and a worm hooked there will become lifeless far sooner than it should. If you avoid this critical life-support area, a worm can live for hours. So hook a worm above the collar or below it—never through it.

A Gang of Crawlers for Lunker Largemouth

One reason worms have been an all-time favorite bait among anglers for centuries is that fish like them. And the reason fish like them, we must assume, is because they taste good. But taste is closely related to the sense of smell, and the fact is that worms emit an odor that is enticing to fish. This makes them one of the best baits to use when fish are finicky or sluggish.

During the heat of summer and the chill of winter, when bass aren't as inclined to go chasing after a fast-moving bait as they might be during the spring and fall months, worms can be the answer to filling a stringer. One technique I have used successfully for big bass during the sluggish times of the year is the presentation of a gang of nightcrawlers that I move at a snail's pace in search of fish.

For this technique, I use spinning tackle and 6-pound-test line. The light line is important because fish have time to look a slow-moving bait over; I want a line that's hard to detect. I use a three-hook nightcrawler harness. In roily water, I use the commercial harnesses that come with bright beads and flashy, spinner blades. But if the water is clear, I tie my own harnesses, using only 10-pound-test monofilament and bronzed hooks, with 8 inches of line above the top hook to function as a shock leader.

I impale a large and lively nightcrawler on each of the three hooks by running a hook into the upper body of each worm, about an inch from the tip of the head. A foot up the line from the harness, I squeeze on a split-shot sinker, and above that I add one or two slender stick floats that can be adjusted to fish at various depths. If I'm fishing depths of more than 8 feet, I use a small sliding float.

I like to keep the bait about a foot or two off the bottom, and I work it parallel to the shoreline. After determining the depth of the water—with a depthfinder, sounding line, or past experience—I make a long cast parallel to shore, preferably where there is visible cover. When the bait has settled to its proper depth, I begin a retrieve that consists of one slow turn of the reel handle, followed by a pause of approximately 10 seconds, another turn of the handle, another pause, and so on until the bait has been retrieved. My next cast will be farther out from the first one by about 5 feet, with the float adjusted, if necessary, to keep the bait at the right depth.

Rather than a savage strike, this technique encourages a gentle pickup. Usually you will only notice your float moving off slowly and often without even sinking beneath the surface, unless the bass is heading for deeper water. The fish should notice no resistance. That's why you should open the bail of your reel and give him plenty of line, because he may have only picked up the bait to carry it off somewhere to be devoured. It takes a lot of patience, but I find it helps to count to fifteen before setting the hooks, and I hook more than I miss by doing this.

This is one of my favorite methods on shallow lakes and farm ponds, where the bass, unable to escape temperature extremes by moving to deeper water, become lethargic and difficult to catch. A small pond or a small cove of a larger lake can be worked completely in this manner, but it might take a couple of hours to do it right. Chances are, though, if there are bass in the area, they'll end up on your stringer.

A Gob of Crawlers for Big Catfish

Large catfish also like their worms in quantities but seem to prefer them presented a bit differently. Instead of a harness, I use a big, long-shank hook—usually a Carlisle in #1/0, #2/0 or #4/0 sizes. I fill this hook up completely with fat nightcrawlers, impaling each worm twice. Each hook can hold as many as a half-dozen crawlers. This bait can be used with fish-finder rigs (see Chapter Three). For night fishing it can be quite effective in shallow water, held just off the bottom with a fluorescent-painted float.

Mealworms—No Fuss, No Muss, Year-Round Bait

One of the cleanest and easiest live baits to use is the mealworm. It is an excellent bait for trout, whitefish, smallmouth bass, and all sorts of panfish.

To hook a mealworm, use a small, short-shank hook—size 8, 10, or 12, depending on how big the worm is. Insert the hook point just beneath the worm's head, and slip the worm up around the hook gap all the way to the hook eye, entirely concealing the hook. Another way particularly well-suited to persnickety stream trout is to use a #14 or #16 light-wire hook tied to a fine tippet. Impale the worm once just beneath the head, and drift this bait as you would a nymph or wet fly.

Mealworms are as neat and easy to raise as they are to use. My own mealworm farm consists of two pipe tobacco tins with plenty of tiny air holes punched in the tops. Any sort of container will do nicely, as long as it is kept in a cool, dry place. Add an inch or two of corn meal, wheat flour, or just about any other kind of finely ground meal or cereal to the bottom of the container. Then add two dozen or so mealworms that you might have left over from a previous fishing trip.

The mealworm that is used as bait and is available at most bait shops is the larval stage of a rather large beetle. Bait worms should be kept refrigerated, as refrigeration retards the metamorphic process. Worms kept for breeding purposes will do best in the 60°- to 70°-temperature range and within about two or three weeks will pupate into large grubs. (And incidentally, these grubs make great trout bait, too.) The grubs will remain motionless in this stage for about another week or two until they are transformed into full-fledged beetles. The beetles will burrow into the meal, lay their eggs, and die soon after.

I check my mealworm farm about once a week and remove discarded shells and dead beetles. I move newly hatched worms to a second tobacco tin where they grow to bait size. The fully-grown worms go into small containers—little margarine tubs with lids or mealworm containers that come from bait shops—with about a ½-inch of meal in the bottom and four dozen worms per container. I keep these in the refrigerator where they will remain healthy and ready for use for months. When I need more breeder stock, I just transfer some of the worms from the refrigerator to the worm farm, and the process begins all over again.

When I'm going fishing, I can stick a container with four dozen live mealworms into a pocket of my fishing jacket and scarcely even notice that it's there. Mealworms are dandy little baits that can be used year-round. And once you start your own farm, you'll never have to buy them again. The fact is, you'll probably be able to keep all your fishing buddies supplied with bait.

Tips on Fishing with Grasshoppers

I discovered the worth of grasshoppers quite by accident some years ago when my family was visiting my uncle's farm. I had my fishing gear with me and planned to fish a neighbor's farm pond, but I hadn't brought any bait with me. It was August, hot and dry, and I don't think there were a dozen worms within miles of that farm. But the pastures were alive with fat grasshoppers. So, on the way to the pond, my brother and I caught a couple of dozen of them.

In the heat of the day, the bass and bluegills in that pond weren't about to take grasshoppers on top, and I wasn't having much luck with them fishing deep, either. I decided to try to make them a bit more appealing. As I hooked my next grasshopper, I removed its back legs and took the bobber off my line, leaving only the grasshopper and two split-shot on my line.

I cast the bait out toward the center of the pond and let it sink to the bottom. Then I retrieved it with short twitches of the rod tip, jigging it across the bottom. A bass of about 4 pounds smashed it, and six more followed in the next hour and a half.

Since that time, I have used the same technique in hot weather to catch largemouth, smallmouth, bluegills, catfish, and trout. When I'm fishing a grasshopper on top—usually in the morning and evening hours—I use a #6 or #8 extra-fine wire Aberdeen hook on which I have wrapped a tiny rubber band. By lifting the loops of the rubber band and sliding them over the body of the grasshopper, the bait stays alive and kicks around on the surface much longer than when impaled with the hook.

Grasshoppers are excellent hot-weather bait. When worked on the surface, they should be kept close to shore near overhanging bank grasses and tree branches. Undercut banks are other likely spots to work live grasshoppers on top, but you can also drift a legless hopper beneath the surface and into the pool under the bank.

Try Belly Meat Strips

Next time you clean a mess of fish, use a sharp fillet knife to trim a bunch of strips off the bellies of the fish to use on later fishing trips. The strips should be about ½-inch wide and can vary in length from 1 inch to 3 or 4 inches. Pack the belly-meat strips in plastic sandwich bags, a dozen or so to each bag, and keep them in the freezer until your next fishing trip.

These strips can be used in lieu of pork rinds on weedless spoons and spinners. They can be attached to spinner baits and are great for dressing jigs and jig heads. Or they can be used by themselves as strip baits for catfish.

When fish are sluggish and appear disinterested in your offerings, try adding a belly-meat strip to a streamer. Use light line on a spinning outfit and only enough weight to allow for casting ease. Work this bait very slowly around likely cover, across the bottom, and in other usual haunts. This is a deadly technique when fish are choosey.

Kisses for Fishes

Although it isn't likely that the Borden Company had fishermen in mind when they introduced their bite-size (bait-size), individually wrapped Cheez Kisses, they certainly seem to be made to order for the cheese-bait fisherman. Before heading for your favorite cheese-dunking spot, make a half-a-handful of monofilament leaders, 12 to 24 inches long. On one end of the leaders tie loops; on the other ends attach small snap swivels.

At your fishing hole, unwrap a Cheez Kiss, push the eye of a #10 treble hook through it, concealing the tines in the cheese, and attach the hook to the loop end of the leader. Snap the swivel at the

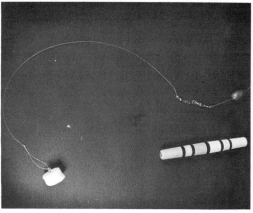

A #10 treble hook can be concealed in a Cheez Kiss and attached to the loop end of a monofilament leader. The snap swivel at the other end of the leader fastens to a barrel swivel tied to the terminal end of your fishing line.

For bottom fishing, use an egg sinker or dipsey sinker above the barrel swivel. For keeping the bait off bottom, use a sliding float above the sinker.

other end of the leader to a barrel swivel that has been tied to the terminal end of your fishing line.

If you are fishing on the bottom, use an egg-type slip sinker or dipsey sinker above the barrel swivel. To keep your bait off the bottom, use a sliding float above the sinker with a piece of rubber band tied to the line above a plastic bead and the float.

Another Use for Nylon Stockings

Not long ago, I read one fisherman's recommendation for keeping warm while wading in cold water. He suggested slipping on a pair of panty hose before donning britches and waders. Now, I don't consider myself the macho type, but I do draw a line when it comes to dressing up in women's underthings. Besides, I'm not sure I would be able to convice my fishing partners that I was only trying to keep warm. Furthermore, my wife told me I certainly could not borrow her hose and would have to buy my own. I think I'll stick to my longhandles and wool socks.

There is, however, a dandy use for discarded nylon stockings, and

I make sure that my wife saves all those that get runs or holes in them. I use them for tying bait sacks when I'm using soft bait that refuses to stay on the hook. Soft, ripe, and smelly cheeses and chicken livers are some of the best catfish baits there are, but they will fall off the hook on all but the gentlest of casts. So I make tidy and tenacious packages of them with pieces of nylon stocking.

I shape a ball of soft cheese or wrap one or two chicken livers around a #2, #1 or #1/0 treble hook and place this in the center of a patch of nylon stocking, 4 or 5 inches square. I gather the edges of the nylon stocking patch up around the hook shank, just beneath the eye, and twist it several times. Then I start wrapping nylon thread around the top of the sack and hook shank until it is held fast. I finish the wrap with several half hitches and trim off excess stocking material with a pair of scissors.

I like to make these baits up in advance and store them in the freezer. When I'm tying up chicken-liver sacks I do so over a shallow cake pan that will catch all the drippings. I pack the finished baits in plastic containers and pour all the chicken blood over them before freezing.

Baits prepared in this way will stay on the hook, yet the mesh of the nylon allows them to "bleed" in the water and attract fish. This technique can be used for any soft baits, including tainted fish and meat that is used for catfish and sturgeon or egg clusters used for trout and salmon (see also, "Sure-Fire System for Salmon/Trout/Steelhead," Chapter Eight). For the ability to replace baits of this sort quickly, use leaders similar to those described above for the Cheez Kiss baits.

A Jug of Wine, a Loaf of Bread and . . .
a Doughball Not for Minors

When I was a youngster, my ancient Aunt Minnie used to visit us every few months. She always brought with her several bottles of port wine, which she enjoyed sipping in the evening. She invariably left behind a half bottle or so when her visit ended. One day I was getting ready to go carp fishing and was searching for doughball ingredients when I spotted some of Aunt Minnie's wine. After convincing my mother that I only wanted the wine for carp bait, I made a doughball that caught a stringer full of carp, including one that went 12½ pounds.

An excellent dough bait can be made by trimming the crust from several slices of rye bread, dampening the bread with port or another sweet wine, and kneading it into a doughball.

Carry a pack of small snelled hooks and use them with pieces of bread crust when fish rise to such offerings.

Since that day this recipe has proved superior to all others I have tried—and it is the easiest to make, too. Simply trim the crust from several slices of rye bread, dampen the bread with port or any other sweet wine, and knead into a doughball. Keep it sealed in a plastic bag to prevent it from drying out.

Surface Dough Bait

Ever take a lunch break while fishing, pinch a corner of bread crust off your sandwich to toss in the water, and watch a hungry fish gobble it up? This has happened to me often enough on otherwise fishless days to cause me to go prepared now. I keep a pack of #12 snelled, single salmon-egg hooks with me. When a fish decides to join me for lunch, I embed a tiny salmon-egg hook in a piece of crust, tie the leader to 4-pound-test line on my ultralight-spinning rig or to a light tippet on my fly-line leader, and float the crust toward the previous rise. More often than not, one or several of the fish that have come for lunch end up being the entrée for dinner. This trick has worked for me on panfish, trout, and catfish.

How to Make Super Catfish Bait

If you like catching catfish and enjoy fishing in solitude, here's a bait that is suited to your preferences. Not only do catfish find this a whisker-licking treat, but it smells so bad that you're sure to have your favorite fishing hole all to yourself.

To about a pound of lean ground beef, add a small jar of processed Limburger cheese. Make sure that the meat and cheese are at room temperature so that they can be mixed thoroughly. The bait, at this point, will have all the flavor and smell that will attract catfish, but it will be too gooey to stay on a hook. Solve this problem by adding enough cotton to the mixture so that a small wad of bait will cling to a #6 or #4 treble hook. If you separate the strands of cotton, it is easier to mix.

It's also a good idea to take several wads of extra cotton along when you head for your catfishing spot. Warm weather can cause the meat and cheese to soften considerably, so you'll want to add more cotton to the bait. And if it's a particularly hot day or night, you might want a little extra cotton to plug your nostrils.

Some Fish Like Sweets

Most fishermen know that small marshmallows are good bait for a number of species, including most panfish, catfish, carp, trout, and even grayling. But there are other sweets that work well—not only because fish will take them, but also because they will stay on the hook. Small gumdrops that come in assorted colors and flavors will sometimes take fish when everything else has failed. While lemon, lime, and licorice gumdrops are good baits for warm-water and cold-water species, cherry and orange ones that resemble small egg clusters can be drifted for salmon or steelhead.

At least one tackle manufacturer has made the same discovery. Tom Mann of Mann's Bait Company produces plastic worms and grubs that come in all the gumdrop flavors. He sells his Jelly Worm flavoring in aerosol cans for use on other soft plastic baits.

A Different Kind of Egg Bait

Here's another bait you can prepare ahead of time and store in your freezer. It's a bait that will take panfish, catfish, and carp. I have never used it for trout, but there's no reason that it won't work for them, too, as I have caught whitefish and grayling with it.

Separate the yolk from the white of a fresh egg and put it into a small bowl. Heat some cooking oil in a small frying pan. On another burner of the stove, heat a small hook that you can hold with a pair of longnose pliers. Dip the heated hook into one of the egg bowls—either white or yolk. The hot hook will sizzle a bit and a thin coating of egg will be literally fried to it. Now dip the hook into the hot oil in the frying pan. Make sure you're frying over a medium heat, and watch out for splattering oil.

It takes only a couple of seconds for the egg on the hook to fry solid on both sides. Now dip it back into the egg and fry again. Keep doing this until a bait-size ball of egg has formed on the hook. You can use different-size hooks to prepare different-size baits. And you can make baits from yolk and from egg white as well. You can also use tiny #12 and #14 hooks and fry on just a thin coating of egg white. These will resemble tiny grubs and should be fished as such. These little egg grubs can be used through the ice for bluegills, too.

CHAPTER 6

Fishing Methods

Tips On Practice Casting

It should go without saying that practice will improve any fisherman's casting accuracy. Veteran anglers will tell you that accuracy is essential to the sport. Yet while many serious anglers practice their casting during the off-season, too often they limit themselves to conventional techniques and one type of practice plug. Just as the tennis player who hasn't mastered his backhand is limited in his sport, so is the fisherman whose casting accuracy is restricted to ¼-ounce plugs and overhand casts.

Once you have attained an acceptable degree of accuracy with the conventional overhand cast, learn the sidearm cast. This is sometimes the only practical one to use. With spinning and spin-casting tackle, learn how to cast backhanded and how to simply flip a lure out for a short distance. Master, also, the bow-and-arrow (otherwise known as catapult) cast.

Vary the weights, sizes, and shapes of your practice lures, just as you would vary the baits when you are fishing. Use small, dense, and heavy practice lures that rocket through the air like a jig. Then try light and bulky plugs that approximate the surface lures and balsa wood or plastic minnows.

Small pails and coffee cans make excellent practice targets, but don't make the mistake of using just one. Place a dozen of them at different distances, near and far, and learn to accurately cast to each with a variety of practice lures. Put some obstacles in your way, too. You might place one can next to a bush and another beneath an overhanging tree branch. Make it tough on yourself.

When you practice your fly casting, use practice flies to keep the leader from bullwhipping. You can tie your own practice flies or use any fly that has had the hook gap snipped off. Or you can just tie a bright feather or piece of yarn to your leader. For bait-casting and spinning practice you can make your own practice plugs from a variety of materials, or you can use old plugs and spinners with the hooks removed.

Don't restrict your practice sessions to calm days. Get out on windy days and learn how to cast crosswind and into the wind, as well as with the wind to your back. In short, when you practice, you must simulate the kinds of conditions and obstacles you will face in actual fishing situations. The tougher you make it, the better you will become. It makes practice more of a challenge, too.

Tips for the Beginning Fly Fisherman

If you have avoided getting into fly fishing because of the endless amount of entomologic knowledge the sport seems to require or because of confusion over lines, leaders, tippets, knots, and balanced tackle, stop fretting and start fishing. Don't worry about stuffing a fly box full of all the various sizes and patterns that will coincide with insect hatches. Don't concern yourself with the vast store of literature on the ancient art of angling with artificial flies. That will all come in due time.

Meanwhile, read a good book on the basics of fly fishing and get started. As you become proficient with a fly rod, you will find that you have a desire to learn more and more about your quarry and the ways to take him. Expertise is gradually acquired, and patience is an absolute necessity—especially for the novice fly fisherman.

Buy a good 7½- or 8-foot fly rod to begin with—the best you can afford, within reason—and a single-action reel. Too many beginners go with level line, because it is so much cheaper than the tapers. This is a mistake. Start with a double-taper line, as it will shoot easier and will present a fly so much more delicately. A good line for starters that balances with many trout action rods is DT7F—that is, Double Taper, size 7, Floating.

Short leaders—say, 6 to 8 feet in length—are easier to handle. As you gain confidence and finesse, you can gradually work up to longer leaders for fishing with dry flies. If you plan to fish with streamers, bass bugs, and poppers, you'll want to use shorter leaders anyway. Practice casting in your yard or in a nearby park, and don't worry about shooting 60 or 70 feet of line. Work with short casts until you can consistently place them where you want them. Gradually add distance to your casts, a few feet at a time. For much of your fly fishing, shorter casts will prove the better choice, particularly when you're using dry flies where the current will cause your line to bow on long casts and will thus require constant mending.

As for the complicated subject of the right flies to use, there are numerous kinds that have little or nothing to do with local hatches and others that will nearly match up with a variety of hatches. Start by stocking your fly box with a few basic patterns such as the mosquito, black gnat, McGinty, Adams, and renegade in sizes 12 and 14. Add to that a few woolly worms, hoppers, variants, and bivisibles, and you'll be ready for top water action. Several streamers, grubs, and nymphs will get you started on the underwater patterns. Ants, beetles, and muddlers are other good patterns that will produce under various conditions. All of these flies will catch trout. If you fish for bass and panfish, they will do that job, too. But you will want to pick up a few poppers and bass bugs as well.

Eventually, you will learn the fine points and complexities of the sport. The most important part of fly fishing, however, is getting started. I learned how to fly fish in precisely the same manner. While I lay no claims to expert status, I do catch a respectable share of fish with fly tackle—and I doubt that there is a fly fisherman anywhere who has more fun at it than I do.

Spin Fishing—The Most Versatile Method of All

According to A.J. McClane, retired executive editor of *Field & Stream* magazine and the dean of modern angling, "No one event during the last century did more to promote fishing as a sport in America than did the introduction of the spinning reel." Nothing influenced my own fishing more than McClane's early articles on spinfishing and spinning tackle. I suppose, out front, I ought to confess to having fishing heroes and prejudices—McClane fitting into the former slot, and a preference for spin fishing comprising the latter.

I started out with bait-casting gear, but after reading McClane's articles about the intriguing fixed-spool reels, I was determined to have my own spinning tackle. I was still a youngster in my pre-teens when I bought my first spinning reel and a one-piece, solid-glass spinning rod. It was really a clunker of an outfit, the whole rig—rod, reel, and line—costing me less than ten bucks. But I gave it an abundance of hard use and caught many pounds of fish before it was passed on to my younger brother.

My bait-casting tackle still saw a lot of action. With it, I could use the heavier lines so often necessary for fishing midwestern rivers and lakes for hefty catfish. In those days, monofilament lines were stiff and kinky; so we used light lines that were small in diameter and a bit more limp. In fact, for my first ten years of spin fishing I used nothing but 6-pound-test line. I only rarely came upon another fisherman who used anything heavier, and then it was usually 8- or 10-pound test. Heavier monos took a set on the reel spool and came off in unruly coils that turned to hopeless bird's nests and clogged the guides of the rod. Or, at best, they created far too much drag through the guides for casting distance and accuracy.

The transition, and my growing preference for spinning tackle, took place during my early teens. By then I owned a fine bait-casting rod and one of the Cadillacs among bait-casting reels. It was kept in fine tune at all times and was my most prized possession. But for my fourteenth birthday, I received a Garcia CAP spinning reel that I later coupled up with a two-piece, tubular, glass Shakespeare Wonderod. By that time I was fishing for anything that swam and was learning the differences among various species. I was learning, too, of the necessity for versatility under various fishing situations. I ventured to more distant fishing waters and made new discoveries on nearly every outing. And my spin-fishing tackle got most of the action.

Since those early days I have owned enough tackle to stock a fair-sized sporting goods store. I have fished throughout North America for just about every fresh-water game fish from bluegills to king salmon. I have tried practically every method of modern angling. While I can't say that I have disliked any, spinning is certainly the one that has proved to be the most versatile—it's a system that will do it all.

Ah, but there's the word that explains my prejudices: system. While most of the early spinning reels differed greatly from manufacturer to manufacturer, nearly all of them were middleweights—what we now refer to as fresh-water or medium-duty reels. It wasn't long, though, before a big bruiser of a spinning reel that found favor among salt-water anglers and surf casters was introduced. Although ultralight reels were to be found among the early designs, they didn't catch on until the middle 1960s. Now spinning reels, from tiny ultralights to big, heavy-duty, salt-water machines—and every size in-between—are offered by all the major manufacturers. They have been greatly refined over the years, and all of the better-known brands are truly precision pieces.

Spinning rods come in just about any length or action that a fisherman could want. Some serve as ideal general-purpose rods, and others are more specialized in design and application. And with today's premium-quality fishing lines, limper, tougher, and smaller in diameter than their predecessors, the angler can put together the right combination to take any fish that swims in fresh water. The serious spin fisherman will have a system that will meet the demands of variable fishing situations.

It's not my purpose, here, to sell any particular brand of spinning tackle, but rather, to promote top-quality gear. There are a number of reputable manufacturers who offer complete selections of superb spinning rods and reels: Berkley, Daiwa, Garcia, Heddon, Orvis, Shakespeare, and Wright & McGill, to name a few. While any good spinning outfit will perform the basic functions of spin fishing, features found in the tackle will differ according to manufacturer.

The best advice I can give to any angler is to shop around and find the brand of tackle that feels best and functions best according to your own personal needs; then begin building a system of tackle of the same brand. There are several advantages to building a system from one line of tackle, one of which is the simplification of tackle maintenance and repair. Also, if you prefer to have the factory or factory-authorized repair station clean and check your tackle for you, you need only ship the tackle off to one place.

Perhaps the most important reason for systemizing your tackle in this way is that you will get to know your gear more intimately. Various models of reels, for example, from one particular series will be virtually identical in design, only scaled up or down in the different sizes. My own spinning system happens to be Garcia-Mitchell. My Mitchell 308 ultralight reel is basically the same as my Mitchell 300, only smaller. My Mitchell 406 and 302 reels are from the same series, but are larger. The similarity of these reels allows me to get to know them entirely. There is a sameness in the feel of each outfit. Most importantly, drag adjustments on each reel are identical and are located in the same place, which keeps me from fumbling around making crucial adjustments when a fish is on.

When it comes time to retire one of my old, battle-scarred veterans, I replace it with a new reel of the same make and model. This allows me to use the old one for backup or for spare parts. I nearly always have three or more rigs with me when I fish the lakes and reservoirs for bass. One will be a bait-casting outfit that I use almost entirely for worms and jigs. Two of them will be spinning rigs that I use for plugs and spinner baits, each equipped with a Mitchell 300 reel. I have no difficulty switching from one to the other.

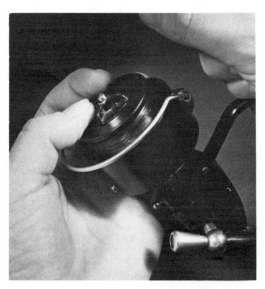

By using matched spinning tackle and reels made by one manufacturer and from one series, there's no fumbling around in search of drag adjustments. All reels in the series will be similar in design, and the transition from one to another will be simple.

Any complete fresh-water spin-fishing system will be comprised of more rods than reels. The most basic of systems would include a medium-duty reel, such as the Mitchell 300, at least two extra spools, and three rods. For light fishing, one spool should be filled with 6-pound-test line, and the rod should be a light-action 6-footer with a fast taper. This outfit would be ideally suited to fishing for all types of panfish as well as trout and smallmouth bass. The short rod would be an asset on any small stream, and the fast taper would facilitate the casting of tiny lures.

A 7-foot medium-action rod—one with a large diameter butt and plenty of backbone—will fare well in the toughest of bass-fishing situations. It can also be used for light trolling and many types of bait fishing as well. An 8-foot salmon/steelhead rod can be used with a reel such as the Mitchell 300 for steelhead, smaller salmon, pike, and musky fishing.

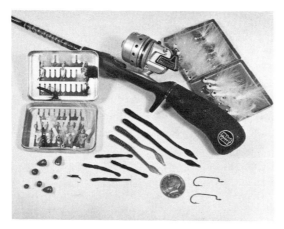

For fishing with tiny jigs and plastic worms, a miniature spin-casting outfit, such as Daiwa's Minicast, is perfect.

The other two spools should be filled with 10- and 15-pound-test line and can be used interchangeably with the 7-foot and 8-foot spinning rods, depending on water clarity, snags, and the size of the fish being pursued. Ideally, though, the most versatile system will include several different reels, an assortment of extra spools, and rods to be matched with conditions. I consider my own collection of spinning tackle to be a complete fresh-water system; I can't think of any way I should add to it.

Matched with my ultralight spinning reel are two rods. One is a two-piece, 5½-foot, ultralight-action fiberglass rod, which is suitable only for the lightest of fishing. The other rod is nearly identical, except that it has more backbone and is rated as light action. For use with my Mitchell 300 reels I have two rods. Each is two-piece, fiberglass, and 7 feet long. One is a medium-action, fast-taper rod that is suitable for most types of fresh-water fishing and can handle a wide range of lures. The other is a medium-action rod with a stiffer tip. I use this one for heavier lures and for fishing in snag-strewn waters where I might need to horse in a hefty bass or pike. I have also used this rod for plastic worm and jig fishing, but I prefer bait-casting tackle for this.

Although the two 8-foot spinning rods I use are called salmon/steelhead rods, each is distinctively different from the other; and both are suitable for a variety of fishes and fishing situations. The lighter one is nearly identical to my 7-foot, medium-action, fast-taper rod, except that it is a foot longer and has a longer handle. This is the rod I use for summer steelheading and for winter steelheading in small streams. It's also good for low, clear waters, because I can use lighter lines and smaller baits with it. I often use a Mitchell 300 reel with this rod instead of the larger-capacity and heavier Model 406.

The other 8-footer is a medium-heavy action, fast-taper rod. Coupled with a Mitchell 406 reel, it is a heavy-duty rig that is ideal for big waters and big fish. It's the outfit I use for most winter steelheading and all of my stream-salmon fishing, but it is equally suited to big-lakes fishing for such species as lake trout and musky. The fisherman who goes after lunker catfish or sturgeon better have gear that will handle such brutes. For this kind of fishing, I use a 10-foot, heavy-action spinning rod and a Mitchell 302 reel. This is normally considered salt-water tackle, but it has fresh-water applications.

Spools for my ultralight reel are filled with 4- and 6-pound-test line. Most often I use 15-pound-test line on the Mitchell 300 reels, but I carry extra spools of 6- and 10-pound test. On the Mitchell 406, I use 10-, 15-, or 20-pound-test line, depending on water conditions and the fish I'm after. On the big Model 302, I generally use 30-pound-test line, but I'll switch to 20-pound-test if I need to make long casts or am using less weight and smaller baits.

Of all the fresh-water fishing methods, only spin fishing is the system that can be adapted to any situation or species, from tiny mountain brooks to the Great Lakes, from panfish to sturgeon.

Spin-Casting Myths Dispelled

In the early days of spin fishing, some anglers found difficulty in the transition from bait-casting tackle to spinning tackle. A reel that dangled from the underside of the rod handle was a cumbersome thing for some fishermen who were used to bait-casting reels that rode topside. The development of the spin-casting reel was supposed to provide the best of both worlds—it would cast the light, spin-weight lures, yet could be used with a bait-casting rod. To such purposes, spin-casting reels are well suited, and those who prefer a reel that rides upright should select such tackle instead of using spinning gear.

But something went awry early on, when some writer wrote something to the effect of: "most experts prefer open-face spinning reels to closed-face or spin-casting reels." Other writers followed the leader, repeated this statement, and embellished it until it was so distorted and turned around that it came to mean: "If you're not an expert, you better start out with a simple spin-casting reel instead of the more sophisticated and complicated spinning reel." And that's probably one reason why so many wives and children get stuck with spin-casting tackle when they are introduced to fishing.

I must confess that I believed in the myth of spin-casting simplicity for a long time and even started my wife out with such tackle. Since she had nothing to compare it to, she had no complaints for a long time. I even graduated her to bigger and more expensive spin-casting reels, and ultimately introduced her to "the tackle that experts prefer." Within a half-hour after she first picked up a spinning rod with an open-face reel on it, she was handling it like a veteran. It wasn't long after that that she told me she really didn't care to use her spin-casting tackle any longer, because the spinning gear was so trouble free and easy to use. In fact, it took me a while to convince her that there are, indeed, some fishing situations to which spin-casting tackle is particularly suited.

Another myth of nebulous origins is that casting accuracy is greater with spin-casting tackle than with spinning gear. Since we are told that bait-casting reels afford the angler better control and accuracy than do open-face spinning reels, someone probably assumed it would only follow that spin-casting reels would be more accurate, too. Bunk!

By virtue of design, a closed-face spin-casting reel must have a narrower spool than an open-face spinning reel. This means a reduced line capacity in the former. So spin-casting reels are best suited to the lighter-weight lines, from 6- to 10-pound-test. With the proper weight line, a spin-casting reel should be just as accurate as an open-face spinning reel. In the hands of an expert spin-caster, it might even be a tad more accurate. But load a spin-casting reel with 15- or 20-pound-test line, and you can bet that accuracy and distance will be greatly impaired. The heavier lines will be stiffer and will cause much more drag as they uncoil and try to get through the small hole in the front of the spool cover. Since heavier lines tend to lay unevenly on spin-casting reel spools, they also foul more frequently.

Although spin-casting tackle is not nearly as versatile as spinning tackle, it does have its place in the scheme of angling. The angler who has trouble switching from bait-casting to spinning tackle and prefers the similarity between bait casting and spin casting should let his preferences guide him in the selection of tackle. But he must remember to limit his use of spin-casting tackle to light duty and to use conventional bait-casting gear when heavier lines are required. And, of course, the fisherman who never uses anything heavier than 10-pound-test line for all his fishing could get by with nothing but spin-casting tackle. Even the well-rounded angler who fishes far and wide for a variety of species under all sorts of conditions would do well to cash in on the specialized advantages of spin-casting tackle.

The singular drawback with the open-face spinning reel is that it is not well suited to fishing with jigs and plastic worms. As long as a relatively even tension is applied to the line during the retrieve— such as when using crank baits, spinner baits, spoons, and spinners —the spool on an open-face reel will load evenly and will cause no problems. But if the tension on the line is uneven, as it is when a bait is jigged during a retrieve, line will load unevenly. In subsequent casts, line will spill from the spool several loops at a time, creating bird's nests of the worst kind.

One way to alleviate this problem is to run the line between the thumb and forefinger of the rod hand, applying even tension during the retrieve. But for many of us, this is awkward and cumbersome. A far better solution is to match the tackle to the situation. So when I'm using light jigs or small, plastic worms with light sinkers, I prefer spin-casting tackle over anything else. Since I palm a bait-casting or spin-casting reel during the retrieve anyway, it's no trouble to apply even tension to the line with my thumb and forefinger. Consequently, the line loads evenly and poses no problems when casting. And on those days when pickups are light, a finger on the line is one of the best ways to detect a nibble.

For fishing with the tiniest of jigs and plastic worms, I recently acquired one of the Daiwa Minicast outfits. With 4- or 6-pound-test, premium monofilament line, it will handle these nearly weightless lures; and its operation is trouble free.

Bait Casting Revisited Realistically

Since revolving-spool reels are more forgiving of uneven tension applied to line during the retrieve than fixed-spool reels are, they are better suited to jig and worm fishing than spinning reels are. For this reason, I use bait-casting tackle for nearly all such fishing. Just as I prefer to use spinning tackle for most other types of fishing, there are many fishermen who prefer bait-casting tackle for all or most of their fishing. It is largely a matter of personal preference and comfort, and that should be the major guiding force in selecting one kind of tackle over another—except in the instance of restrictive design limitations.

Some misconceptions have grown out of facts, however, and can cloud the issue of tackle selection. One is the idea of accuracy. All other things equal, bait-casting reels are generally considered more accurate than spinning reels. But there are many variables to consider before accepting this as gospel. First, a cheap clunker of a casting reel will be no match for any spinning reel, since the functioning of a casting reel depends on precision mechanics that have little to do with the casting ability of a fixed-spool reel.

Secondly, even the finest of casting reels will be clumsy and inaccurate in the hands of someone who finds such tackle uncomfortable. I can cast accurately with bait-casting tackle, but I am every bit as accurate (if not more so) with spinning tackle, mainly because I am more comfortable with the latter. Besides, there are some casts that I make with spinning gear—such as the backhand flip and the bow-and-arrow cast—that I couldn't begin to do with bait-casting gear. So the degree of accuracy has no bearing on my personal choice of fishing tackle. Rather, I let the application dictate which type I will use.

Another misconception—one that was born of the bass boom of recent years—is that a worm rod should have all the action of a broomstick. Too many anglers think of worm rods as bass rods and use them for all their bass fishing, compounding an erroneous idea into an even more serious problem. Granted, there are times when

If you are most comfortable with casting tackle, by all means make that your choice, but don't base your selection on fads and myths.

a heavy-action rod and a casting reel filled with 20-pound-test line are the only choices. But bass don't spend all their time in the lily pads or stickups.

If you're a one-rod fisherman, the so-called worm rod is a poor choice, indeed. You are far better off to pick a medium-action, fast-taper rod—one with a stout butt end and plenty of backbone for horsing out lunkers, but with enough tip action to facilitate casting some of the smaller and lighter lures. In short, no matter what kind of tackle you prefer to use, it is wise to match it to the fishing conditions. And don't let fads cloud your thinking.

What Speed for Trolling?

There was a time when, according to all of the experts, there were but two speeds at which any lure should travel—slow and slower. But times have changed and so has our thinking. There are occasions when only slow trolling will entice fish and other times when we must troll fast to get strikes. The primary consideration in determining trolling speed is the action of the lure being used.

Some lures that are especially suited for slow travel have hideous action when trolled too fast, while some that are designed to be trolled or retrieved fast have little or no action at all at speeds that are too slow. The only way to match the trolling speed with the bait being used is to trail the lure alongside the boat and study the action while the throttle of the motor is adjusted for the speed that imparts the best action to the lure.

Ever Try Backtrolling?

Sometimes idle speed still isn't slow enough for trolling, especially if you want to bounce your bait along the bottom when tail winds cause your craft to move too fast. Next time this happens to you, try backtrolling. That is, move your boat through the water stern first. The increased drag of the water against the blunt stern, as well as the effects of the tail wind now lessened as it strikes the narrower bow, are usually enough to sufficiently slow your craft down. This technique should never be used in rough water, though, since a wave breaking over the stern could scuttle the boat.

The Versatile Winneconne Rig

When I used to fish Wisconsin's Lake Winnebago for walleyes, I learned about a dandy light-trolling rig that was known locally as the Winneconne rig. It is excellent for getting small, light lures, such as Rapalas and Rebel Minnows, down near bottom in waters that are 15 to 30 feet deep. The Winneconne rig is easy to make, too. You will need some three-way swivels, a spool of line that tests lighter than your fishing line, another spool of line the same as your fishing line, and an assortment of dipsey sinkers. Tie the tag end of your fishing line to one of the eyes of the swivel. Then tie a 24- to 36-inch leader of the same strength line to another eye, and attach your lure to it. Now tie an 18-inch dropper of the lighter line to the remaining eye of the swivel, and tie a dipsey sinker to its end.

As the dipsey sinker bounces along the bottom, the lure will swim just above bottom. The design of the dipsey sinker keeps it from getting snagged too often. When it does get hung up badly, the weaker line to which it is tied will break off, allowing you to retrieve your lure. I have added my own touch to this rig to allow the quick changing of sinker weights until the right weight for the depth and conditions is determined. I tie a small snap swivel to the end of the dropper line, and attach the sinker to the swivel.

How to Rig Keel Weights

Another handy item for light-to-medium trolling is the keel weight—a sinker molded around a chain swivel that is weighted off-center to keep it from turning in the water and twisting line. It's a must when using lures such as spinners and spoons. Some swivels on keel weights have snaps; some don't. All require a leader for attaching the lure. I keep several such leaders tied up and readily at hand in my tackle box. For keel weights without snaps, I have leaders with snap swivels on each end. For weights with snaps, I use leaders with snap swivels on the lure ends and barrel swivels on the other end. Having these leaders made up in advance saves precious fishing time.

Diving Planes for Trolling

If you don't have a boat outfitted with downriggers and don't like dragging excessive weight through the water to get your bait down deep, there's another alternative. Several types of diving planes that will get your bait down deep are on the market. When a fish strikes, the plane is tripped so that it can be reeled toward the surface. Although these planes are relatively light in weight, when set in their diving attitude, they do create quite a bit of drag. So a fairly hefty rod should be used. Any medium-heavy-action trolling and boat rod will do nicely.

Flashers, Dodgers, and Other Attractors

If your trolled lures are collecting few fish, you can make them more visible and attractive to finicky fish by using flashers, dodgers, or other attractors in conjunction with them. There are a number of such items available commercially, or you can make your own from spinners and spoons. All such attractors must be used ahead of the bait or lure, which is attached to a monofilament leader from 18- to 36-inches long.

Although most of the store-bought attractors come equipped with swivels, it's a good idea to attach one or two extra swivels to each rig; and use only top-quality swivels. Since I have had problems with severe line twist while using various attractors, I now tie a snap swivel to the end of my fishing line to which I attach the attractor. At the leading end of the monofilament leader, I tie another swivel. Here I use a barrel swivel if the attractor is equipped with a snap, or a snap swivel if it is not so equipped. If I'm using a spinner or spoon as a lure, I tie another snap swivel at the trailing end of the leader.

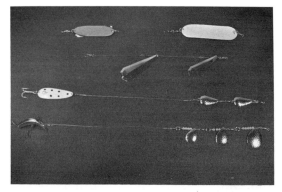

Pictured at the top are store-bought herring dodgers and Ford Fender flashers. The two bottom rigs are homemade from spoons and spinners purchased on sale. One trails a Daredevil spoon, the other a silver Flatfish.

One type of homemade attractor can be assembled from two or more old spinners that have had the hooks removed. Attach them to one another in a series with split rings, and add swivels to the trailing and leading ends. Another type of attractor can be made from two or more spoons with the hooks removed. Attach a split ring to each end of each spoon, and separate each spoon in the rig with a barrel swivel.

I always use top-quality spoons and spinners as lures. But when I'm making attractors, I use the cheapest ones I can find. Whenever I find the bargain basement imitations of top-brand spoons and spinners on sale at a good price, I buy a batch to use in making attractors. For this purpose, they work fine.

Still Fishing

The term still fishing has been widely misconstrued. The word still, here, refers to the stationary position of the fisherman, not of the bait, as so many of the bait dunkers throughout the country seem to think. No matter whether you're bait fishing for brim in some southern lake, lunker catfish in the Ohio River, or bass in a midwest farm pond, you'll catch more fish if you move your bait periodically. A bait suspended beneath a float, or one resting on the bottom, will certainly catch a fish—if one happens by. But a bait that is moved every few minutes covers a lot of territory and has a far better chance of finding a hungry fish.

Reels Sans Sand

Still fishing can be tough on tackle. Anglers often prop their rods on rocks, tackle boxes, or in the crotch of a forked stick and let their reels lie in the mud or sand. Fresh-water fishermen would do well to learn from their salt-water brethren who still fish along the coast. To keep sand out of their reels, they seat their rods in sand spikes. There's no rule prohibiting the use of sand spikes by fresh-water fishermen. Yet I rarely ever see a fresh-water fisherman using one. I wouldn't be without mine in any part of the country where I happen to be fishing.

If you live inland, you might have a hard time finding sand spikes for sale at your local tackle emporium. No problem—make your own. All you need is a piece of PVC pipe (available at plumbing supply stores) about 30-inches long. Cut the bottom of the pipe off at an angle to form a point. When you reach your favorite fishing hole, shove the pointed end of the pipe into the ground, angled slightly toward the water. After you cast out your bait, slip your rod handle into the top of the sand spike, and enjoy your fishing sans sand in the reel.

How to Foil a Fish

Each year in late June or early July, when the ice moves out of Summit Lake on Alaska's Richardson Highway, bait fishermen set up camp on shore. Here they fish for big lake trout with whole smelt or small grayling. Since most of the fishermen usually sit around camp, playing cards and drinking beer while waiting for lakers to come by and take their baits, they use a nifty trick to detect bites from the distance of their camp stools.

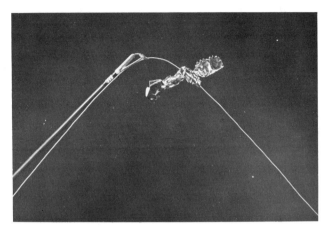

When still fishing in a lake, wrap the foil from a stick of chewing gum around your line near the rod tip-top and open the bail or trip the free-spool on your reel. If the foil moves toward the lake, you have a taker.

After casting out his bait, a fisherman will prop his rod up and open the bail of his reel. Then he unwraps a stick of chewing gum and twists the foil wrapper around his line next to the tip-top. Between poker hands, he need only glance at his rod to see if the foil is still in place. If the foil is moving or has disappeared, he usually asks to be dealt out of the next hand.

The Night Beat

During the summer doldrums, there's nothing we enjoy more than packing a cooler full of beer and sandwiches and heading for a favorite catfishing spot about sundown. We fire up our lanterns, bait our hooks, and settle back to enjoy the cool of the evening and, usually, some great catfishing.

Having done a lot of night fishing, I've learned a few tricks that help to make the sport even more enjoyable. We always get to our fishing spot by sundown, so we can set up camp without groping in the darkness. This is when we fill our lanterns and position them for the best lighting. We find a good spot to put the stringers while it is still light, and we get all our gear laid out conveniently.

There are a few things we do at home, too, before setting out for a night of fishing. For example, we put spools of high-visibility fluorescent line on our reels. This line is excellent for night fishing as it is easy to see, even in the fringe of the lantern light. We put fluorescent tape to good use, too. Several strips around the tip sections of our rods make them highly visible and helps us to detect bites. We also wrap strips of fluorescent tape around the flashlight and landing-net handle to make them easier to locate in dim light.

CHAPTER 7

Fishing Strategies

How to Fish a Lake for the First Time

Fishing a strange lake or reservoir can be an exasperating experience, especially at day's end when you return to the dock tired, sunburned, and fishless only to find some of the local experts loaded down with fish. On any fishing trip to unfamiliar waters, money spent to hire a competent guide for the first day can be the wisest investment you will make. When you consider the cost of transportation, food, lodging, and tackle, the guide's fees will shrink in comparison. What you can learn from a good guide in a morning of fishing can make the difference between a successful venture and a dismally disappointing trip.

On some lakes, guides can be hard to find or nonexistent. And certainly, many fishermen prefer to strike out alone to pit their wits against their quarry. In such cases, the best aid to fishing is a reliable map—preferably a fishing map that shows depths and underwater structure. Some states offer maps and structure charts of lakes and reservoirs within their boundaries. Prior to your trip, you should write to the fish and game agency in any state where you plan to fish and request a list of available maps. There is usually a slight fee charged for each map.

There are also commercial sources of fishing maps, and these maps can be found at local marinas and tackle shops. For fishing the southeastern states, some of the best maps are available from the Alexandria Drafting Company, 417 E. Clifford Ave., Alexandria, VA 22305. Lakes Illustrated has more than 100 different maps of popular lakes and reservoirs throughout the U.S. Their address is Box 4854 GS, Springfield, MO 65804.

Although topographical maps—such as those offered by the U.S. Geological Survey—do not indicate bottom structure or accurate bottom contours, they can be valuable fishing aids and are better than having no maps at all. In the case of some relatively new reservoirs, older topo maps that show buildings, roads, bridges, stream beds, and other types of structures that existed before the land was

When fishing any lake or reservoir for the first time, seek out a high vantage point from where you can view the water from above.

inundated are sometimes available. Any topo map is useful when talking to local anglers or proprietors of marinas and tackle shops. Locating a good fishing spot by following verbal directions is difficult at best. But if you have a map that someone can point to and you can follow later, any hot spot becomes easy to find.

Large-scale topographical maps will also show many dirt roads and trails that would not appear on typical road maps. So topo maps can aid you in locating and reaching access points. In the case of smaller lakes and ponds, and especially high mountain lakes, the topo map is an aid to finding the body of water itself.

Whenever I plan to fish an unfamiliar lake for two days or more,

I always arrive early enough the day before so that I can conduct a systematic investigation to determine where and how I will fish the next day. My first stop is always at a local marina or bait and tackle shop. As sources of fishing information, the operators of such businesses are generally reliable, but they're also reliably general. "They're taking a lot of bass up on Cutter's Arm," a tackle-shop owner might tell me. That's a useful bit of information, but when I look at a map and find that Cutter's Arm is 3 miles long and a mile wide, I'll want this guy to be more specific and to point out some spots on the map that have been productive.

If the lake or reservoir is large enough to have numerous tackle shops and marinas along its shores, I'll talk to as many proprietors as possible. I will also seek out local anglers, and tackle shops and marinas are good places to locate them. Public boat-launching facilities are other spots I always check. The afternoon hours often find fishermen returning to the boat ramp; naturally, I look for the ones who have fish.

About one out of ten fishermen will be a competent angler, and fully half of the competent anglers will be reluctant to disclose their fishing spots and techniques. But I rarely ever go to a strange lake without finding several fishermen who enjoy talking about their methods and bragging a little about their abilities.

In the course of an afternoon of chatting with local folks, I can begin putting together a good bit of valuable intelligence. It doesn't take long for patterns to start forming. Certainly a large portion of the yarns have to be discarded, but a few tips here and there and some corroborative stories give me an indication of where to begin looking for fish. For example, of a half-dozen marina and bait-shop owners, perhaps three will tell me about the bass fishing "up on Cutter's Arm." Then, maybe several cooperative fishermen will tell me that they did well in the same area. One person might tell me about a rip-rap bank to try. Others might point out weedbeds, reefs, spring holes, creek channels, roadbeds, feeder streams, and other areas worth trying. Eventually, the size of Cutter's Arm becomes much more reasonable and fishable. Those areas recommended by several persons are the ones I try first.

I never rely on my memory when I'm involved in such an investigation. I take notes and I mark my map. If a person is a bit reluctant to offer information, however, I never let him see my notebook and map. But as soon as I'm out of sight, I jot down all I can remember.

It's amazing how these little tidbits eventually fall into place to form a wealth of valuable data. When I find a good fisherman who is willing to talk, I make sure I pinpoint as many spots as possible and ask for landmarks. More than once, a cooperative angler has pulled out his own map and shared his notes with me.

Whenever possible, I investigate a lake from as many vantage points as I can find. When there are roads along lake shores, I drive them, stopping frequently to observe the lake and the people fishing it. I use binoculars to study shoreline features and to watch fishermen. I'm always on the lookout for concentrations of fishermen, and I pay particular attention to those who are taking fish. I always search for the highest point of land from which I can study the lake from above and for great distances. There I use binoculars as I do elsewhere, but I also look for visible structure that will show up even at moderate depths in reasonably clear water. Reefs, shoals, points, and sharp drop-offs are easy to spot from above, and it is also easy to locate concentrations of fishermen from this vantage.

Armed with as much data as I can gather in an afternoon, I am able to spend an hour or so that evening studying my maps and notes and planning a strategy that is likely to put some fish on my stringer the next morning. If I am planning to fish a particular body of water for several days, I continue to gather notes and to talk to other anglers.

Depth finders, oxygen probes, and thermometers are great aids to fishing, but they are little more than expensive gadgets unless they are used in conjunction with the kind of data that a systematic investigation will provide. A few hours of chatting with local fishing folks, taking notes, studying maps, and observing the waters you plan to fish can mean the difference between a successful trip and coming home with an empty stringer.

Fishing by Aerial Reconnaissance

There are thousands of farm ponds and small lakes throughout the U.S. that go virtually unfished, simply because fishermen are unaware of their existence. Farm ponds and quarries, especially in the midwestern, southern, and eastern portions of the country, provide some of the most fertile and productive bass and panfish waters to be found. But only the ones within sight of a road get substantial pressure. Those that are within view and easy reach, particularly ones near population centers, are often overfished.

Since many older topographical maps will show only the old ponds and might omit the smaller ones altogether, the best way to locate unfished waters is from the air. And don't be frightened off by the cost of renting or chartering a small airplane. First, you should be able to charter a single-engine, four-place plane (such as a Cessna 172) for about $40 to $50 an hour. If you have a friend who is a licensed pilot, rental for the same type of aircraft should run about $25 or so an hour. These costs can be trimmed even more by getting in touch with someone in a local flying club where hourly rates for the planes are usually $20 or less and where members are always looking for an excuse to go up.

By splitting the costs with one or two fishing partners, you can cut the price of aerial reconnaissance to $20 or less an hour for charter and $8 to $12 or so an hour for rental. My recommendation would be to make this a joint effort anyway—not only as a means of saving money but also as a way of increasing efficiency. As with any other aspect of fishing, you must approach this project systematically.

Before going up, you will want to secure a good road map and a topo or surveyor's map of the area you plan to fly over. Find roads and landmarks that are easy to spot from the air, and work out a route for your pilot to follow. For example, you might want to follow an interstate highway since it would be easy to identify from the air. Get familiar with all intersecting state and county roads so that when you spot a pond from the air you can mark it on your map.

It helps to have a camera with you, as enlargements of your aerial photos will help you precisely locate any ponds or quarries that you find from the air. You will want to keep accurate notes, too. Whenever you spot a pond that looks like it would be worth investigating, note, as nearly as possible, its exact location and any nearby land marks—such as roads, railroad tracks, grain elevators, and the like— that will help you find it from ground level. If a pond appears to be a part of an identifiable farm from the air, mark the road access on your map. During a well-planned, 1-hour flight, you should be able to locate several new fishing spots that are out of the way and rarely, if ever, fished. Then all you need to do is find out who owns the ponds and secure permission to fish them.

Stream Savvy

In some ways, creeks and rivers are easier to fish than large lakes and reservoirs. This is because the knowledgeable fisherman usually will find typical fish habitats easier to locate on a stream. Of course, there will be times when the most likely looking spots will be devoid of fish, and other times when the ordinarily nonproductive areas will give up fish after fish. But most of the time fish will be found in their typical habitat.

Except during seasonal migrations, I avoid the heavily fished portions of a stream, especially those that are easily accessible or are near roads or parks. Often, though, these same places can be highly productive at night or during the fall of the year when there are bigger fish actively feeding and fewer anglers pursuing them. Frequently, a mere half-mile upstream or downstream from an access area will show few signs of fishing pressures and will provide the angler with plenty of activity.

The topo map can be an even greater aid to the stream fisherman than it is to the lake fisherman, especially for the angler who is willing to wade and work for his fish. On such a map, you may find a winding river that meanders roughly parallel to a road. You might find two points, a mile apart by road, where the stream crosses beneath bridges or comes close enough to the road for easy access. By following the stream instead of the road, however, you might have to cover two, three, four, or more miles, much of it virtually unfished, except by other wading anglers.

My brother Phil and I used to fish such a stream in southwestern Ohio when we were in college. Despite the fact that this creek was within easy reach of several million people—and certainly countless thousands of anglers that reside in that area—it provided some of the best smallmouth and rock-bass fishing to be found anywhere.

On the section that we fished the most, the creek passed beneath four bridges, each less than a mile apart from the next by road yet separated by two miles or more by creek. We would park at one bridge and fish our way upstream to the next, with an easy walk back to the car afterward. Although we sometimes saw other anglers fishing near the bridges or within several hundred yards of them, we never encountered others on the long, clear pools we found on those stretches between the bridges where the creek wended its

First targets on any stream should be rocks. Fish above them and below them.

way through woods, meadows, and farmlands. It was hard to believe that this creek lay within a half-hour's drive of two major population centers, numerous smaller towns, and an interstate highway.

When I am fishing any stream for the first time, I seek out the typical habitat. I don't waste time fishing the kind of waters that are normally barren of fish. Since most fish will be found near some sort of shelter or structure where they can wait for food that passes by, I am watchful for the kinds of cover that fish prefer. Rocks of all sizes and shapes and at various locations on a stream are the first fish indicators that I look for. Individual boulders, rocky banks and ledges, and rocky bottoms are all likely spots that I never pass by.

Most anglers realize that the classic midstream boulder will harbor fish, and they will fish the rich waters just below such a rock. Many, however, overlook the equally productive water immediately above boulders. When approaching any boulder, it is best to make the first casts well above it and to allow the bait or lure to drift down onto the rock. If you fail to interest a fish above the rock, the current will wash your offering alongside and finally behind the boulder where you stand another chance of hooking up.

Submerged boulders are just as productive as exposed ones and should be fished as meticulously. They can be located by bulges in the surface currents. Where water is moving fairly fast, the bulge over a submerged rock will break just below the downstream side of the rock. Rocky banks and streambeds and rock ledges are other places I look for. I always try to fish as close to the rocks as possible. This results in a lot of snags and breakoffs, but it also makes for plenty of hookups.

Visible springs are always good places to try, especially during the warmer summer months when fish will congregate in the cooler water near the spring. Submerged springs can be located by the lush foliage that grows near them. Deadfalls, log jams, and overhanging willows provide shade and are often excellent spots for finding fish in the summertime.

The confluence of any feeder stream is a good place to try just about anytime. Often deep pools where fish will lie in wait of food that is washed down from the tributary are created in such places. In the case of spring and fall migrations, fish will often school up briefly in such pools before entering a tributary. Sometimes a check of the feeder stream will show that its waters are several degrees cooler than the main stream, making the pool at the mouth of the tributary and the tributary itself a good choice for summer fishing.

My approach to any bend in a stream is always a cautious one, because here I often find a gently sloping bank on one side and a deeply cut bank on the other. Where there are enough trees to prevent drastic erosion along the cut bank, currents will wash the bank away well beneath the trees, creating deep, cool holes that almost always harbor fish.

Whether you are fishing a stream for the first time or returning to one of your favorite creeks, a systematic approach to the kind of water and cover that is likely to hold fish and the avoidance of barren waters will mean more fish and less time wasted.

Fishing the Comfort Zones

Water temperature is important to fish, so it ought to be important to the angler pursuing them. Rest assured that the serious angler is going to be equipped to determine the temperature of the water he is fishing, and he is going to know the temperature range within which he is most likely to find the kind of fish he's after. For most stream fishing, any good thermometer will suffice for determining water temperature. But if you're looking for a good thermometer to carry in your fishing vest, pick one that is designed to give rapid temperature readings. Most fishing thermometers will fill the bill, but so will photographic thermometers used to record temperatures of chemicals and washes in the darkroom. For fishing lakes and reservoirs, electronic thermometers are best. They will give instant readings at any depth, whereas a conventional thermometer lowered to a given depth and then brought back up again may be affected by differing temperatures nearer the surface.

Since fish are cold-blooded animals, their body temperatures will be the same as their surroundings. By taking the temperature of a fish as soon as it's brought aboard, you can determine the temperature of the water where the fish struck. And usually more fish will be found in that same temperature range. Here, again, the photographic thermometer is handy; its long slender probe can be inserted into the throat of the fish for a quick temperature reading with no harm to the fish.

Fish are generally divided into cold-water species and warm-water species. But in some parts of the country, and in large, deep res-

ervoirs and lakes, warm-water and cold-water fish can be found inhabiting the same waters. During the spring and fall of the year, in
fact, mixed catches of bass and trout might occur in the same depths
and at the same water temperatures. At my favorite lake on the Oregon coast, for example, any spring morning might produce a mixed
stringer of rainbow trout, largemouth bass, bluegills, and bullheads.
Fall fishing is just as likely to produce cutthroat trout as bass and
panfish. And November is the time when anglers take bass and coho
salmon from the same waters.

One reason for this is that the temperature ranges that fish tolerate are fairly broad and will overlap from species to species. Within
these tolerant temperature ranges are preferred temperature ranges
that are narrower and will not overlap as often. These are the temperatures that fish seek out whenever possible and are the ones that
the angler should look for, too. There are times when fish will be
found in waters that are colder or warmer than what they normally
tolerate, but generally they will be less active then and might entirely cease ingesting food.

The chart opposite lists some of the most popular American freshwater fish and shows the temperature ranges that they will normally
tolerate and the temperatures they prefer. If you are fishing outside
the tolerant range, you are probably wasting your time. On the
other hand, if you can locate water within the preferred range and
couple that with suitable habitat (preferably near bottom) you're going to catch fish—and probably plenty of them.

Know What the Fish Are Eating

Examining the stomach contents of the fish you take home with
you can help you learn a good bit about what the fish in any body
of water feed upon generally and at specific times. I keep records
of what such examinations disclose, often basing my fishing strategy
upon the data I have gathered previously. When I am planning to
fish an unfamiliar lake or reservoir, I make a concerted effort to find
out what sorts of forage fish exist in those waters. Such knowledge
often helps me determine what sort of lure or bait I will first use.
When I'm checking out any water and find fishermen cleaning their
catches, I will ask to examine the stomachs of the fish they've
caught. I have never had anyone refuse my request.

Species	Tolerant Temperature Range (°F.)	Preferred Temperature Range (°F.)
American Shad	55 to 70	64 to 68
Bluegill	60 to 80	67 to 75
Brook Trout	47 to 68	55 to 60
Brown Trout	47 to 68	60 to 65
Bullhead Catfish	55 to 85	65 to 80
Chain Pickerel	60 to 75	64 to 68
Channel Catfish	67 to 85	70 to 75
Chinook Salmon	50 to 63	52 to 54
Coho Salmon	45 to 60	52 to 54
Crappie	60 to 75	64 to 68
Lake Trout	45 to 55	50 to 52
Landlocked Salmon	40 to 55	45 to 50
Largemouth Bass	65 to 80	70 to 75
Muskellunge	60 to 75	64 to 68
Northern Pike	50 to 75	64 to 68
Pumpkinseed Sunfish	65 to 80	70 to 75
Rock Bass	60 to 75	60 to 70
Sauger	45 to 70	59 to 61
Smallmouth Bass	60 to 75	65 to 68
Rainbow Trout	47 to 68	60 to 65
Walleye	45 to 70	59 to 61
White Bass	58 to 75	58 to 64
White Perch	55 to 70	58 to 60
Yellow Perch	45 to 70	45 to 55

In some waters, predatory species may feed predominantly on shad; in others they might feed mostly on bluegills. In still others, perch might be favored, or suckers, chubs, smelt, and any of a number of other forage fish as well as the fry of game fish. At various times of the year, fish might show a preference for one kind of food over another. You might find that the predator species you're after is gorging on crawfish, newts, leeches, or some kind of insect life. This important knowledge can help you catch fish while other fishermen just wonder what they ought to try next.

More Tackle Can Mean More Fish

It may sound terribly elementary to say that the more time you spend fishing the greater are your chances of catching fish, but think about it a moment. In two hours of bass fishing, you will be lucky to have a lure in the water for more than one hour. Consider the time you spend moving from one place to another, changing lures, working snags loose, pulling weeds off your hooks, positioning your boat, anchoring, and all the other activities and motions that are attendant to the sport. In fact, on the average cast, your lure spends about 20 to 25 percent of the time out of the water. So beneath this seemingly rudimentary statement lies the fact that on any fishing outing you might spend half your time (or less) fishing and half your time (or more) doing something else.

One way to better utilize your time and to become a more efficient angler is to go better prepared—and that means with more tackle. On any morning that my wife, Patty, and I head for our favorite lake for a day of bass fishing, all our tackle has been checked over and made ready the night before. Tackle boxes are orderly and contents are untangled and in place. Rods are strung and lines have swivels, snaps, or worm hooks attached and ready for action.

Once our boat is launched and we are on our way to our first preselected fishing spot, Patty and I each have four rigged rods and reels readily at hand. We each have a pair of medium-action spinning rods and reels, one of which is rigged with a surface or shallow-running lure and the other with a spinner bait or weedless spoon. We each have a worm rod rigged with worm hook and slip sinker and an ultralight spinning outfit for panfishing with tiny lures. We're usually fishing by the first hint of dawn and spend a couple of hours working shoreline cover, lily pads, and weedbeds with surface plugs, shallow runners, spinner baits, and weedless spoons.

In any of a number of productive coves or along stretches of shoreline that have either given up fish in the past or look as if they ought to be worth trying, our strategy is to work partially submerged logs, tree stumps, and other visible cover with surface and shallow-running lures. As we approach weedbeds, lily pads, brush, stickups, and flooded timber, we work those snag-strewn areas with spinner baits and weedless spoons. Switching from one type of lure to another is a simple and speedy matter of laying aside one rod and picking up another. Then, as we move on to a different area, we repeat the process, leaving behind a stretch of bass habitat that has been efficiently probed.

We let the fish dictate the course of our tactics. As long as they continue to take our offerings, we keep tossing the plugs to the shallow-water cover and the weedless hardware into the snags. There have been times—especially on heavily overcast or rainy days—when the bass have hugged the shore all day. But most often, as the sun moves toward its zenith, the bass head for cover in deeper water. That's when we swap the surface lures and shallow runners for deep-diving lures and get our worm rods ready for action. We each leave one rod rigged with a spinner bait, since this versatile lure can be worked at any depth and in any kind of cover with a minimum of snagging.

It sometimes takes a while to find bass in the deeper water and, to be certain, there are days when they elude us entirely. But before we leave any area, we have thoroughly worked in search of bass. We'll take up the ultralight tackle to fish for panfish for a quarter of an hour or so, and we'll continue fishing this way until we're ready to call it a day.

This has become our standard strategy whenever we are fishing bass waters, and it has proven highly productive. Certainly, there have been days when we've run through the full range of lure types, have covered every bit of likely habitat that we could find, and have come up bassless or with only a small fish or two to show for our efforts. But more often, we catch our share of bass, mainly because we are able to cover a lot of water without wasting time. As for the panfish, we usually catch as many as we want. Sometimes we get so involved in the panfishing that we give up the bassing tactics altogether. If we were only toting our heavy bass gear, we would miss out on a lot of panfishing fun.

CHAPTER 8

Fishing Systems

Introduction to Drift Fishing

Drift fishing is a popular system for taking steelhead trout in the streams of the Pacific Northwest and in the Great Lakes region. The system need not be confined to steelheading, however, as it is effective on a wide range of fish that dwell in free-flowing streams throughout the country. It will get a bait down to the bottom where the fish are, and it will cover a lot of territory.

The effectiveness of the system is dependent upon the casting and presentation of the bait as well as upon the terminal rigging. Quite simply, casts are made diagonally upstream, and the bait is allowed to sink to the bottom where it will drift downstream with the current. When the bait has drifted to a point where the line runs diagonally downstream, the drift is generally terminated, and the angler makes another upstream cast to start another drift.

After making a cast, the angler should allow the bait sufficient time to sink to the bottom—a matter of a few seconds—and then he should take up any slack in the line. During the drift, it is important to keep the rod tip pointed upward, at about the 10-o'clock position, to prevent any excessive drag on the line caused by the current.

There are numerous ways to rig a line for this sort of fishing, several of which employ pencil sinkers. The rigging I prefer calls for a three-way swivel to which a piece of surgical tubing has been added. Such swivels are available with the tubing already attached, but it is far cheaper to buy swivels and surgical tubing in bulk quantities and to make your own.

Use the T-shaped swivels (not the Y-shaped ones), and slip a 2-inch piece of surgical tubing onto the dropper eye of the swivel. Secure the tubing to the swivel eye by wrapping fine wire around the upper end of the tubing. Twist the ends of the wire, and bend it back against the wire wrap. Then fold the upper end of the tubing back over the wire. Attach your fishing line to one of the remaining eyes of the swivel. The other eye is where the monofilament leader (usually 18- to 24-inches long) is attached.

The pencil sinker, which can be cut to any weight to suit the current, is simply pushed into the open end of the surgical tubing. And it need not be pushed in far to secure it—about a quarter of an inch or so will do. During the drift, then, the pencil sinker should bounce along bottom. When it gets snagged—and it will if you're fishing in the right places—a steady pull on your line will cause the sinker to pop out of the tubing, thus saving the rest of your terminal tackle.

At the business end of the leader, where the hook is attached, steelheaders will use any variety of baits. These can include cured salmon eggs, worms, and artificial egg clusters, such as Gooey Bobs and Okie Drifters. If you are fishing for other stream-dwelling species, use the kinds of baits they prefer. For example, during the early part of trout season, when waters are often high and roily, worms are favored by many anglers and can be effectively drifted in the manner described. By tying a salmon-egg hook to your leader, you can drift a single salmon egg in the same way.

Smallmouth-bass fishermen will find the same system far superior to other methods of bait fishing for these fine game fish. Minnows, helgrammites, crawfish, and night crawlers are all good choices for smallmouth drift fishing. Walleyes, sauger, white bass, rock bass, channel cats, chinook and coho salmon are a few of the other kinds of fish you can take by drift fishing. It is among the most effective ways to present a bait to any stream-dwelling fish.

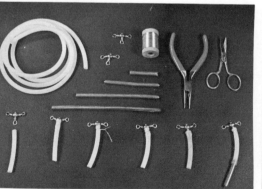

Pictured at the top are all materials required to make your own drift fishing rigs: surgical tubing, crossline (T) swivels, fine wire, pliers, scissors, and pencil sinkers. Across the bottom, each step in the assembly of the rigs is shown.

To fish the deadly Mepps/spawn sack combination, you'll need fresh eggs, nylon stockings or maline cloth, monofilament line, scissors and a supply of Mepps spinners.

Sure-Fire System for Salmon/Trout/Steelhead

My good friend Jim Martin taught me a variation of drift fishing that he learned in the Midwest and that has proved to be the most consistent taker of salmon, trout, and steelhead of any system I have ever used. I was living in Fairbanks, Alaska, when I met Jim and learned about this unusual technique, and, frankly, I was skeptical about it at first. But before I even had a chance to try it out, Jim made a trip to southeastern Alaska where he and his partner used this system to catch and release dozens of steelhead in less than a week. They returned to Fairbanks with several 15-pounders on ice and one brute of 20½ pounds that ended up as the state record for that year.

This system is unique in that it is a compatible marriage of artificial lure and salmon-egg cluster that is not only deadly, but also far easier to employ than conventional drift-fishing techniques. Drift fishermen usually must contend with two problems when using salmon eggs. First, fresh eggs—those that milk the best and are the most appealing to salmon and trout—refuse to stay on the hook on all but the gentlest of casts. Even the more durable cured eggs are delicate baits at best. Secondly, anglers new to drift fishing, and even some veterans, frequently experience diffficulty in detecting the gentle pickup common to this type of fishing. Rather than striking savagely, the fish will often merely stop the bait momentarily, the only indication being a slight tick in the line or a brief hesitation in the drift.

This system solves the first of these problems by enclosing the salmon eggs in a tough mesh sack. Spawn sacks are nothing new, and, in fact, tackle shops in salmon and steelhead country generally carry maline cloth patches designed for tying them. Bridal-veil cloth is another suitable material, but most often we use sheer nylon stockings. To make a spawn sack, we we put a pinch of eggs in the center of a 4-inch by 4-inch patch of nylon stocking or maline cloth, and, holding the corners, we twist the sack into a snug, quarter-size cluster. We tie off the top with monofilament, and trim excess line and nylon with scissors.

The other half of the lure/bait combination is a Mepps Aglia spinner with a plain treble hook, one tine of which is inserted into the spawn sack beneath the monofilament wrap. The size of the Mepps to be used is determined by the current of the pool where it will be drifted. This is because the spinner not only acts as a fish attractor, but also as the weight that will sink the spawn sack to the bottom.

Casts and drifts are made in the same way as those described in "Introduction To Drift Fishing" above. During the drift, the lure/bait should bounce along bottom about every couple of feet. If it drifts freely without touching down, it's too light; if it rolls along the bottom and consistently hangs up, it's too heavy. We have found that the #3, #4, and #5 Mepps Aglia spinners that weigh, respectively, ¼, ⅓, and ½ ounce, suit the various currents of the pools in which we fish.

We have tested different spinners for this system and have tried various colors, blade finishes, and designs, with hooks both plain and dressed. The plain-hook, gold-bladed Aglia has outfished all others. The same lure with a fluorescent-red blade has proved tops in roily water. The Aglia blade is designed to revolve at about a 60° angle from the spinner body on a normal retrieve, and it will revolve on extremely slow retrieves. When it is drifted for salmon or trout, the blade twirls lazily, even in relatively slow currents. Other blades we've tried just don't function as well.

There's no problem detecting the pickup with this system, because it's about as delicate as a karate chop and sometimes as disarming. For some reason, most fish attack the Mepps/spawn sack with startling ferocity. I first thought the mesh of the spawn sack was catching on their teeth, preventing them from discarding the bait and, thus, giving the appearance of a strike. But that theory proved faulty when we tried drifting J-Bait, Gooey Bobs, and other plastic cluster eggs hooked on the Mepps spinner. Strikes weren't as frequent as with fresh roe, but they were just as wild.

I came up with several more theories on why fish would assail this unlikely duo, but I finally decided it made no difference as long as it worked. After all, who cares why pike will engulf a wobbling hunk of steel painted red and white, or why a bass will suck up a piece of purple plastic?

Jim and I thoroughly tested this system on Alaska's Gulkana River for two seasons, and the records I compiled certainly convinced me that this simple system has to be one of the best to come along in years. During our first season, the best run with this system was when Jim caught and released 35 chinooks in two days and returned to Fairbanks with one of a pair of 49-pounders.

The following year, when Jim and I were teaching our outdoor-workshop course called "Sport Fishing in Alaska," we took six students to the Gulkana River during the peak of the run. There the eight of us caught and released 201 chinooks in one week, 200 of which fell for the Mepps/spawn sack. By excluding the largest fish (a 51-pound trophy taken by one of our students) and the smallest (a 4-pound jack caught by yours truly) from our records, the average weight of the salmon we caught worked out to 30.4 pounds.

It doesn't stop with salmon and steelhead, though. I have taken a number of trout incidental to salmon fishing, but I have also intentionally caught other fish with a scaled-down version of the system. For spring trout and grayling fishing, this system is unexcelled. While many spring fishermen use spinners or bait, a conventionally fished spinner often fails to get down to the fish. And a bait that is plunked into a pool to wait for passing fish doesn't cover sufficient territory. A drifting Mepps with eggs, however, bounces along the bottom and seeks out the fish.

I use #0, #1, and #2 Mepps Aglia spinners for this light-tackle fishing and narrow-diameter, premium 6-pound-test line that resists water drag and sinks the lures quickly. To these spinners, I either attach miniature, nickel-size spawn sacks, or I impale a single, cured salmon egg on each tine of the treble hook. It's a super system that will produce fine catches wherever it's legal to use salmon eggs.

Five handsome grayling that fell for the
Mepps-and-egg combination.

A New Twist for Bass Fishing

Quite by accident one evening, I stumbled onto a lure combination that later became the foundation for a system that, in two seasons of testing, has netted more bass for my wife and me than all other techniques combined. At the time, I was experimenting with various crank baits used in conjunction with soft, plastic twister tails in hopes of coming up with an effective and inexpensive eel-like lure to use on striped bass when they migrated up the coastal rivers to spawn. What ultimately resulted was a system of lures that will snake through the water and drive largemouth bass wild. Color combinations are nearly infinite for adaptation to all weather and water conditions. And the system will cover a broad range from shallow to medium depths.

Although we tested about two dozen different kinds of lures, those that proved the best for the system are the Rebel Humpback Deep Runner, and the Norman Little Scooper, Super Scooper, and Magnum Scooper. All of these lures must be modified slightly be-

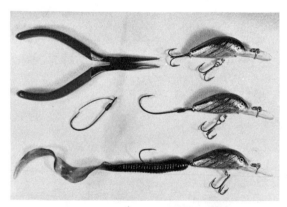

Conversion of a Norman Little Scooper is shown here. Rear treble is replaced by a #2/0 weedless hook with weed guard removed. Up-riding rear hook is then dressed with a 6- or 7-inch twist tail.

fore they can be used in the system. The first step in the modification is to remove the rear treble hook from each lure by unscrewing the screw eye that holds it. Use pliers to bend open the screw eye just far enough for hook removal.

The trailing treble will be replaced by a #2/0 single hook. We use Eagle Claw weedless hooks for replacement, because the large ring eyes allow full movement when the hooks are attached to the screw eye. But we remove the weed guard from each hook by clasping it with pliers near the plastic retainer on the hook shank and pulling toward the hook eye. When the single hook has been attached to the screw eye and the eye has been clamped shut with pliers, we mount it in the rear of the lure with the hook point riding up.

The final step in the modification of the lure is the addition of a 6- or 7-inch, soft, plastic twist tail, such as a Mister Twister or Burke Wig-Wag Worm. Color combinations of lure bodies and tails are nearly limitless. Tails and lures can be mixed and matched, or they can be color coordinated. We usually match up the color of the lure body to the color of the tail. For example, to a chartreuse lure with a black back we will attach a chartreuse tail; a silver-sided lure with a purple back gets a purple tail.

Although we carry a good supply of red, black, purple, yellow, pearl white, blue, amber, and chartreuse tails with lure bodies to match—all of which have caught fish—we have our favorites. For early morning, evening, and heavily overcast days, the highly visible chartreuse lure has been the number-one bass getter. Pearl white has proved to be the next best choice under those same conditions. In clear to slightly colored water, red and purple have been the best producers; in roily waters, pearl white and black are top choices.

The best all-around producer of bass, and the one that Patty has outfished me with nearly every time out, is a silver-sided Little Scooper with a red head that fades to yellow on the back. To this is attached a translucent red tail. This lure has caught bass at all times of the day and under all the conditions we have faced, but it has been particularly effective in water of average clarity on overcast days when bass are active well after daybreak in waters that run 6- to 10-feet deep.

In different waters in other parts of the country, perhaps other colors and color combinations will shake out on top. That's why you might have to do some experimenting of your own. However, if you want to try the system out, I would recommend chartreuse and red as good colors to begin with. You might want to add black and purple to provide a good selection that can be adapted to nearly any conditions you will encounter.

The first time you see one of these lure combinations move through the water, you will realize that few lures produce such exciting action. But you're in for a few other pleasant surprises, too. For example, you will find these lures to be remarkably snag resistant. The lure's retrieve attitude is such that as it dives toward bottom and approaches sunken logs, branches, rocks, and the like, the protruding lip will bounce the lure over the snag and will usually keep the belly treble from hanging up. And the up-riding single hook in the rear will run through all but the worst cover without snagging. The lures are not weedless, however. So when you are working weedbeds and lily-pad patches, it is best to cast parallel to them and to work the edges.

Another plus with this system is that these lures are extremely easy to control. One of our favorite techniques is to cast to visible shoreline cover, such as deadfalls, tree stumps, partially submerged logs, and brush piles. Since the lures will float until they are retrieved, we can cast slightly beyond the target and, by holding the rod high and retrieving slowly, we can inch the lure over any potential snags. Then, when the lure is precisely in the right spot, a few quick turns of the reel handle, with the rod tip pointing downward, drives the lure to its depths.

The Norman and Rebel lures have the added advantage of neutral buoyancy. When the retrieve is stopped at any point, the lures will hold their depth. This feature not only adds to the control of the lure, but it also helps to coax some bass into striking. After diving the lure with a fast retrieve for a few feet, it can be slowed in an enticing slither that often evokes savage strikes. The built-in action of these lures, coupled with the writhing twister tail, makes this combination highly visible. But since these baits are equipped with rattles, bass are attracted by sound as well as sight.

If you decide to try this system out, there are a few precautions you should take to keep from impairing the lure's deadly action. If you have lures of similar design in your tackle box and plan to convert them for adaptation to this system, make sure that there is a split ring attached to the screw eye at the front of each lure. Tying your line directly to the eye will impede the lure's action. If there is no split ring, either add one or attach your line via a lure snap. Do not, however, use a snap swivel, because the bulk of such hardware will also influence the action of the lure.

The action also can be negatively affected by weeds or algae, especially if such debris clings to the diving lip. And if the screw eye at the front of the lure is bent in any way, the lure will not run true. Instead, it will side-plane to the surface. Use a pair of longnose pliers to adjust the screw eye so it is perpendicular to the surface of the diving lip. One last word of caution: Be sure to keep the lure bodies separate from the twister tails in your tackle box, as the soft plastic of the tails will react with the paint on the lures.

Since beginning our experiments with this system, we have accumulated several dozen converted lure bodies and a drawer full of matching twister tails. We wouldn't dream of going bass fishing without them.

The Old Popper-Dropper Trick

In waters where both large and small fishes—such as bass and bluegills—are found, or in coastal rivers where stripers and shad might be sharing the same haunts, you can increase your chances of filling a stringer by fishing for the big ones and little ones simultaneously. Carry an assortment of tiny jigs and shad flies for the small fish and large surface lures for the lunkers. Tie a leader, 12- to 14-inches long, to a jig or shad fly. At the other end of the leader, tie a small snap. Attach the snap to the eye of the rear hook on the surface plug, and cast this popper-dropper combination to the usual kind of cover you fish with surface lures—shoreline weeds, lily pads, deadfalls, boulders, boat docks, and the like.

As you retrieve the surface lure in a jerk-stop-pause fashion, the proper action is automatically imparted to the jig that trails behind and just below the surface. Often, the surface commotion will attract schools of panfish which will take the trailing lure with relish. In turn, the smaller fish will sometimes catch the attention of a nearby lunker, which will usually opt for the surface plug that appears to be a wounded, struggling fish and an easy prey.

Hammer Handles on a Fly Rod

Some years ago, my partners and I were on one of our Wisconsin fishing trips where we spent early morning and late evening hours prodding the pockets and pools of a nearby duck marsh for bass and pike. The bass there were stocky fish and full of fight. Many of the pike were small and known locally as hammer handles.

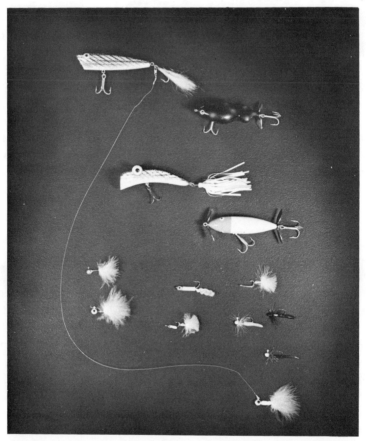

A large surface lure trailing a tiny jig or fly from a 12- to 14-inch
leader can be a winning combination for lunkers and panfish.

One particularly pleasant spring evening, I was casting a big bass
bug with an 8-foot fly rod, hoping to fool one of the resident large-
mouths. Just as the deer hair and steel settled next to a pile of brush
near the mouth of a small creek, the water erupted, and a cartwheeling pike kept me wondering why I hadn't tried this sport
before.

Since that evening discovery, I have fished for small pike with a
fly rod in Michigan and Canada and have found few experiences as
exciting. Small pike are great fighters that seem to spend more time
out of the water than in. They will eagerly take a variety of fly-rod
lures and will rival any bass or trout in their antics.

Any good, bass-weight fly rod will suit this sport. I prefer a bass-bug, tapered line, such as WF8F. Leaders should be relatively short —about 6 feet—stiff at the butt, and tapered abruptly to a 6-pound tippet to assure that the bulky, wind-resistant flies will turn over with ease. Check leaders frequently for fraying.

All big bass bugs and poppers will take pike on top. Large trout and salmon streamers will work well beneath the surface. Small pork-rind skirts can be added to any of these flies for extra attraction. Although I have rarely had my leader parted by small pike, flies do get chewed up. So it pays to carry plenty of extras. When the pike are running small, don't despair. Make the most of the situation by trying hammer handles on a fly rod. You'll be in for some big surprises.

Lessons Learned from Grayling

One of the most delightful of all fresh-water fishes is the American grayling. In my estimation, no other fresh-water fish can rival its beauty and grace, and few will take artificials as eagerly. During spring and fall migrations, grayling will strike small spinners and spoons. In the warmer months, they are a dry-fly fisherman's joy— rising readily to black gnat and mosquito patterns, often with an un-orthodox strike that is nothing short of spectacular.

There are times, however, when grayling—like any other fish— can be downright persnickety. They're notorious for being ex-tremely tippet-wary and, consequently, grayling fishermen have learned to change their approach when floating flies to these fish. Instead of casting upstream in the traditional manner, flies are drifted downstream so that the fly appears to the fish before the tip-pet does.

The important lesson learned from the finicky grayling is this: An approach that is contrary to tradition can sometimes mean more fish in the creel when the quarry is being spooked by leaders and tip-pets. Too often, the instructional literature of angling either forces us into a rut or lulls us into a belief that there is only one system for angling with certain kinds of tackle or for certain species. For ex-ample, we are told that fish normally lie in a stream with their heads pointed into the current and that the way to approach them is from downstream, making casts upstream. This approach also allows for a more natural presentation of the dry fly, because it will not usually be affected by drag on the fly line.

When such an approach fails, it only makes good sense to try something else. Since fishing for grayling, I have tried the downstream cast to tippet-wary trout and have found it to be quite effective. The technique calls for a stealthy approach, so as not to alarm the already skittish fish, and careful wading that will not roil the water.

For two reasons, casts should be short with a minimum of false casting. First, the activity required for long casts will spook the fish. Secondly, there's no need to cast any great distance, since the current will help you drift your fly down to the fish. You need only pay line out as the current demands, making sure that you feed the line fast enough for the fly to drift naturally.

The only thing that takes some getting used to with this system is the strike. Usually, when casting upstream in the conventional manner, your position, relative to that of the fish, aids you in setting the hook. So a quick strike most often results in a connection. But when you are drifting a fly downstream, you should hesitate for a split second after the strike in order to avoid yanking the fly away from the fish.

A System for Summer Bluegills

Generally speaking, few fish are as easy to locate and catch as bluegills. One reason that they're easy to find is that they never stray far from where they were hatched. And since their numbers increase rapidly wherever they are, they must compete with one another for available food. This is one reason why they will eagerly take baits and lures.

As the water warms in the summer months, however, all but the smallest bluegills will move to slightly deeper waters to seek out temperatures from 67° to 75°. So, to catch eating-size fish you might have to search a bit. Because bluegills never travel too far, a systematic search will usually turn up schools of catchable fish.

A thermometer is always helpful for locating the right temperature range. Usually the fish will be found near some kind of structure or where the water of the preferred temperature is near the bottom. Although schools of bluegills sometimes can be found suspended above bottom, they will never be too far from some kind of

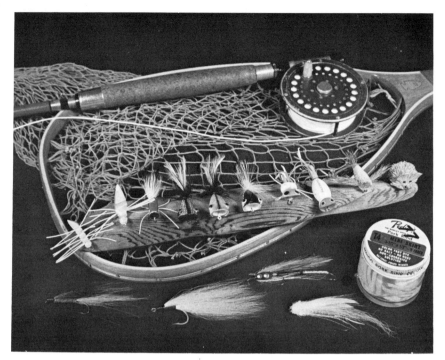

Small pike are great fun on fly tackle. Use a bass action rod, bass taper line, and large bass bugs, poppers, and streamers. For added appeal, hang a pork-rind strip on streamers.

protective cover. While the spots that give up plenty of saucer-size bluegills in the springtime will seldom produce large fish during the warmer months, they are nonetheless good places to begin searching out the schools.

I use ultralight tackle for this kind of fishing, and, most often, I will use tiny jigs to probe the depths. I begin fishing near weedbeds, brush piles, deadfalls, and other cover that normally produces bluegills. If I catch only small fish, I begin slowly and methodically moving farther away from the shore, jigging vertically just off the side of the boat.

A 4½- or 5-foot ultralight rod and a small reel filled with premium quality 4- or 6-pound-test line is just right. Any 1/16- or 1/32-ounce jig will produce fish, but those dressed with a half-inch piece of a small, plastic worm will usually outperform all others. Another excellent combination is a tiny jig head dressed with a mealworm.

Once a school of good-size fish is located, fishing will be fast for the first ten or fifteen minutes. Then, as the fish become accustomed to the lure, they will usually stop hitting as eagerly. That's when I move off the spot and begin casting to them with tiny spoons, spinners, and spinner baits. If I have reason to believe that the school is a large one and that it contains some big bluegills, I will anchor my boat within casting distance and will give them a thorough workout with small lures.

Once I'm anchored near a school, 4-inch plastic worms often produce some dandy bluegills. I use an ultralight spin-casting outfit for this light worming, and I rig the worms Texas style on #2 worm hooks. I pinch on a small split shot just above the hook eye and fish it just as I would work a plastic worm for bass. Big bull bluegills on such tackle are every bit as sporting as bass are on heavier gear. They will provide steady action all day long, and they are certainly fine table fare.

CHAPTER 9

The Fisherman Afloat

Try Before You Buy

If you had never driven a car, a number of steps would have to be taken before getting behind the wheel and before you could prove enough proficiency to be legally licensed to operate a vehicle. So presumably, before you invest in an automobile, you would know how to operate one and might even be at least vaguely aware of the mechanical principles that enable the vehicle to function.

Such is not the case with watercraft. No authority is going to watch over you to make sure that you know how to operate a boat or know how to avoid the potential perils of water travel. Common sense dictates that we take on the responsibility of learning something about boat handling, water safety, and the limitations of various kinds of watercraft before venturing into the purchase of one.

If you have had little or no experience at the helm, you will find it helpful to go with a friend who is an experienced boatman. Have him teach you all he can about boat handling. Then log a few hours at the helm so you can get the feel of running a boat. Try to gain such experience in a variety of situations and under different conditions, in calm and rough water.

Courses in boating skills are offered throughout the country by the Coast Guard Auxiliary and the Power Squadron. A local boat dealer should be able to put you in touch with someone in one of these organizations. A bonus to the successful completion of one of these courses is a discount on boating insurance policies. With some knowledge of boat handling, and perhaps a bit of experience, you should be better able to determine what sort of craft will best suit your fishing needs.

On the Merits of Modest Beginnings

While most of us probably have dreams of owning or plans to own that ultimate fishing boat some day, there are some distinct advan-

151

tages to starting out with a smaller craft—not the least of which is cost. Beyond the aspect of initial investment are the other monetary considerations, such as the cost of maintenance, repairs, and operation. Certainly, the small cartopper is far more economical to own and operate than a fully outfitted bass boat.

There are other advantages to consider as well. For the beginner, the small craft offers an excellent way to gain experience and confidence on the water and to learn how to handle a boat. Furthermore, the fisherman who starts out with some sort of small fishing boat soon learns that it has some characteristic advantages over larger craft. It can be launched just about anywhere, for example. When launch ramps are crowded with fishermen, boaters, and waterskiers clambering to get into or out of the water, the guy with the cartopper needn't wait in line. Also, there are some lakes and streams that are either fished from shore or from small watercraft that can be carried by two persons, because no facilities exist for launching trailered boats. More than one fisherman has decided to keep his old cartopper when the time came to buy that new bass boat or runabout because of the small boat's versatility and the larger boat's limitations.

I think one of the best reasons for owning one or more smaller boats before finally investing in that dream boat is that the fisherman gradually learns what he wants in that more expensive boat. After all, a well-equipped, high-performance fishing boat can cost as much or considerably more than the family vehicle, ranking it among the largest investments that a person is likely to make. It only makes sense to know precisely what you want before you buy.

For instance, after a long day of fishing and hauling up a pair of anchors by hand a dozen or more times, it is easy to recognize the merits of anchor-retrieval systems that require less physical exertion. Or after a couple of years of fooling around with stringers and bait buckets, aerated live wells seem more necessary than frivolous. Through such experiences, the ideal boat begins to take a mental shape. So when time comes to buy, outfitting that new boat will be more certain and less risky.

Tips on Anchoring

While any fisherman with some time logged at the helm can become a competent boater—as, indeed, many do—too many know too little about the seemingly simple task of anchoring a craft. One reason many of us get some faulty notions about anchoring is that we get our first introduction to boating when we rent a boat and motor at a local marina. The rented craft most often will be equipped with one anchor to which 10 or 15 feet of rope is attached.

Ideally, the anchor rode (boatman's jargon for the anchor line) should be seven times the depth of the water where the craft is to be anchored. You can get by with a rode that is five times the depth, but anything less will be ineffective, even in a slight breeze. So, the boat that you rent is usually set up to be anchored effectively in 2 or 3 feet of water.

When you outfit your own boat for anchoring, use two anchors, and make sure that your anchor rodes are at least five times the depth of the water in which you will normally anchor. The effectiveness of your anchor is increased as the rode becomes closer to parallel to the bottom.

If you use your boat mostly for fishing and you normally anchor in water no deeper than 10 feet, your anchor rodes should be at least 50-feet long. If you often anchor in 20-foot depths, your rodes should be at least 100-feet long. If your boat is large enough for sleeping aboard and anchoring overnight, you should stick to the seven to one rule—7 feet of rode for every foot of depth.

Make a Pair of Brush Anchors

When fishing in flooded timber or near brush piles and deadfalls, the simplest and quickest way to anchor—and the method that will not disturb the fish below—is with a pair of brush anchors. You can make a pair of these anchors in less than five minutes for less than $5. All you need are two pieces of quarter-inch nylon rope about 5-feet long and four snap hooks. Tie a snap hook to each end of each piece of rope.

Attach one of the anchors near the bow and the other near the stern of your boat, via the snap hooks. To anchor your boat to a tree branch, just loop the rope around the branch, bring the snap hook back, and fasten it to a cleat or to the other snap hook. Anchoring the bow and stern in this fashion takes about two or three seconds, and the boat can be set free again just as quickly. And best of all, it doesn't spook nearby fish.

Simple, inexpensive brush anchors can be made in minutes with a 5-foot length of rope and two snap hooks for each anchor.

Care of Paddles and Oars

Among the most neglected of all boating gear are paddles and oars. The fisherman who pays close attention to maintaining his cartop boat or canoe and who adheres to a strict maintenance schedule for his outboard motor too often overlooks the necessary upkeep of his paddles and oars.

As soon as varnish or paint is chipped away, water begins to deteriorate the wood of paddles and oars. As moisture seeps deeper into the grain of the wood, it swells the wood. This causes the remaining finish to crack and peel, exposing more raw wood to the destructive elements. And, before you know it, your paddles or oars will take on the characteristics of driftwood; they will begin to rot and weaken and will fail when you need them most.

Minimum maintenance of oars or paddles calls for annual refurbishing. During the off-season, sand them down first with medium-grit sandpaper and then with fine-grit sandpaper. Wipe them clean with a slightly damp cloth or sponge, and apply two coats of marine varnish, polyurethane, or paint. If you have neglected your paddles or oars for two years or more, and they are showing signs of severe wear, use a paint or varnish remover to take off all of the old finish. Then apply two coats of preservative paint or varnish. A little attention during the off-season can prevent problems when the fish are hitting. Oars and paddles that are properly cared for will last virtually indefinitely.

Ballast for Your Square-Stern or Cartopper

If you use a cartop boat or square-stern canoe and outboard for your fishing, you'll run bow-light when you fish alone if you don't put some kind of ballast in the bow. Of course, you can put all your tackle in the bow, but that wouldn't be enough to offset your weight and that of the motor. Besides, it would put your gear out of reach.

A simpler solution is to make up some sandbags that you can lay in the bow to weigh it down. Sandbags can be made from the legs of old, worn-out jeans. A pair of men's jeans will yield enough material for two bags per leg. Each bag will weigh about 20 pounds when filled with sand.

Simply cut the pant legs off at the crotch, and cut each leg in half. Sew up the bottom of each bag, and fill with plastic bags full of sand before stitching the tops of the sandbags closed. Putting the sand in plastic bags not only makes it easier to do the final stitching on the sandbags, but it also keeps the sand from getting wet. Four of these bags will put an extra 80 pounds in the bow of your boat.

How to Carry an Outboard for Long Distances

Toting your kicker from a car trunk to the boat dock usually isn't much of a chore, since you can normally park near where you are launching a cartopper or renting a skiff. But if you have to carry any outboard motor for a long distance, the handles that the manufacturer provides will dig into the flesh of your hands, and the weight of the motor will severely strain your shoulders.

Instead of carrying the motor by the handle, get it up on your shoulder where the weight will cause a minimum of fatigue and no pain. Put a flotation cushion or life jacket over your shoulder for padding. Then rest the leg of the motor atop the padding—propeller pointing forward, engine aft—and drape a hand over the forward portion of the leg to maintain balance. With the motor so balanced, you'll be able to carry it for some distance, even over rough terrain.

Author's square-stern canoe rigged for shallow river running with extension clamped onto transom and outboard fastened to the transom extension.

If in Doubt, How Much Oil?

In two-cycle outboard motors, the oil must be mixed with the gasoline to keep the engine parts lubricated. If you have purchased a new engine, your operator's manual will tell you what proportion of oil to mix with gas. In the event that you have bought a used motor and have no manual, or if you just can't remember how much oil to mix with the gas—in short, if you are ever in doubt—use more oil than what you think you need. While too much oil can cause your engine to run rough, smoke too much, and will foul plugs, it will cause no permanent damage. Using too little oil, on the other hand, can cause expensive damage to your engine.

Gas to oil ratios for most two-cycle engines will range from 16:1 to 50:1—that's 1 pint of oil per 2 gallons of gas (16:1) to 1 pint of oil per 6 gallons of gas (50:1). So if you're stuck somewhere, need to refuel your boat, and have no idea how much oil to use, mix a pint

of oil with 2 gallons of regular gas. That will get you back to the dock
of the launching ramp without harming your engine. Later you can
check with a nearby boat dealer to find out what mixture you should
be using.

Discarding Outboard Fuel

Invariably at season's end, I have at least one six-gallon tank of
outboard-motor fuel left. Sometimes my auxiliary tank and spare
fuel cans have fuel remaining in them, too. Since gasoline can begin
turning to a gummy varnish after sitting in a tank or can for as little
as ninety days, I used to fret about what to do with this leftover fuel.

Finally I asked a friend of mine, who is one of the largest boat
dealers in the Midwest, about this problem. "Pour it into your car,"
he said, and apparently detecting my skeptical look, he added, "and
don't worry about the oil mixture. That outboard oil is top-quality
stuff and will probably be good for your car's engine. At least it
won't hurt it."

Since then, I have poured all my leftover outboard fuel into my
car's gas tank. Before doing so, however, I take advantage of the opportunity to inspect my outboard tanks and spare gas cans. After I
transfer the outboard fuel to a clean G.I. gas can, I check the inside
of my fuel tanks and spare cans with a flashlight to make sure they
are clean and free of corrosion, dirt, or any other visible contami-
nant. There's always a little fuel left in the bottom of the cans. By
sloshing it around, I can see if there is any foreign material that
would clog a fuel line or carburetor.

If you end up with a tank or spare can of outboard fuel that is
more than 90 days old, don't chance using it—either in your outboard or your family car. Get rid of it. Discarding as little as a gallon
of gas, however, might pose a bit of a problem. Generally you can
dump it at a local refuse area or sanitary-landfill operation, but be
sure to tell the dumpmaster what you intend to do. He will probably want you to discard the flammable liquid in some out-of-the-
way area. If he won't let you dump it at all, phone your local fire
department, and ask them what to do with it.

Poor Man's Riverboat

Easing through snag-filled shallows at idle speed generally poses
no problem for the outboard-powered craft, since the motor will

kick up on impact with obstructions. Run those same waters at full throttle or at cruising speed, however, and you will not only stand the chance of doing serious damage to your engine and boat but will also place yourself and your passengers in the path of peril.

On a lake or reservoir, there's no reason for navigating such waters at any but the slowest of speeds. But against the swift currents of a free-flowing river, power is essential. And it is usually in the worst stretches of any river—the shallows and rapids where boulders, submerged logs, and shifting gravel bars are constant threats to navigation—that power is most important.

Consequently, sportsmen who use such waterways prefer a craft with a shallow draft and flat bottom. Favored among river runners are aluminum or wooden jon boats in lengths from 16 to 20 feet, equipped with powerful outboards and engine lifts or jet units. These boats can safely navigate swift and shallow rivers and can put outdoorsmen into otherwise inaccessible areas. Two problems with the traditional riverboats, however, are cost and launching restrictions. The person who plans to buy such a craft can count on spending $3,000 or more for a no-frills boat, motor, and trailer, and the average is probably closer to $5,000 for a well-equipped riverboat. Furthermore, some sort of launching facilities are required to get the boat into and out of the water.

I first saw the solution to each of these problems when I was on a duck-hunting trip with a friend in his 18-foot riverboat on a slough of Alaska's Tanana River. The local Grumman boat dealer, Hal Dinkens, and two of his hunting partners had reached the same remote area we were hunting in a 19-foot square-stern canoe that was jury rigged for shallow running. I only caught a glimpse, then, of the extended transom on Hal's canoe, but I talked to him later and was convinced that this was one way I could afford to own a boat that was suitable for river running.

The following summer, I met several other members of the square-stern set and spent some time running rivers with them, learning what these versatile craft could do. By fall, Hal had sold me a new Grumman Sportcanoe—a 15-foot, 3-inch craft that is remarkably stable and well-suited to river duty. Some of the square-sterners have their canoes equipped with small motor lifts, but most simply fit their canoes with transom extensions that sufficiently raise their motors for running rocky shallows and moderate rapids.

My own extension is a copy of the one that Hal Dinkens uses. To duplicate it, you will need two 12-inch by 8-inch pieces of ¾-inch plywood that will be joined together to form one strong 12-inch by 8-inch by 1½-inch slab. Use a paintbrush to apply a liberal amount of waterproof glue or waterproof contact cement to the joining surfaces of the plywood. After sandwiching them together, lay them on a flat surface and put something heavy (such as a tool box) on top of them while the glue cures—generally about 24 hours.

Fill all holes and gaps in the plywood laminations with wood filler. When the filler has cured, remove excess with medium-grit (#120) sandpaper and wipe the extension clean with a slightly damp sponge. Finally, apply two coats of polyurethane or marine varnish.

To attach the extension to the transom of your boat or square-stern, you will need two heavy-duty 4-inch C-clamps. Adjust the height of the extension so that your outboard propeller extends just below the bottom of the hull, and make sure the C-clamps are screwed as tightly closed as you can get them.

With your engine so situated, you can safely run the rocky shallows of rivers. Even if you do hit a barely submerged rock or log from time to time, it will usually be a glancing blow rather than a head-on collision with your lower unit. This minimizes the chance of serious damage.

While I might not be able to run a river as quickly as the riverboaters do, my "poor man's riverboat" still gets me there and back. Furthermore, I have been able to use the same craft for hunting, camping, fishing, and exploring on rivers, creeks, lakes, ponds, and duck marshes. My canoe is light enough for cartopping and short portages and can be launched nearly anywhere. Since it is easy to paddle, it is perfect for float trips, too. Best of all, my initial investment was a fraction of the cost of a traditional riverboat, and the same is true with operational and upkeep expenses. It's the kind of riverboat I can afford to own.

Four Uses for Plastic Jugs

Although it is normally a good idea to attach a safety chain to a small outboard to prevent the loss of the engine, river running calls for other measures. In the event that my engine were to vibrate loose, break off the transom, or in any other way depart from its rightful position, I don't want it dangling from a chain attached to the stern of my canoe where it might hang up in the rocks and ultimately capsize the craft.

Instead, I attach one end of a 25-foot rope to my outboard and the other end to a marker buoy that is nothing more than a plastic half-gallon jug with a tight cap glued closed. Theoretically (and I hope I never have to test the theory), in the event of an accident that would cause me to lose my engine, it would fall free of the craft, and the buoy would mark its position for later retrieval.

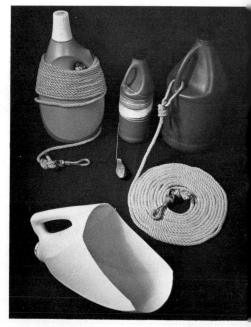

Plastic jugs from bleach, detergent, water softener, cooking oil, and other liquids have numerous uses. Attach one, via a length of rope, to your small outboard when running rivers to serve as a marker buoy in case you lose your engine. Small jugs make great buoys for marking underwater structure. A large jug filled with sand can be used as an anchor for a small boat or canoe. A jug with the bottom cut out at an angle is a dandy boat bailer.

A half-gallon jug can be turned into an anchor for a small boat or canoe, too. Just fill it with sand, attach one end of a rope to the jug handle and the other to your boat, and you have an anchor that will hold your boat fast on small lakes and ponds in fairly calm weather.

A quart, half-gallon, or gallon jug makes an excellent marker buoy. Just attach one end of a line to the handle of the jug and the other end to a small anchor, such as a large bank sinker, pyramid sinker, or a decoy anchor. Then wrap the line around the jug. When you tie into a fish while trolling, toss the marker buoy overboard, and troll in the vicinity of the buoy to pick up other fish in the school. Marker buoys are also handy to use in conjunction with a depth finder to mark underwater ledges, drop-offs, reefs, old roadbeds, creek channels, and other rich fish habitat. For this purpose, carry several buoys with you.

A plastic jug also can be turned into a boat bailer. Just cut off the bottom diagonally to form a scoop with a convenient handle, and you can use the bailer to scoop water out of the boat.

Slip Rental Can Save You Time and Money

When gas was 23¢ a gallon and uncrowded fishing spots were numerous and nearby, renting a slip for my boat was the farthest thing from my mind. But, as Dylan so prophetically sang, "The times they are a-changin'."

Although my wife and I travel extensively and enjoy fishing throughout the country, we do much of our fishing near home. Our favorite lake is thirteen miles from our front door. Pulling a boat and trailer with our truck costs us about $2 a round trip for gas. We can make the same trip in our compact car, without the boat, for less than 50¢ worth of fuel. Slip rental at the lake costs us $16 a month.

If we fish the lake three evenings a week and two full days a month and have to pull the boat with us, that's about 14 trips a month for a total of $28. With the boat in its slip, however, we can use the little car and $7 worth of gas. Add that to the slip rental fee, and we're paying $23 a month. That can be viewed as a savings of $5 a month or ten extra trips to the lake.

If the money savings alone isn't enough to convince you that slip rental is worth investigation, consider the time savings and convenience. Launching a boat and retrailering it after a few hours of fishing isn't my idea of fun. Furthermore, it cuts an hour of fishing time off every trip we make. With the boat already in the water, though, we can leave our home and be cranking up the outboard in about twenty minutes.

Of course, the idea of owning a trailerable boat is mobility, but we're no less mobile with our boat resting at its moorings. If we want to fish another lake, we just pick up our boat on the way there and drop it off at the lake on the way back. We have rental space available at a number of places, from our local coastal lakes, bays, and rivers to the large mountain lakes that are open only during the summer months. In checking around, I have found that rental fees range from 50¢ to $1 a foot per boat per month. Even greater savings can be had on an annual lease basis.

So if you have a favorite lake or bay where you do most of your fishing and get no particular thrill out of launching your boat and dragging it back and forth with you on each trip, check into slip rental. It could save you money and, moreover, add many hours to your fishing time.

Front-End Hitch

Normally, the bolt-on, bumper-type trailer hitch is looked upon as a flimsy and unreliable link between trailer and towing vehicle. To be sure, no one recommends such hitches for use with any trailer with a Gross Vehicle Weight Rating (GVWR) over 1,000 pounds. And I would not trust these hitches for any long-range trailering or extended trips.

There is, however, one use to which these hitches are ideally suited—for mounting on the front bumper of your towing vehicle. With a front-end hitch, launching and retrieving a trailerable boat are greatly simplified. The obvious advantages of full, head-on visibility of boat, trailer, and launching ramp are, of course, paramount. Additionally, rear drive wheels of towing vehicles are kept high and dry during launching and retrieving.

When a motor home or pickup camper is used as a towing vehicle, visibility is severely impaired on any boat ramp when the boat is launched and retrieved in the conventional manner. Front-end hitches on such vehicles are great safety advantages then. Use of a bumper-mounted, front-end hitch should be restricted to trailers with a maximum GVWR of 2,000 pounds. For heavier rigs, a frame-mounted hitch is recommended.

How Much Boat Can You Tow?

Whether you are planning to buy a boat and trailer that you can pull with the family flivver or to buy a new vehicle capable of pulling the kind of boat you want, you should have an idea of how various types of cars and trucks stack up as towing vehicles. The following chart shows the basic capabilities of different types of cars, pickups, and vans. In addition to considering the size of the towing vehicle and its engine, you should investigate the possible need for such additional equipment as heavy-duty suspension, heavy-duty cooling system, engine- and transmission-oil coolers if your rig will be a fairly heavy one. Keep in mind that the GVWR of a trailer includes the weight of the trailer itself, as well as the boat, motor, and everything you will load into it.

Maximum Trailer GVWR	Type of Car	Type of Truck
500 pounds	Smallest sub-compact, such as Toyota Corolla, Datsun B210, VW Beetle, etc.	
1,000 pounds	Sub-compact, such as Toyota Corona, Datsun 610, Ford Pinto, etc.	Mini-pickup, such as Chevrolet LUV, Datsun Lil Hustler, Ford Courier, Toyota, etc.
2,000 pounds	Compact, such as Chevy Nova, Dodge Dart, Ford Maverick, and others with six-cylinder or small V-8 engines.	Half-ton pickups and vans with six-cylinder or small V-8 engines.
4,000 pounds	Mid-size sedans and station wagons with mid-size to large V-8 engines.	Half-ton pickups and vans with mid-size to large V-8 engines.
over 4,000 pounds	Full-size sedans and station wagons with largest V-8 engines.	Three-quarter-ton pickups with largest V-8 engines.

CHAPTER 10

Fishing Attire

How to Select the Right Wading Footwear

In the selection of wading footwear, there are a number of variables to consider. The first consideration is the type of bottom that exists in the waters you will wade. This will determine the type of soles your wading footwear should have. If you spend most of your time wading streams where much of the bottom is comprised of slippery rocks, the felt-soled wader or hip boot should be your choice. If you wade mostly on sand or mud bottoms, the cleated soles will better suit your needs.

Ideally, if you wade a variety of waters, you should have a pair of waders with felt soles and another pair with lug soles. If you don't care to own two pairs, buy the lug-soled waders and fit them with a pair of felt-soled wading sandals when you are fishing rocky streams with slippery bottoms.

Another decision a fisherman must face when buying wading footwear is whether to pick hip boots or chest waders. The latter would seem the logical choice, since chest waders are more versatile—they will do all that the hippers will do and more. But your own personal needs must be considered first. I got by very well for years owning only a pair of hip boots. I lived in the Midwest then, and the streams I fished were mostly small. Although there were many pools that were too deep to wade with hip boots, shallower riffles were frequent enough to allow stream crossings. And the deeper pools were usually small enough that long casts were not required. If your needs are similar to what mine were then, by all means, buy hip boots instead of waders.

If you're an inexperienced wader, or if you are outfitting a beginning fisherman, you should certainly start with hippers. The place to learn how to negotiate currents and uncertain stream bottoms is in knee-deep water, not the waist-deep water where a simple loss of footing can be disastrous.

Another consideration is cost, and chest waders will always be more expensive than hip boots of comparable quality. With the chest waders, attention to quality is always of paramount importance. The simple rule of buying the best you can afford applies to all outdoor gear, but is doubly important in the purchase of chest waders. In fact, I would further recommend that you avoid the cheap, off-brand waders altogether, as they can be more trouble than they're worth. Cheap ones are likely to be heavy and uncomfortable, and they will take little abuse. Often it takes no abuse at all for the crotch seams to split on the cheapies.

On the other hand, you might be able to find a pair of bargain hippers that will serve you well for years. But you will probably have to shop around a bit. The cheap hip boots are almost always heavier than the better-quality ones, but by shopping around you should be able to find a pair that is sufficiently lightweight and comfortable. Unlike chest waders, a cheap pair of hip boots is better than none at all.

Another decision that you will face when buying waders or hippers is whether to purchase insulated or noninsulated boots. Again, your own personal needs will dictate your choice. Insulated boots are always more expensive and are of limited worth for many anglers. I prefer to wear thermal underwear and an extra pair of heavy wool socks when I'm wading during the colder months. Then later in the year, when the weather and water are warmer, I just shed one of my layers of clothing to maintain comfort. For wading the warmer waters during summer months, I just wade wet in tennis shoes and jeans.

Some anglers like the stocking-foot wader, over which a pair of wading shoes is worn. Generally, these waders are not as tough as conventional chest waders, but they are great for air travel and for packing into remote fishing areas. The stocking-foot wader also can be a good choice for the angler who wades both mud-bottom and rocky-bottom waters, as he can simply switch from cleat-soled wading shoes to those with felt soles to fit the situation.

If I had to cover all my wading needs with one type of wading footwear, though, I would pick a top-quality pair of chest waders with cleated soles. And I would carry felt-soled wading sandals for use on slippery rock bottoms.

Patching Waders and Boots

Waders and hip boots without patches are either relatively new, or they aren't getting much use. Those that get plenty of use are going to get punctured from time to time. If you punch a hole in your waders on the way back to the car after a day of fishing, no problem. You can use any of a variety of tire-patch kits to make repairs at home. The hot-patch kits, available in the automotive departments of most discount department stores, are great for making repairs on waders.

If a mishap occurs on your way to your fishing spot or while you are fishing, you need something that will make a fast and efficient emergency repair. Hot-melt patching sticks that will permanently repair small holes and will make good temporary repairs on longer tears in waders and hippers are available at most sport shops and department stores. Whenever I'm wearing any kind of rubber (or synthetic rubber) boot, I carry one of these patch sticks with me. A disposable cigarette lighter that I keep in my fishing vest comes in handy for heating the patch stick.

To make a patch with one of these sticks, you need only hold it over a flame until the patch material softens. You then dab it over the puncture; it cures instantly as it cools. It is important that you thoroughly dry the area to be patched. And if the puncture is anything more than a small hole, you should put a larger permanent patch over it when you return home.

Drying Wet Footwear

One reason for hanging rubber boots, hippers, and waders upside down is to allow for proper air circulation so the interior of the boots will sufficiently dry. You can purchase wader hangers through sporting-goods stores and some mail-order companies, or you can easily improvise your own with sturdy wire coat hangers.

During normal use, boots will dry sufficiently as they hang, soles up, in a closet, garage, or dry basement. But during several consecutive days of fishing, boots might not totally dry overnight. And there are few things worse than donning cold, damp waders or boots on a chilly morning. Boots dampened from perspiration can be dried out in a few hours with an electric hair dryer. It also helps to hang them above a floor register overnight where rising warm air will dry them.

If your boots have gotten drenched because you waded too deep, fell in, or because they developed a leak, you should try to get as much moisture as possible out of them before using a hair dryer on them. While the uppers will normally dry quickly, the boot portions will be tougher to get entirely dry. You can stuff them with absorbent paper towels or dry newspaper and let them stand for about an hour so that much of the moisture will be drawn out. Then remove the paper, and dry them with a hair dryer.

Other Fishing Footwear

Other types of footwear that I use while fishing include tennis shoes, 9-inch high-top hunting boots with Vibram lug soles, and 14-inch neoprene pacs. Besides using the tennis shoes for wet wading in the summertime, I also like them when I'm fishing from a boat or canoe during hot weather. First, they keep my feet cool, but they also offer sure footing. They are easy to get off—an important consideration whenever you go afloat, especially if by canoe where water might get a bit rough.

For most backpacking and portage trips, a top-quality boot built for hiking or hunting is best. I do not, however, like the so-called hiking boots with the relatively short uppers. I like the additional ankle support offered by a high-top hunting boot, especially if terrain is hilly or mountainous. My hunting boots are fully insulated and fully lined with soft leather, and I wear them year-round. I always wear heavy wool socks with them. The cushioning of the lining and insulation, as well as that of the heavy socks, keeps me from wearing blisters on my feet. And in addition, the wool socks absorb perspiration well.

I bought these boots large enough to accommodate heavy socks. The fit is just snug enough when I first don them to keep the boots from slipping and rubbing blisters on my feet. Then, during the course of a few miles of hiking, there is enough cushion to allow my feet to swell naturally without cramping them. These boots are also equipped with cushioned tongues and cushioned collars at the tops to prevent binding and to aid circulation when they are snugly tied. They have quick-lace eyelets, which make them easy to get off in an emergency, should one occur during a portage trip.

Another kind of boot I have grown very fond of since I was introduced to it in southeastern Alaska several years ago is the Uniroyal neoprene pac. These boots are about the most popular kind of footwear to be found in the soggy Alaska panhandle and, in fact, the locals refer to them as "Juneau boots." They're the most comfortable rubber (synthetic rubber) boot I have ever used and are the only ones I have been able to wear for extended periods. I once wore them every day for two months when we were staying on Chichagof Island off the coast of southeastern Alaska.

These pacs have hard toes, and the supple neoprene uppers allow for maximum comfort, preventing chafing and cramping. The soles have a deep tread which assures sure-footed movement in the roughest of terrain. As is the case with any rubber boot, though, they do not breathe like leather boots. So they can be uncomfortable in extremely hot weather. But for eight or nine months of the year, these are the boots I prefer for backpacking, portage trips, and for fishing from a boat or canoe in the rainy Northwest. They keep the feet dry, and as a safety measure, they're easy to slip off.

Buy the Right Rainwear

I have lived in or visited the soggiest sections to be found in North America. And since I am an outdoorsman, I have been out in the rainiest weather this continent has to offer. Furthermore, I have owned enough foul-weather clothing to open my own rainwear shop. But, truth be known, I have been sopping wet and miserable more times than I care to count.

Some of the most rainproof clothing I have used also has been the heaviest and least ventilated. Often when I wore it, I got nearly as wet from perspiration as I would have from the rain. In addition, it was so bulky that I only used it when I headed out on a rainy day. Many times, I was caught without rainwear when a sunny day turned into a downpour.

Because of these bad experiences, I reasoned that a lightweight suit would not only be more comfortable, but could also be rolled into a compact package that I wouldn't mind packing with me on all my fishing outings. So I began using the light backpacking rainsuits. I tried several cheap ones and found that they were okay for keeping you dry during a little shower, but in a heavy downpour or a steady, all-day rain they would soak through.

My next lightweight suit was higher priced, but not much better. The material was more waterproof, but the seams leaked in all but the gentlest of drizzles. About the time I was ready to give up on the light backpackers' suits, I discovered the Uniroyal Dryfast Suit. This is an extremely tough suit, but is light and compact. It has heat-sealed seams and the zipper front of the jacket has a storm fly that snaps shut to keep water from seeping in through the zipper. My wife and I each have one of these suits, and we take them with us on every fishing outing. We wear them with our neoprene pacs and keep warm and dry in the rainiest of weather.

In the spring and fall, when a chilly wind can make you miserable, these suits make great windbreakers. Furthermore, the jackets are made with plenty of room in the shoulder area so there is no binding across the shoulders while casting, paddling a canoe, or engaging in any other rigorous activity. We have used these suits for four years now, under some of the most severe conditions, and they are showing no signs of wear.

It's not my purpose, here, to peddle Uniroyal rainwear. Rather, I want to recommend the best foul-weather clothing I have come across to date. This company caters to outdoorsmen in the design of their clothing, and they listen to what hunters and fishermen have to say about what they want in quality rainwear.

My wife and I each have several other Uniroyal rain garments of a more specialized nature. Our Flexnet parka jackets, for example, are cut 34-inches long. This means that they are perfect for wearing with hip boots, since the bottoms of the jackets hang several inches below the tops of the hippers to keep us totally dry. Uniroyal offers a variety of suits and other specialized garments, ranging in price from about $20 to about $65. All are marketed under the Royal Red Ball trademark.

Dressing for Warmth

It is universally accepted among outdoorsmen that the best way to stay comfortable outdoors most of the time is to dress in layers. The fisherman so dressed can stay warm during the chilly, early morning hours; then, as the day grows warmer, he can peel off a layer or two to remain comfortable. There seems to be some disagreement, however, about what should comprise these layers.

The first rule, regardless of what sort of garments, materials, or insulation you choose to keep you warm, is that all clothing should be fairly loose-fitting. Tight-fitting clothes inhibit circulation. During the chilly spring and fall, you might want to wear some sort of long underwear. In the coldest of weather—while ice fishing or winter steelheading—two layers of long underwear can keep you toasty warm. The layer next to your skin should be the Scandinavian-type fishnet underwear that promotes air circulation and quick evaporation of perspiration.

The type of clothing you should use for additional layers will depend upon the kind of cold you are trying to combat—wet or dry. If you're not troubled by rain, down-insulated garments are tops. In moderately cold weather and dry climate, I use a down-filled vest that affords plenty of warmth to my torso yet allows me sufficient freedom of movement. When it gets down near zero or below, I use a full-length down parka with a down hood.

Most of the time, though, I am trying to keep warm and dry at the same time, because the chilly months are often the wet months. That's when wool is best. Even if it gets wet, wool will still keep you warm. Heavy wool socks keep my feet warm, and a long-tailed wool shirt, which I wear outside my pants, keeps my torso warm and protects the vulnerable kidney area. To keep damp and cold air from sneaking in around my collar, I wear a lightweight turtleneck shirt beneath the wool shirt. Over all that goes my fishing coat, and if it's raining, my rainwear.

Gloves and fishing just don't go together, but there are times when it gets so cold that I have to slip on a pair of gloves to keep my fingers from getting numb. For most situations, wool gloves are best; again, they will be warm even when wet. In the severe cold that ice fishermen often encounter, protection of the hands and fingers is of much greater importance. A pair of knit gloves will allow the fisherman to handle most of the fishing chores, but a pair of heavy over-mittens hanging from a cord around the neck provide additional protection when needed. The fisherman need only plunge his hands into the mittens for total protection, and they can be slipped off whenever necessary with no fear of losing them.

A Daypack for Fishing

Dressing in layers does create one problem for the fisherman on foot—that is, where to put those garments that get peeled off in the noonday heat. I have a small, inexpensive daypack that is perfect for this purpose. When it is not in use, it folds into its own self-contained, zippered pocket to make a tidy 4-inch by 8-inch package that weighs a mere three ounces and can either be worn on the belt or tucked into a pocket. In use as a pack, it will hold as much clothing as I need to remove. These handy little packs are available at most camping and department stores for less than $5.

Good Fishing Is Out of Sight

If you were to use photographs of fishermen appearing in the national outdoor magazines as a guide to selection of the right color clothing to wear while fishing, you would certainly conclude that bright red is the best color, and that bright yellow and blaze orange are other good choices. The fact is, however, that these colors make for better color photographs, not better fishing.

Certainly, there are times when clothing color makes no difference at all. If the fish are unable to see you—because of water depth, clarity, or angle of view—wear what you want: If you are fishing the gin-clear waters of a trout stream or are probing the shallows of a relatively clear lake or pond, it is best to be dressed in subdued colors that blend with your surroundings.

It has been proven that fish not only see colors but are also able to distinguish shades of red, yellow, green, and blue. So it only stands to reason that if fish can be spooked merely by a shadow cast on the water, a fishing line that is visible to them, or even the delicate tippet to which a fly is tied, something 6-feet tall and colored bright red is going to appear unnatural to them.

The Sensible Fishing Hat

A fishing hat should be something more than just a place to hang flies to dry. It should be something that will help to keep you comfortable and healthy regardless of the weather or time of year. In cold weather, a lot of body heat can be lost through an uncovered head. In hot weather, a hat can do much to reflect the burning rays of the sun and can, in fact, protect you from heat exhaustion or, worse, heat stroke.

It doesn't make much difference what kind of hat you wear, as long as it offers the kind of protection you need. It is best to choose light-colored hats for summer use, as they will reflect sun rays and keep you cool. A long-billed hat will keep the sun out of your eyes, and a hat with a wide brim can shade your eyes and the back of your neck as well. But these hats can be a bit of a problem in a wind.

My own preference for summer wear is a Jones-style hunting hat.

It has enough of a brim to shade my eyes, yet it will stay on even in strong winds. For the cold, wet time of year, my vote goes to the knitted wool watch cap. There's never a problem with this type of cap blowing off. If my ears get cold, I can pull the cap down over them; when it's raining, I can wear the watch cap beneath my rain parka hood with no interference.

Flies in Your Fishing Hat

Since Cornelia Crosby first started sticking flies into her felt fishing hat in the 1870s, fishermen have followed the tradition. But there's more to flies in a fishing hat than fashion. A fishing hat is an excellent place to let flies dry before returning them to a fly box, where a wet fly can rust hooks in short order.

The mistake that many fishermen make is to stick their flies into any old kind of material with no regard for the consequences. Hooks poked into felt, wool, poplin, or any other type of material that hats might be made of can cause a number of problems. Once the barb sinks into the fabric, the flies will be nearly impossible to extract without damage to the hat. More important is the damage to the fly. Hook points, especially on tiny dry flies delicately tied to small, fine-wire hooks, will be dulled when stuck into most fabrics.

The best material for this purpose is fleece. So fit your fishing hat with a fleece hat band if that's where you plan to keep your flies. Such hat bands are available at most fly shops, or you can mail-order one from the Orvis Comapny.

CHAPTER 11

Fishing Comfort and Safety

File a Plan

When I was living in Alaska, I was astounded by the number of residents of and visitors to the state who got lost in the vast, north-country wilderness each year. Many of them found their way out or were found by others. But a shocking number of outdoorsmen perished because they failed to take the necessary precautions.

The best survival measure any outdoorsman can take is to file a trip plan with someone before embarking into the boondocks. If at home, most of us can simply call a neighbor and tell him of our plans—where we're going, how long we plan to stay, number of persons in our party, and estimated time of return. If we're overdue, the friend can call authorities and see that a search-and-rescue mission is initiated.

The traveler in a strange locale need not feel that such precautions are impossible, though. In coastal areas, a float plan can be filed with the U.S. Coast Guard. Inland, a trip plan can be filed with the state police. Information to be provided when filing a plan includes your name, address, phone number, destination, number and names of persons in your party, identification of vehicle or watercraft, and estimated time of return. If you fail to return by the projected time, a search will be set in motion. Of course, if you do return on schedule, you must close your trip plan by phone or in person.

Even if the country or waters you are trekking into are as familiar to you as your own backyard, something as simple as a broken leg or mere engine trouble could be disastrous. To go afield or afloat without filing a plan with someone is foolhardy. Do yourself a favor, and let someone know of your outdoor ventures. It could literally save your life.

Who Needs Flotation Devices?

Common sense and the law require you to have a U.S. Coast Guard-approved personal flotation device aboard for every person on board whenever you go afloat. It never hurts to have a few extra buoyant cushions along, too. In the event of an accident, the more floating items left on the water, the better the chance of avoiding fatalities.

There are other common-sense rules to follow that will keep you and your fishing partners safe while afloat:

1. Make all nonswimmers aboard your craft wear approved life vests at all times.
2. Be sure that everyone wears a life vest while the boat is underway. Something as simple as a steering failure can thrust a person overboard.
3. In rough water or storm conditions, everyone on board should be wearing a life vest.
4. When floating any but the gentlest of rivers in a canoe, jon boat, or inflatable craft, everyone on board should be wearing life vests.
5. If you take children out in a boat, be sure that they are wearing small, child-size life vests. Adult-size life vests will afford them little protection in the event of an accident.

Sometimes You Need Double Protection

A friend of mine who is an avid riverboat racer in Alaska was involved in a boat accident on a particularly rough stretch of the Yukon River, and he almost didn't live to tell about it. Although he and two others aboard his boat were wearing Coast Guard-approved life vests, they were in the water for a while before anyone could reach them. By the time they were rescued, their life vests were no longer keeping them afloat. It seems the extremely fine particles of silt suspended in the water penetrated the life vests and eventually rendered them useless.

From that day forward, my friend never ventured onto silty waters without the double protection of a life vest and a flotation jacket. If you travel on silt-laden rivers to reach some of your fishing spots, you would do well to go doubly protected by wearing both a flotation vest and a flotation jacket.

Carry Salt Tablets

Many outdoorsmen exert themselves as much as athletes or infantrymen might, yet most of them fail to take an important precaution that coaches and platoon sergeants demand of their men: They don't adequately guard against heat exhaustion. Whenever an outdoorsman is involved in any sort of activity that causes excessive perspiration—exertion, heat, or a combination of both—he should be consciously aware of the loss of important body salts that can cause fatigue, muscle cramps, and heat prostration.

The proper precaution is the replacement of salts, and the best means to accomplish this are regular doses of salt tablets with water. Naturally, the person who climbs mountains in the Mojave Desert in the middle of July is going to require more salt tablets and water than the average outdoorsman will. But you can perspire excessively by just sitting in a boat, trolling, on a hot day. In addition, you can be walking across a frozen lake or chopping through 2 feet of ice with an ice spud at 10° below zero and still be sweating too much. A bottle of salt tablets should be in your pocket, pack, or tackle box on every outing, at all times of the year. They're available at drugstores and cost a little over a buck for a bottle of 100.

The necessary replacement of body salts is overlooked by many outdoorsmen who partake in outdoor activities during hot weather. Carry salt tablets along.

Two products that every angler with sun-sensitive skin should carry are Bain de Soleil and Surfadil.

Sunburn: Prevention and Cure

If you're one of those fortunate folks who begin turning a golden bronze at the first hint of sunlight, or if you're one of those leather-skinned outdoorsmen whose epidermal layer defies the penetration of the sun's ultraviolet radiation, you can skip these tips. If you're still reading, chances are you are well acquainted with the unmitigated agony of sun-emblazoned skin and the blisters, itching, and peeling that accompany it. Fellow sufferers, have I got news for you!

There are two products you shouldn't be without—one for sunburn prevention, the other for cure. First is a suntan creme called Bain de Soleil, introduced to me some years back by one of my similarly afflicted fishing partners. It is not one of those watery creams or oils that affords people like us all the protection of a coating of gasoline. Rather, it is a thick, but comfortably spreadable, grease that coats and penetrates the skin. Best of all, it works.

Sunburn has always been my number-one outdoor problem. I burn instantly—hell, retroactively! I've sported blisters the size of Hula Poppers, and I'm not ashamed to admit that the itching has brought tears to my eyes. I have tried most of the suntan goops with varying degrees of success—first degree, second degree. . . . But with Bain de Soleil, I have fished from sunup to sunset—whole days trolling in the beating summer sun—and haven't burned. In fact, I have tanned for the first time in my life. It's great stuff.

When using any kind of suntan lotion or sun screen, remember to use it liberally and to apply it heavily to particularly sunburn-prone parts of the anatomy—ears and nose. During the worst part of the day—from 10:00 AM to 2:00 PM—or whenever you are sweating profusely, you'll need to reapply the lotion or cream every hour or so.

If you doubt my word or fail to take my advice on the Bain de Soleil cream, you will want to know about Surfadil lotion. This is the only product I have found that gives me instant and long-lasting relief from sunburn pain and itching. A pharmacist in South Carolina introduced me to this one after I had stupidly spent about three hours fishing in swimming trunks. I didn't know whether to go to the hospital emergency room or to turn myself over to local authorities as a fire hazard. I was charred.

A liberal application of Surfadil brought comfort in minutes. I was soon able to wear clothes again and was out fishing the next day—

but in long pants and a long-sleeved shirt. I still blistered and peeled, but it was a nearly painless affair, without the usual unbearable itching. I now keep tubes of Bain de Soleil in my tackle boxes, and I carry several tubes on extended fishing trips. I also carry a bottle of Surfadil along for fishing partners who try to tough it out without protection.

A Repelling Combination

After living for more than five years in Alaska—the mosquito capital of North America—I have learned to appreciate effective insect repellants above all else when the bugs are bothersome. I have also tried a wide variety of commercial sprays and dopes and have settled on two that do a superior job.

For protecting bare skin from the probing proboscis of mother mosquito, nothing beats Cutter lotion. I find the 1-ounce squeeze bottles particularly handy, as they take up little room in a tackle box or fishing vest. On a backpacking trip, one of these bottles can be kept handy in a jacket pocket.

Where biting insects are a particular problem, though, the fisherman needs to protect more than his exposed skin. He needs to spray clothing, especially in such areas as collars and cuffs. For this purpose, I have found Off aerosol spray to be the most effective and long-lasting.

So on any fishing trip where I am liable to be bugged by bugs, I use Cutter lotion on face, hands, neck, and ears. Then I liberally spray Off onto my pant legs, shirt sleeves, around my ankles, and on the brim of my fishing hat. This repelling combination has kept mosquitoes from biting me even in some of the most mosquito-infested areas to be found on this continent.

Fisherman's Clean-Up Kit

Fish slime, worm goo, outboard gas, and the like make grubby hands the bane of the fisherman. Solve your clean-up problems with a simple kit you can put together at home and carry along on every outing. Dampen a clean washcloth with isopropyl alcohol, and seal it in a plastic bag. Carry it in your tackle box, fishing vest, or rucksack.

Your alcohol cloth will cut dirt, grease, slime, grime, and blood. It also helps to prevent infection of those numerous cuts, scrapes,

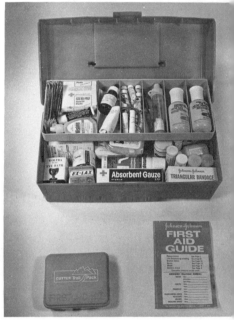

For quick clean-up, carry an alcohol-damp-ened washcloth in a plastic bag on every fish-ing outing.

Assemble your own first-aid kit according to your personal needs and medical history, as well as potential accidents and illnesses. Such a kit can be housed in a small tackle bo͏ For day trips and backpacking, use a trail kit —but cram as many more items as you can into it.

and scratches that result from rigorous outdoor activity. It will help to relieve the itch of many insect bites and rashes. Since it evapo-rates fast, and thus cools, it is particularly refreshing in hot weather; in cold weather, it won't freeze. And in a survival situation, it can be used as an emergency fire starter.

Fishermen's First-Aid Kits

For one-day outings, the small first-aid kits that are available commercially are really all a fisherman needs. These kits are mar-keted for backpacking. Although weight is of primary concern to the backpacking fisherman, you can get by with one of these kits on longer trips. But for this purpose, you should repack the kit to in-clude as many more essentials as you can cram into it.

My own trail first-aid kit was fairly well stocked when I bought it. It included an assortment of adhesive bandages, several sizes of sterile gauze pads, adhesive tape, moist towelettes, alcohol sponges, two ammonia inhalant ampules, burn ointment, a small scalpel, and four aspirin tablets—all packed into a small plastic case that fits handily into a pocket of a pack or fishing jacket.

Since four aspirins aren't enough to combat even a mild hangover, much less a lingering headache or a cold, the first addition I made to this kit was a tin of twelve aspirin tablets. In what little space that remained in the small case, I put a roll of Rolaids antacid tablets, a pair of tweezers, two safety pins, a needle, and a book of matches. Tweezers have numerous uses, such as removal of bee stingers, thorns, splinters, and ticks. Safety pins are always handy for fastening bandages or making slings. A sterilized needle is indispensable for use in removing deeply embedded thorns and splinters, and the needle tip can be sterilized with the flame of a match.

For extended fishing trips, fishing vacations, camping/fishing, and float trips, your first-aid kit ought to be more substantial. You can buy one of the larger first-aid kits that are designed to be carried in a car or a boat, but even these will need to be customized to fit your personal needs and the needs of your family or fishing partners. Perhaps the best practice is to assemble your own kit, as my wife and I did.

The problem with most larger first-aid kits I have seen is that while they might prepare you for the less likely mishaps—from dog bite to nuclear holocaust—they don't help you combat the most common ailments and discomforts. Chances are, when you head out into the boondocks, you are not going to be bitten by a snake; even in snake country the odds are against it. You probably won't fall into a hole and break a leg or arm. It isn't likely that you'll sever an artery, whack off a finger with an axe, fall off a cliff, or get mauled by a bear. I know it doesn't sound very macho, but you are much more likely to catch a cold, get poison ivy, or to suffer from diarrhea, constipation, indigestion, hay fever, sinusitis, a sore throat, or toothache.

It only makes sense to go prepared for these more mundane ailments, but you need not do so at the expense of the more serious accidents. Your first-aid kit ought to contain materials for bandaging a serious cut or burn. You should have something for tying a splint to a broken limb, but any cloth can be torn into strips for this purpose in an emergency. And if you will be in snake country, you should have a snake-bite kit along. But mainly you should have the medications along that will help relieve the symptoms of more common illnesses and the pain of less serious accidents.

When my wife and I began assembling our big first-aid kit, we considered all the usual little ailments that might ruin a fishing trip, and we began stocking our kit accordingly. What we ended up with was something of a mobile medicine chest with an assortment of the kinds of medication we keep on hand at home. It all packs into a small plastic tackle box that is easy to carry along on any extended trip.

The nonprescription medicines we carry in our first-aid kit (with target ailments in parentheses) are as follows: aspirin (headache, toothache, etc.), Alka-Seltzer (overindulgence, upset stomach), kaopectate (diarrhea), Ex-Lax (constipation), Allerest (hay fever, upper-respiratory allergies), Contac (common cold), Chloraseptic aerosol spray (minor throat soreness), Sucrets lozenges (minor throat soreness), Visine (minor eye irritations), Aeroaid aerosol-spray antiseptic (minor cuts and scratches), Aerotherm aerosol spray (minor burns, scalds, and abrasions), oil of cloves (toothache), Ben-Gay gel (muscle aches and pains), Chap Stick (chapped lips), Rolaids (heartburn, acid indigestion), calamine lotion (poison ivy, poison oak, poison sumac), Surfadil lotion (sunburn), After Bite (insect bites and stings), and Dristan nasal spray (nasal congestion).

Also in our kit is a small bottle of liquid medicated soap for cleaning cuts, scratches, scrapes, and burns. We have a small plastic bottle of isopropyl alcohol that can be used for cleaning and sterilizing. And we carry an assortment of different-sized Band-Aids and sterile gauze pads, as well as a roll of sterile gauze, adhesive tape, and sterile cotton.

The useful tools we carry include a small pair of scissors, tweezers, oral thermometer, safety pins, needles, stainless-steel razor blades, and an eye-wash cup. The last item—the eye-wash cup—is something I have never seen included in any of the commercial first-aid kits, yet I consider it one of the most important items to carry on any outing. Several times I have been unable to remove a tiny object from an eye in the conventional manner and was only able to do so with an eye wash.

On one occasion when we were staying on Chichagof Island, a young lady was preparing to transfer gasoline from a 55-gallon drum to 5-gallon cans. When she opened the full drum, the pressure inside sprayed gasoline into her face and open eyes. My wife immediately drenched her with buckets of water, and then thoroughly cleansed her eyes with lots of fresh water. Finally, to make sure that all traces of gasoline had been flushed from the girl's eyes, Patty used an eye-wash cup to rinse her eyes repeatedly with lukewarm water.

One last suggestion I would like to make regarding the assembly of your own first-aid kit is that you ask your family physician to make some suggestions. Since he should be fully familiar with your family's medical history, he can recommend the kinds of medications you ought to have along. Chances are, he might even have some drug samples that he will give you to include in your kit. He can give you directions on the proper use of such medications as well as advice on selection and use of nonprescription medications.

Tips on Buying Sunglasses

Today's serious angler probably owns at least several hundred dollars' worth of quality tackle. And to help him enjoy his favorite sport, he might own waders, boots, backpacks, and camping gear that have set him back several hundred dollars more. If he owns a boat, its price tag may have been in the hundreds of dollars—but more likely thousands. Then, of course, throughout the year, he will spend money replacing tackle, driving to and from his fishing spots, and maintaining and repairing his gear and boat.

He buys the best tackle he can afford and spends a lot of time browsing through catalogs and shopping at tackle stores. He seeks the advice of experts and the recommendations of other knowledgable fishermen. Yet, he buys his sunglasses at the corner gas station, where they hang from a cardboard display card between the plastic windshield scrapers and auto-emblem key chains. The cheap frames of such sunglasses will often fit improperly, the lenses will usually exhibit some sort of peripheral distortions, and their soft plastic will usually be sporting many scratches in short order.

If you want to give your eyes adequate protection while outdoors, there are some facts you should know before buying your next pair of sunglasses. Your eyes, under normal conditions, consume about one-fourth of your body's daily energy supply. Subject them to glare and strain, and this energy consumption will increase greatly. You

Men who make their livings outdoors know the value of good sunglasses.

Whether you're fishing or building a fishing cabin, optical-quality sunglasses will protect your eyes.

may become exhausted much faster without even realizing why you are suffering from increased fatigue.

For the fisherman, glare is a particular problem. Light reflected from water surfaces with constant fluctuations in intensity can keep you squinting and blinking all day long if you aren't wearing adequate eye protection. The way to eliminate glare and eyestrain is to wear optical-quality sunglasses, not those $1.98 specials found on racks in supermarkets and gas stations. Such cheap and flimsy eye wear is sold more for fashion than for eye protection.

Sunglasses should be comfortable, and frames should be adjustable to the contours of the wearer's face. So the best bet is to see a professional eye specialist, pick the frames you like, and have them properly fitted. An advantage of buying quality sunglasses from an optical shop is that if a lens is broken or damaged, or if frames should ever give you problems, you can have these glasses repaired or readjusted at a minimal cost.

A true sunglass lens is neutral gray or green. Any other color is of less value or no value at all as a sunglass. I prefer the neutral gray, because there is no color distortion with this lens. Green lenses cause very little color distortion and offer a bit more contrast, which some might prefer. Sunglasses should allow between 19 and 30 percent light transmission. Any lens that allows more light to pass through it is not giving the user maximum protection.

In addition to eliminating glare and reducing brightness, sunglasses should also filter out potentially harmful ultraviolet (sunburn) rays and infrared (heat) rays. Unprotected eyes exposed to these rays for long periods of time may suffer discomfort ranging from varying degrees of burning and stinging to intense pain. Optical-quality glass, and now even some optical plastics, are capable of filtering out these possibly harmful rays. The cheap plastic lenses, however, do not filter any of the infared radiation and do little to filter ultraviolet rays.

As long as you pick optical-quality lenses, the choice of plastic or glass is largely a matter of personal preference. Plastic lenses scratch more readily than glass, but they can be coated with a diamond film

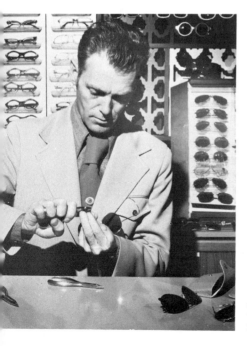

Buy your sunglasses from an optical specialist, not from the corner gas station.

that makes them about as scratch resistant as glass. Furthermore, plastic lenses are nearly unbreakable and are always lighter than glass of similar thickness.

All glass lenses made since January 1, 1972 have had to be heat-treated for impact resistance, so they're tough enough to withstand plenty of abuse. And glass lenses filter out all potentially harmful radiation. If you wear prescription glasses, you should own a good pair of prescription sunglasses. Since some prescription glass lenses can become very heavy, though, you might prefer optical plastic. Ask your optometrist or ophthalmologist for his recommendation.

When you buy sunglasses, make sure they have lenses that are large enough to fully protect your eyes. Besides all the reasons I have already stated for wearing good sunglasses, you ought to consider the protection they afford you from flying dust and debris, misguided fish hooks, and snapping tree branches. Any of these can damage or destroy eyesight.

Another reason for wearing quality sunglasses is that unprotected eyes that are subjected to sunlight for an extended period of time will lose a major portion of their night vision. Often, we must drive great distances to get to our favorite fishing spots, where we spend all day in the bright sunlight and then drive home again at night. Energy-sapping eyestrain can cause drowsiness. Additionally, if you spend the day in bright sunlight without sunglasses, you can lose from 50 to 90 percent of your night vision and not even know it. Studies have shown that after a full day in the sun without adequate eye protection, it takes a week to fully regain that lost night vision. One note of caution, though: Don't wear any kind of sunglasses while driving at night. When the sun goes down, put them away.

But don't take my word for any of this. Shop around, and try on a variety of sunglasses, including the cheap ones. You will surely appreciate the quality sunglasses in comparison. Visit your local optical shop, and request literature on sunglasses. Talk to an eye-care specialist and find out what his recommendations are. If you do all this, I really doubt that you will be buying your sunglasses from the corner gas station in the future.

CHAPTER 12

The Mobile Fisherman

Planning the Fishing Vacation

While most of us complain about the dollar that doesn't go as far as it used to and our busy lives that don't allow nearly enough time for fishing, the fact is that the average American angler has far more money and time to pursue his favorite sport now than at any other time in history. Furthermore, the efficiency of private and commercial transportation has effectively reduced the distances to many of those hallowed fishing grounds that, in the past, were familiar to many of us only through books, magazines, films, and dreams. Such fishing Meccas as Florida, Maine, Wisconsin, Minnesota, Montana, Idaho, Oregon, and even Alaska and the wilds of Canada are now within reach.

We're a mobile society, and most of us can manage to get away at least once a year for a fishing trip of a week or more. But time and money are still precious, so we want to get the most for our efforts and expenditures. One way to assure maximum enjoyment of any trip is to plan and organize the trip methodically and to allow plenty of time for the planning stages of any trip.

Whether fishing is the sole purpose of your trip or only part of a variety of activities that you and your family will engage in during a vacation, you should begin serious planning for such a trip six months to a year in advance. If it is to be a group or family trip, get everyone involved in the planning stages. Surely half the fun of any trip is in the molding of it and in the anticipation of the excitement yet to come. Chances are, you already have an idea of where you would like to go—the general geographical region, that is. But it's a good idea to have one or two alternative trips to fall back on, because you may learn during your preliminary investigations that the trip that was foremost in mind would not be the best choice.

Once you have a general idea of the area where you want to spend your fishing vacation, you should write to the fish and game departments and bureaus of tourism in the states where you will be fishing. You will want to request a copy of the current fishing regulations and all other pertinent literature on fishing in each state. If you have a particular region of a state in mind or a specific body of water, be sure to ask for all available information on that, too. And don't forget to ask about the availability of contour fishing maps of any lakes or reservoirs you plan to fish.

Something else you ought to ask for when you write to any of these state agencies is the addresses of state and regional outdoor magazines. Subscriptions to such magazines can be invaluable aids to learning about the fishing that is available in any region and the tackle and techniques required for successful angling. To help you in your mail research, addresses of the pertinent state agencies in all 50 states can be found in the appendices in the back of the book.

Once you have established a preferred spot for your fishing vacation and several alternatives, write to the chambers of commerce in the nearby towns to request information on local recreational attractions. Because the purpose of chamber of commerce literature is to promote local enterprises, it is often full of material ranging in character from hyper-optimistic advertising copy to unadulterated puff. But it can lead you to some interesting and enjoyable activities that will complement your trip. For example, you might find that a local brewery has an excellent public aquarium where you can observe a variety of live fishes in well-designed and natural-looking tanks. Or you might learn that there is a nearby hatchery you can visit, or a sport show scheduled for when you will be there.

It is important that you determine the best time to visit the vacation spot you have chosen, because the fishing is never at a peak year-round anywhere. If you're restricted to summer travel, you may miss some of the best seasonal fishing in many parts of the country. There are some places, however, that have an excellent summer fishery, so you may wish to seek those out.

Regardless of where you fish, though, summer poses another problem: You won't be the only person looking for a place to wet a line. There will be plenty of tourists and locals crowding the waterways. You can avoid some of the crowd problems by planning to fish mostly between Monday and Friday. On weekends, the numbers of tourists are joined by the local residents, and fishing waters can become less than pristine. By all means, avoid timing your vacation around any of the summer holiday weekends—Memorial Day, Independence Day, and Labor Day. Even people who hate to fish and can't stand the sight of water and wilderness feel an obligation to swarm into every corner of the outdoor world then. Save the weekends and holidays for visiting aquariums, museums, sport shows, and the like. These are also good activities to have in mind if the weather drives you off the water for a day or two.

Lodges, Guides, and Outfitters

Even if you plan to stay at a fishing camp, or if you intend to hire the services of a fishing guide or outfitter, you still have plenty of planning to do beforehand. In fact, this kind of fishing trip might even take more planning and correspondence. It will cost you more than the do-it-yourself fishing trip, and you will want to be assured of getting your money's worth.

You will still want to write to the various state agencies for information. Since many states maintain rosters of guides, lodges, and outfitters, be sure to ask for such material. The state officials will not recommend any particular individual, but they can usually put you in touch with a number of folks in the guiding and outfitting business. Other sources of information are the advertisements in the "Where To Go" sections in the back of such magazines as *Sports Afield, Outdoor Life,* and *Field & Stream.*

You should write to all the lodges, guides, and outfitters you can locate that operate in your area of interest. In addition to requesting all available information about their facilities, rates, and such, ask for a list of former clients to whom you can write for recommendations. The brochures you receive from these businesses should tell you when to come for the best fishing, what kind of tackle to bring, what the weather is like, and what kind of clothing to pack. But as you read through this literature, keep a list of questions that aren't answered by the brochures. Don't be afraid to ask questions and to demand explicit answers. After all, it's your money and your time. Any guide or outfitter who is reluctant to answer any reasonable question isn't worth hiring. Also make sure that all charges are clearly explained to you and that there are no hidden costs. Keep copies of all your correspondence, just in case there should be any sort of misunderstanding later.

Most sportsmen will be happy to tell you about their own experiences with a particular guide or outfitter. But when you write to former clients for recommendations, make it easy for them to respond. With your letter, send a large, business-size (No. 10) self-addressed and stamped envelope. Tell the person that if he or she doesn't have the time to reply, you would be happy to phone some evening or weekend (when long distance rates are cheaper). Then ask for the phone number and a convenient time to call. A few dollars spent on correspondence and phone calls could keep you from wasting hundreds or thousands on a bad trip.

See Your Travel Agent

No matter where you plan to go or how you plan to get there, a travel agency in your locale is a good source of information on the area you plan to visit. Their services cost you nothing, so it only makes good sense to take advantage of what they have to offer. If you plan to use commercial transportation or will require hotel or motel accommodations or car rental, your travel agent can see to these details and can make your reservations for you.

Air Charters Are Cheaper Than You Think

Countless thousands of vacationing fishermen, especially those traveling in the north country, pass within a few miles of waters that are teeming with fish and get very little fishing pressure. They never try these waters out, because they are only accessible by plane. The idea of fly-in trips frightens off most fishermen, not because of a fear of flying, but because of a fear of going broke in the process.

An air charter can get you away from the crowds and can put you in some of the best fishing country to be found anywhere. Furthermore, charter flights can be far cheaper than you might think. Consider first that few charters have to be long-distance trips. Often, a flight of an hour or less from where you parked your vehicle can put you on prime fishing waters.

Rates, of course, will vary from region to region and will differ according to the kind of aircraft used. And just as the prices of everything else rise regularly and significantly these days, air-charter rates will certainly continue to go up. For these reasons, it is impossible to tell you what it will cost you for a fly-in trip. To give you some idea of how cheap it can be, though, I can cite a few examples for you.

Back in 1974, it was possible to hire a pilot-guide in Fairbanks,

A charter flight can put you on highly productive waters that are otherwise inaccessible.

Alaska, for a half-day of grayling fishing that required a total of one hour in the air for a mere $40 per person, with a minimum of two persons required for a trip. A full day of northern-pike fishing that required from one to two hours total flying time cost $60 per person with a two-person minimum. More distant flights into the Alaska Range for lake-trout fishing ran $90 per person.

In 1975, I was planning a trip to a spot thirty-four miles from Juneau in the wild coastal country accessible only by plane or boat. I wrote to two charter services to find out what it would cost us for a charter flight into the area and a prearranged pickup at a later date. David Sheldrake of Southeast Skyways wrote to tell me, "For two people plus 250 pounds to 300 pounds of gear, the total cost of charter, which includes pickup, is $110 in an amphibian Cessna 185. Two people with approximately 565 pounds of gear can charter our Cessna 206 float plane for the same $110, including pickup. We also

These students obviously passed the final exam in their "Sport Fishing in Alaska" course, and enjoyed the test, too.

have the capabilities of carrying nine people and approximately 800 pounds of gear in our Grumman Goose, a twin-engine amphibian, for $232, pickup and all. This comes to a cost of $25.78 per person."

As recently as the early summer of 1977, I checked on charter rates on the south coast of Oregon and learned that I could hire a plane for $40 an hour. So there's no reason to pass within short-flying distances of good fishing waters without giving them a try.

Combine Vacation With Education

In many parts of the country, you can combine a fishing vacation with courses in such subject areas as fly casting, fly tying, rod building, bass fishing, bait casting, spinning, and more. Increasing numbers of colleges and universities are adding outdoor courses and workshops to their curricula. Additionally, a number of other fishing schools—some sponsored by major tackle manufacturers—offer many different courses for fishermen in just about every region of the U.S. These courses can help you become a better fisherman and, in some cases, can quickly familiarize you with the fishing conditions in a particular locale. As a bonus, you might end up sharing a stream, lake, or classroom with such illustrious fishing superstars as Homer Circle, A.J. McClane, Carl Richards, Ernest Schwiebert, or Bob Stearns.

I have been associated with two such programs at a college and a university. When I was in graduate school at the University of Alaska, one of my fishing buddies and I offered a summer-workshop course called "Sport Fishing in Alaska." The first week of this course included classroom lectures and demonstrations, guest speakers, casting instruction and practice, and field trips to local streams. The second week of the course—the final exam, so to speak—was a fishing and camping trip to one of the best salmon streams in North America, where everybody caught plenty of king salmon. At $100 plus tuition, this was about the cheapest salmon-fishing trip that I ever heard of. Last year, I was involved in an outdoor program sponsored by the Oregon Division of Continuing Education at Central Oregon Community College. Included in the curriculum were canoe float trips down the Dechutes River, as well as instruction in rod building, fly tying, and fly fishing.

While you are planning any vacation, be sure to write to nearby colleges and universities for their summer catalogs. State fish and game agencies will often be aware of outdoor courses, so you can inquire about them when you write for other information and fishing regulations. Courses offered by the fishing schools run the gamut from general courses for beginners to highly specialized instruction for the advanced fisherman. Most of these courses are from one day to one week in duration, and the costs range from about $100 to $1,000. Many of them include meals, lodging, and equipment. Some even offer transportation to and from the airport as well as boats for use by the students.

Of the manufacturer-sponsored schools, Fenwick's is probably the largest, with beginner and advanced courses being offered in many fine fishing spots throughout the country. Most of their courses are two-day and three-day sessions that cost from $125 to $145, but several are longer and priced higher. There are new courses being offered every year throughout the U.S. by colleges, universities, manufacturers, sportsmen's organizations, and tackle shops. Including such a course in your vacation plans can add immensely to your overall enjoyment of the trip and the sport. But as with anything else, you should investigate the prospects thoroughly and plan well in advance. A partial listing of fishing schools can be found in the back of the book.

Know Your Fishing Radius

All of us live near to some sort of fishing, and many of us are fortunate enough to live within a short drive of some good angling. We have our favorite spots for those spur-of-the-moment trips as well as lakes or streams that are distant enough to require a bit of planning. The fisherman who hasn't spent some time studying his immediate vicinity and his region of the country for potential fishing areas is considerably handicapped, especially if he is sufficiently serious enough about angling to want to take advantage of every spare moment that he has.

For a thorough study of your fishing radius, you will need several maps. A fairly large-scale surveyor's map or topographical map will help you locate nearby fishing spots. Use a state map for pinpointing areas of potential interest for two- or three-day trips. A regional map or a map of the U.S. will aid you in identifying locations for longer trips. Next you'll need a compass. With the compass set according to the legend on the large-scale map, place the compass point on the map where your home is located and scribe circles with radii reaching 5, 10, 20, 30, 40, 50, 75, and 100 miles. On a regional or U.S. map, your radii should be set for 50- or 100-mile increments and can be carried out as far as you wish.

These circles will enable you to focus your attention on confined areas instead of haphazardly scanning large chunks of the map. Fishing spots located within any given circle will, of course, be farther by road than the mileage indicated by the circle. But at least you will get a rough idea of the distance and can get a more accurate mileage measurement by other means. If you live in an area where you can take advantage of air charters to fly into remote fishing spots, you will be able to accurately estimate distances with the con-

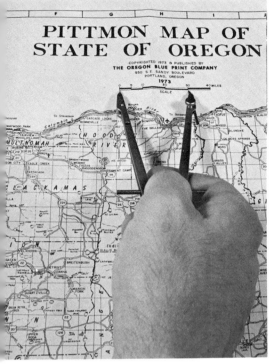

The first step in a systematic search of fishing spots in your area is a thorough study of maps. Set your compass according to the legend of the map you're using.

Then place the compass point where your home is located, and scribe concentric circles on which you can focus your attention.

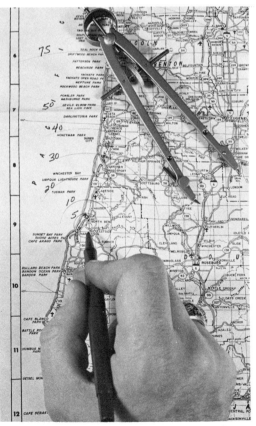

Use a map measurer to determine mileages to the various fishing
areas that you have located on your maps.

centric circles. If you are driving to a remote area, you can use the
same technique to locate potential fly-in fishing spots with the nearest air-charter facilities as the center of the circles.

Knowing your fishing radius helps you to categorize the waters of
various distances. You will be able to list or mark on your map all
of the nearest waters that you want to explore on those spontaneous
trips or when you have a few spare hours after work or after dinner.
Also, you will be able to identify the lakes and streams that are near
enough for one-day trips as well as those that are suitable only for
weekend or week-long jaunts.

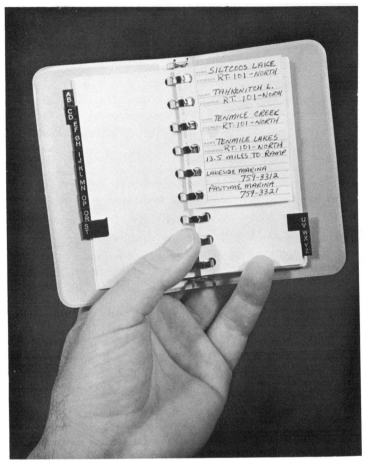

Record mileages and other pertinent information—such as phone numbers for marinas and tackle shops—in a small address book that you can keep in the glove compartment of your vehicle.

The ratio of driving time to fishing time is certainly an important matter to consider, but it is also one of personal preference. I prefer not to drive much more than an hour to get to a spot that I will only fish for the day. If I'm going to fish somewhere for two or three days, I don't mind driving a half-day to get there. If I'm going to be in the saddle for 12 to 14 hours, though, I prefer to split that into two days of driving. That way, I can reach my destination by late morning or noon and have sufficient time to investigate the fishing, set up camp, check into a lodge or motel, or whatever. On that kind of trip, I will be fishing for at least four or five days.

Distance can be fairly well translated into driving time, providing that you consider the types of roads you will be traveling, the number of stops you will be making, towns you will pass through, and the kind of traffic you can expect to encounter. However, you need to know the distance before you can make such calculations. Of course, the best way to determine accurate mileage is to check it with your vehicle's odometer. But if you are heading for a fishing spot for the first time, you will have to use some other method.

The best way I have found to measure the distances on the map is with a map measurer. This handy little tool is designed to give accurate measurements on all types of maps. It is easy to use even on the most winding and irregular road designations. It is not as precise as an odometer, but it will give close enough mileage to estimate driving time. If you use it carefully and correctly, the map measurer will be accurate to within ten miles on a trip of 200 miles. You can pick one up at a local sporting-goods store.

I record my fishing spots and the ones I plan to visit in a small address book in alphabetical order. When I have checked the mileage with a map measurer, I enter the distance in pencil. Then, when I have checked the distance on an odometer, I enter the actual mileage. Other information that I keep in the address book are the names and phone numbers of nearby marinas and tackle shops.

By knowing my fishing radius and systematically keeping track of all the fishing that is available to me, I never waste time wondering where I ought to go on any trip. No matter how long I plan to be gone, I always have a wide selection of lakes and streams from which to choose. And more often than not, I have one or more phone numbers handy that I can dial to check on current fishing conditions.

CHAPTER 13

The Camping Fisherman

Boxes for Campers

If you start packing the trunk of a car or the back of a station wagon or pickup truck with all the gear required for several days of camping and fishing without keeping things organized, it will soon take on the appearance of a junk wagon. Furthermore, gear that isn't packed properly is susceptible to damage.

The organized camping fisherman will keep his equipment in order and stored in boxes, preferably several small ones instead of one huge one. This way, gear can be toted from the vehicle to the camp site with a minimum of effort. Some of the toughest camper's boxes are made of wood. You can make your own from plywood, buy precut kits, or scrounge for usable boxes in places such as junkyards and army surplus stores.

We have two large, homemade camp-kitchen boxes that we bought from a friend who no longer had use for them. They not only hold all of our cooking pots, pans, and utensils, but are also large enough to store plenty of nonperishable foods, plates, cups, aluminum foil, plastic bags and wrap, towels, soap and much more. We have been using these boxes for about ten years now and find them indispensable for camping convenience. We keep them packed and ready to go at all times, which saves us much time in preparing for any trip.

Gander Mountain, Inc. offers three different pre-cut kits for camping boxes, ranging in price from about $25 to $40 each. These kits can be mail-ordered and are easy to assemble with simple tools. Junkyards often have all sorts of old wooden crates that can be used as they are for camping, or can be modified to fit your needs. Some will be simple five-sided boxes to which you can add hinged plywood lids and carrying handles made of rope. Such crates are usually very cheap, too.

Large wooden ammunition crates are also great camping boxes. These will already have rope handles and lids equipped with hinges and hasps. They usually can be found at army-surplus stores and at some junkyards. I bought several a few years ago at a military-surplus outlet for 50¢ each. The hardware on them alone was worth more than that.

Although not as durable as wood, heavy cardboard boxes can be put to many uses by the camping fisherman. They can be made stronger and less prone to water damage by either covering them with self-adhesive, plastic-coated paper, sold in rolls in the housewares departments of discount stores, or by giving them a coat or two of polyurethane finish. The best boxes for this purpose are the cardboard egg crates and fruit boxes that you can pick up at a local supermarket. Other containers that make good boxes for campers are old coolers, sea chests, and footlockers. Auctions, garage sales, and flea markets are good places to look for bargains on these items.

You will find that you can keep all of your camping paraphernalia in several such boxes. You will be able to keep everything organized, systemized, and ready to go at a moment's notice. You'll spend less time rounding up your gear and packing it and more time enjoying your trip.

Another Tent for Your Camp

If you are a one-tent camper, one of the best additions you can make to your collection of camping gear is another tent, especially if the tent you have now is a small one. But no matter what size your tent is, it will easily become cluttered if it is used for both sleeping and storing gear away from the elements. The ideal base camp or fishing camp will have tents for sleeping and at least one other tent for cooking and storing supplies.

For sleeping, I want the best kind of tent to be found—one with a sewn-in floor, mosquito netting, and good ventilation. The cook tent need not be an elaborate one, though. Some of the bargain tents or army-surplus tents are fine for cooking and for keeping rain off the supplies and equipment. The simple addition of another tent can turn your camp into a comfortable and well-organized place to enjoy the outdoors.

Constant Hot-Water Supply for Your Camp

A large pot, capable of holding two or more gallons of water, is one of the handiest items I have toted along on fishing, camping, and float trips. The first person up in the morning at our camps has the duty of starting a fire and filling the water pot. Within minutes, there's warm water for washing up. By the time camp chores are finished and the fire is just right for cooking, boiling water can be added to smaller pots for steeping tea or making camp coffee. After the meal, there is plenty of hot water for washing dishes.

If we are in camp all day, as is often the case when we're fishing, we keep the fire going and leave the water pot near enough to the coals to stay hot. A constant source of hot water makes camp life more comfortable and convenient.

Grills for Your Camp Fire

For cooking over wood fires, there is nothing handier than a good grill. Camping grills are available in a variety of sizes at most camp-

A large pot of water kept on the campfire provides a convenient source of hot water whenever you need it.

ing stores and through some mail-order suppliers, but the alert camper will be able to find suitable grills elsewhere, too.

The shelves of old refrigerators, for example, make fine grills. So a visit to the local junkyard can turn up useful camp grills for a minimum of cash. Grills from old, worn-out charcoal barbeque broilers and hibachis make excellent campfire grills, too.

We keep several such grills in one of our camping boxes. When we need extra space for cooking, we simply add another grill or two. We keep two grills from an old discarded hibachi for preparing steaks and chops over the coals and find them ideally suited for the purpose.

Tote Some Charcoal Along

Even where firewood is plentiful, nothing can be more useful for cooking over coals than charcoal. We always take a bag or two of charcoal briquets along on our camping trips. When we rake the coals away from the fire and into position for cooking, we add several handfuls of charcoal briquets to the embers. Within a half-hour, we have a bed of coals and constant heat for all our cooking chores.

Build a Quasi-Wilderness Smoker

A few years ago, my fishing partners and I were planning a week-long trip to our favorite salmon river. We decided that this year our smoker would have to be more efficient and less time-consuming than in years past. We simply wanted to spend more time catching salmon and less time smoking them.

For smoker construction we have used two designs, employing the same materials in each. One is a tepee with a frame made from three green saplings, about 7 feet in length. Fish racks are made of chicken wire or wide mesh screen stretched parallel to the ground and lashed to the poles with heavy twine or bailing wire. The first rack should be about 3 feet above the ground and the second one about a foot above that.

For walls, we enclose the tripod with heavy-duty polyethylene— the kind used for vapor barriers in home construction. A staple gun is handy for attaching the plastic to the poles. A small opening should be left at the top, and the bottom edge of the plastic should be weighted to the ground with rocks or sand. A small flap for access to the inside can be taped shut.

Our second design, though slower in the cooking and smoking operation, accommodates more fish and requires less attention. For this one, we use green poles to build a rectangular frame, 5-feet tall, 6-feet long, and 3-feet wide. Again, walls are heavy-duty plastic, and racks are chicken wire or screen. We use a light canvas tarp draped over the top to retain heat and allow smoke and moisture to escape slowly.

Our greatest problem in the past has been maintaining an even heat with a good bed of coals and keeping green willow just smoldering to provide the smoke. We solved this by using charcoal briquets and commercially produced hickory chips. An old aluminum saucepan was just right for holding the hickory chips to a slow, smoky burn.

A small charcoal fire provides a surprising amount of heat in an enclosed area. And since no draft blows across the coals, they burn slowly and require a minimum of attention. We dig a shallow pit for the charcoal, filling it first with embers shoveled from our campfire. Since the rising heat and smoke tend to dissipate inside the smoker, the coal pit can be small—about one fourth of the floor space of the smoker. Charcoal should be distributed evenly in the pit.

Coals should be checked about every two or three hours and more charcoal added as required. In smaller smokers (such as the tepee type described), twenty-four to thirty-six hours will be sufficient to cook and smoke a batch of fish. Larger smokers (such as the rectangular one) will smoke fish in about thirty-six to forty-eight hours. Two pans of chips per batch will be enough to impart a good, smoky flavor to the fish.

Preparing fish for the smoker is really quite simple. Since we like a fairly hard-cured fish, we cut fillets into inch-wide strips and soak them in a strong brine for four hours. A new, plastic trash can with a lid is handy for brining and keeps insects away from the fish. The brine is made of one cup of dark-brown sugar and one cup of salt for each quart of water. We also toss in a couple of bay leaves, a tablespoon or two of fines herbs, and a half-a-handful of cracked black peppercorns. We make enough brine to cover the fish entirely.

During the brining process, the fish should be stirred around in the brine about every hour. Just prior to smoking, fillets are removed from the brine, patted semi-dry with paper towels, and air-dried for about thirty minutes, or until they are glazed and sticky to the touch, then placed on the smoking racks, skin side down.

It's hard to beat this tasty treat while you're fishing, or later, in the comfort of your home. We have kept fish, thus prepared, in brown paper bags for as long as three days without refrigeration. At home, I usually keep small packages in the freezer and leftovers in the refrigerator. Smoked fish also can be canned at home. Of course, the added bonus is that this method of wilderness smoking is so simple that it doesn't take up much precious fishing time.

Can Your Axe

In the fishing camp, few tools are as useful as a good axe. Splitting firewood, making rod racks and smoker frames from saplings, and hammering in tent pegs are just a few of the tasks to which an axe can be put. An axe without a sheath, however, is a dangerous item to have around. If you don't have a sheath for your axe (and many are sold without them), you can make one out of an old tin can. With both ends of the can removed, flatten the can with an axe or hammer. Now slip the flattened can over the head of the axe, and hold it in place with a big rubber band.

The Versatile Ground Cloth

One of the most useful items that every camping fisherman ought to own is a good, lightweight ground cloth. Those made of waterproof ripstop nylon are the best. Besides its intended use—to keep a sleeping camper comfortable by combating ground moisture—the ground cloth can be draped over a backpack to keep it dry in a downpour. In a pinch, it can be used as a rain poncho. During a cloudburst, a ground cloth can be quickly laid over camping gear to keep it dry. It can be used as a tent fly or can be turned into any of a number of different kinds of shelters. It can be attached to the side of a pickup-truck camper or motor home, then stretched out to staked poles to function as a shade-giving canopy.

When no facilities are nearby, a ground cloth can be attached to vertical poles to make a good privy or outdoor bathing area. In an emergency, a ground cloth can be lashed to two poles to function as a stretcher. A blaze-orange one makes a good emergency signal flag. And there are probably dozens of other uses for the versatile ground cloth. Make sure you pack one with you whenever you venture into the wilds.

Air Mattress or Pad?

For warm-weather camping, the choice between an air mattress or foam pad is pretty much a personal matter. For a number of reasons, though, I gave up on the air mattresses some years ago. First, a top-quality air mattress will always be heavier than a foam pad. And air mattresses have to be blown up, which can become quite a chore if you are camping at even moderately high elevations. Most importantly, once the air inside an air mattress cools—despite what you may have heard or read to the contrary—it does little or nothing at all to insulate the sleeper from the cold ground; whereas a foam pad provides excellent insulation.

For most of our camping, my wife and I use Woods Trail Beds (available from Gander Mountain, Inc.). These pads are comprised of a 2-inch, high-density foam core enclosed in a heavy-duty, cotton-polyester cover. They are considered by many outdoorsmen to be the best pads there are. For backpacking there are a number of smaller, lighter, and more compact foam pads available from most camping and backpacking supply outlets.

Don't Pack Too Much Too Far

Because we have all heard tales about the mighty he-men who hike 25 miles into the mountains with 70-pound packs on their backs, most of us pack entirely too much weight when we first begin backpacking. It doesn't take a lot of miles on the trail under the burden of an overloaded pack to discover that "this ain't fun!"

More than one person has been soured on backpacking by trying to carry too much too far. So if you are just taking up backpacking or are introducing someone else to it, remember to pack light and not to travel too far. You should be able to find plenty of fishing spots within a five-mile hike; that is sufficient distance for any beginning backpacker to cover. As for pack weights, the average woman should be able to comfortably carry about 25 pounds, the average man about 35 pounds.

No New Clothes for Backpacking

Probably every outdoorsman knows better than to venture out in a new pair of boots that haven't been properly broken in. But it is equally important that other garments be broken in, too. Pants and shirts should never be brand-new, they should be sufficiently worn and softened by several washings. Stiff pant legs or collars can chafe the skin and make the hiker mighty uncomfortable. A couple of washings will usually remove a lot of the itch from wool socks and long underwear.

Light-Packing Light

Something a lot of beginning backpackers overlook when they pack up for a trip is some kind of light. Most flashlights are too heavy, and lanterns are certainly out of the question. But a small, lightweight, disposable flashlight and several long-burning candles can really come in handy on any backpacking trip. A small alpinist's lantern is excellent for burning candles outdoors, as it is both light-weight and compact and will protect the flame from the wind.

Don't Pack Wet Laundry

On any extended backpacking trip, you will accumulate some dirty laundry that will be damp or wet for one reason or another. Towels and washcloths wet from use, underwear and socks damp from perspiration, and any clothing that has become rain soaked will mean additional weight if you pack it away without first hanging it to dry. Bring along several plastic trash bags to keep your laundry separated from the rest of your gear and supplies. Take a length of light rope or heavy twine to use as a clothesline for drying out wet or damp garments.

Keep Your T.P. Dry

When I was a boy, I spent many hours in the out of doors with an Algonquin Indian. From him, I learned much about hunting, fishing, and camping. One sage bit of advice I first heard from him was: "Keep your T.P. dry." His suggestion had nothing to do with that cone-shaped tent used as a dwelling by some American Indians and known as a tepee or teepee. With his tongue poked in his cheek and his black eyes sparkling, he grinned, "Toilet paper, boy. Keep it dry."

One of the handiest items for keeping your T.P. and other nonwetables dry and usable is a drawstring plastic bag. After filling the bag with anything that should be kept dry, pull the drawstrings tight, fold the top of the bag over several times, and tie the drawstrings together with a bow. If you have trouble locating plastic bags with drawstrings, try a local industrial supply house, where they are readily available and cheap. You may have to buy a large quantity, but you should have no trouble convincing some of your outdoor friends to share the cost and the convenience.

How to Clean Your Mess Kit Sans Suds

Next to bad water, improperly cleaned mess kits have probably caused more diarrhea among outdoorsmen than anything else. Food residue, especially grease, left in a mess kit is the culprit that can make you wish you had stayed at home.

About the best way to clean cooking utensils, plates, and silverware without polluting lake or stream is with sand. A handful of dry sand in a mess kit will quickly absorb grease. You can then scour the inside thoroughly with more sand and water until it is squeaking clean. Knives, forks, and spoons can be jabbed into the sandy ground repeatedly until they come clean. If you are en route to your fishing spot and have to overnight away from a water source, sand is about the only thing to use to clean your mess gear, especially if you are packing light and conserving water.

Try Trackpacking for Uncrowded Fishing

The face of North America is woven with a network of railroad tracks, some still in use, some not. In many areas, particularly in hilly or mountainous terrain, railroads were built along streams; that was usually easier and cheaper than tunneling through mountains. These railroads can lead you to some excellent fishing away from the usual crowds. And hiking along a railbed is considerably easier than breaking trail through the boondocks. Chances are that there are some railroads in your own locale that can lead you to fine fishing. If you are traveling to another state, be sure to study topographical maps in search of tracks near streams and lakes.

Packing for Float Trips and Boat Camping

Your major concern on any float trip or boat-camping expedition will be to keep supplies and gear protected from water. Waterproof canoe bags are great for this purpose, but they aren't always easy to find and are never cheap. Anything that needs protection from moisture should be packed in sealed plastic trash bags. Use the heavy-duty bags for this purpose, as they are the only ones that will hold up under the rigors of camping.

It's a good idea to pack food staples such as salt, flour, sugar, and cereals in their own small plastic bags before putting them into a larger waterproof container. Pack each sleeping bag in its own plastic trash bag, and then pack them into another plastic bag. Small, plastic trash cans with lids are also excellent for packing gear and protecting it from the elements. Once packed, they can be securely lashed inside the boat or canoe. Make sure that heavy items are packed at the bottom with lighter items toward the top of the can for maximum stability while afloat. Plastic and aluminum coolers are also great for waterproof storage.

CHAPTER 14

The Organized Fisherman

The Fisherman's Library

Expertise in any area of endeavor requires a certain amount of erudition, plenty of practice, and practical experience afield. The competent angler, then, is going to couple the knowledge gained from reading with the wisdom acquired on lakes and streams. If you are at all serious about the sport of angling, you ought to plan to set up a reasonably adequate library of fishing literature.

Although my own modest library contains a fair number of books that might be considered fireside reading (collections of fishing yarns), those I consider the most important are the how-to books and the reference volumes. For anyone beginning his own fishing library, I would first advise that he consider the kinds of angling that interest him most and begin acquiring reference books in those subject areas—bass fishing, trout fishing, panfishing, fly fishing, spinning, and the like.

To any angler, regardless of his interests, I would heartily recommend that the book with which to begin a library should be *Mc-Clane's New Standard Fishing Encyclopedia and International Angling Guide*. This is the most important fishing book that I own by far, and is perhaps the most definitive volume ever written on the subject of angling. With 1,156 pages in 8½-by-11-inch format, this trophy catch tips the scales at about 8½ pounds and is the most comprehensive and best-organized encyclopedic guide to angling available today.

Since interests and tastes vary greatly, I'm not going to burden you with a long list of book titles. But I think I ought to mention a few other books that I consider important volumes for the modern fresh-water angler. No matter what your favorite kind of fishing happens to be or what area of angling you would most like to explore, one or several of these books should prove valuable.

For the trout fisherman, a well-written volume full of expert advice based on a lifetime of experience is *Trout Fishing* by Joe Brooks. The book covers all aspects of fly fishing for trout in streams, lakes, and ponds and offers helpful information on tackle, casting, wading, and fly selection.

A more specialized book with an unusual approach is Ray Ovington's *Tactics on Trout*, in which he addresses every imaginable aspect of stream fishing for trout. Although his step-by-step instructions assume that the reader is a fly fisherman, much of what he has to say is useful for the spin fisherman as well.

If you are serious about fly fishing, Ernest Schwiebert's classic, *Matching the Hatch*, should be in your library. This is a comprehensive text on stream entomology as it applies to the selection of artificial flies. If fly tying is one of your interests, you will want to know about a new book that I recently added to my library—*Popular Fly Patterns* by Terry Hellekson. This one is strictly for reference, but it is surely destined to become a classic as it is the most complete manual I have found to date. It contains dressing formulae for more than 800 flies with more than 600 detailed pen-and-ink illustrations. I plan to spend a lot of time at the tying bench with this book, come winter.

On the subject of bass fishing, I have found nothing better than Grits Gresham's *Complete Book of Bass Fishing*. If any book can be complete on any subject, this one comes close. I had been bass fishing for a good number of years when I read this book, and I was able to learn quite a bit from it. It also served as a good refresher course in some areas. For the beginning bass fisherman, it would be a perfect choice.

America's Favorite Fishing, by F. Philip Rice, is subtitled *A Complete Guide to Angling for Panfish* and is an enjoyable and informative little book on a delightful kind of fishing. In addition to addressing every facet of panfishing, from finding the fish and selecting the right bait to cooking the catch, Rice adequately handles fly fishing, spinning, and live-bait techniques. He also offers the reader a state-by-state guide to panfishing.

If you are a do-it-yourselfer, the price you will pay for C. Boyd Pfeiffer's *Tackle Craft* will be returned to you many times over by the money you save making your own fishing tackle. Pfeiffer's clear, concise instructions and his crisp, sharp photography make every one of his projects simple to duplicate.

Fishing is a sport that leads one into many related-interest areas or hobbies, such as fly tying, collecting old tackle or angling books, making lures, and such. The allied interest that grabbed my attention most recently is custom rod building, and I probably never would have ventured into this rewarding activity without the urgings of Dale Clemens in his book, *Fiberglass Rod Making*. Here, again, is a masterful guide that simplifies seemingly difficult tasks. With the help of Clemens' book, I can now afford to own fine, custom-made rods, because I can build them myself. This is a book I would strongly recommend if you have an interest in rod building.

Starting a library requires some caution and planning. If it is to be a rewarding adjunct to angling, you should approach the task systematically. Certainly, you will want to spend some time at libraries and bookstores browsing through fishing books. Those that particularly strike your fancy should be added to the list of books you eventually want to acquire.

A good way to get started is to join a book club that specializes in outdoor-sports titles. Not only will you save money by purchasing books that are offered at less than publishers' prices, but the introductory offers advertised by such clubs are real giveaways. And from time to time these clubs offer some outstanding specials on books that they have left over. As long as you are careful to return your notice on any monthly selection you don't want, and to use good judgment in any selections, book-club membership can be a way of adding to your angling library regularly and inexpensively.

Sometimes you may come across titles that you wish to add to your personal library but are unable to find at a local bookstore. If the book is still in print, it is a simple matter to have your dealer order a copy from the publisher. If it is out of print, it may be a bit tougher to locate. A good book dealer will offer to help and, through his connections in the business, will often be able to locate out-of-print books for you. Some book clubs offer the same book-finding service. You need only write them with the pertinent bibliographical data—title, author, publisher.

I know of two book dealers that specialize in outdoor-sports books. Although their inventories are in a constant state of change as they buy and sell books, they always have several thousand volumes on hand at any given time. Some will be rare collectors' volumes, some will be hard-to-find books that are no longer in print, and others will be more current, popular titles.

One of these is the Angler's and Shooter's Bookshelf, Goshen, Connecticut 06756. For $2.00 (refundable) they will send you their catalog in two parts: *A* to *K* in the spring and *L* to *Z* in the fall. After buying a book from them, you will continue to receive catalogs for five years. Sporting Book Service sends their catalogs out in two parts, also, and their's is free. Write tham at Box 177, Rancocas, New Jersey 08073.

You can sometimes find fishing books at used-book stores. As long as you aren't looking for rare first editions or other collectors' volumes, you should be able to locate some good buys.

For bibliographical details on the books I have mentioned here and on a few others I consider worthwhile for most serious anglers, see the "Selected Bibliography" in the back of the book.

Organizing Periodicals

Popular fishing and outdoor periodicals are another source of angling information and reference material that many fishermen like to keep in their libraries. Periodicals have a tendency to accumulate rather rapidly, however, and can pose organizational problems.

Most magazines offer binders or boxes for housing a year's worth of their publication in an organized fashion under one cover. You can also purchase magazine file boxes from most office-supply stores. While such storage receptacles provide convenient storage, you will need some kind of system for ready reference.

One method that some fishermen use is to stick gummed index tabs (available at office-supply stores) to the pages where pertinent articles appear. While this helps to highlight certain topics, the more magazines you acquire, the less convenient index tabs become; you still may have to thumb through many magazines before finding the article you want.

A far better method is to set up a subject-index file on 3-by-5-inch file cards. Buy a small file box, a set of alphabetical file guides, a box of third-cut file guides, and a supply of 3-by-5-inch file cards. For quick reference you can write one- or two-word subject locators on the tabs of the third-cut file guides and place them in their proper alphabetical order. You might have file guides for such topics as bass, trout, fly fishing, catfish, monofilament, rods and reels, to name a few possibilities. Behind the alphabetical file guide lettered B, for example, you would find the third-cut file guide labeled "Bass." A typical file card found in that section might read: BASS, "Six Magic Spots for May Bass," Homer Circle, *Sports Afield*, May, 1977, p. 56.

Such a system enables you to go immediately to the specific periodical and page without searching or thumbing through a stack of magazines. For the system to be an efficient one, it is important that you stay caught up with it. It only takes a few minutes to index any magazine. If you only read one outdoor magazine a month, there's nothing wrong with letting the issues stack up for a few months and doing the indexing during the off-season. But if you read several outdoor and fishing magazines each month, do your indexing monthly to keep it from getting out of hand.

Another advantage of the card index is that cross referencing is a simple matter. In addition to keeping track of bass articles in general, you may want to index material according to geographical location and time of year. For instance, under F in your file you might have a file guide labeled "Florida," with a card behind it that says: FLORIDA, "Six Magic Spots for May Bass," Homer Circle, etc. Or if you are keeping track of the seasonal aspects of bass fishing, you might have file guides for the four seasons or the 12 months of the year—under "Spring" or "May" you would have this same article on another card.

In addition to the information on the file card required to locate an article, you can put other notes—such as highlights from the article or key phrases—that will guide you to the article you wish to review.

The Fisherman's Files

Because of the overwhelming number of periodicals I must go through every month, I no longer index current periodicals in the way I just described. Now, the only magazines that I index that way are the ones I wish to keep intact. This includes old issues that have some collector or reference value, annuals (such as the *Garcia Fishing Annual, Fisherman's Digest,* etc.), and a few others that I don't want to toss out.

Instead, I clip articles from current periodicals that I wish to retain and keep them in files housed in filing cabinets. I realize that as an outdoor writer I must maintain files that might be more extensive than those of the average fisherman, but, on the other hand, I have met some serious fishermen whose files would be the envy of any angling scribe. So it just boils down to what you need to sustain your level of activity in the sport.

Regardless of how you choose to organize and index magazine articles, there are some things that require filing in file folders. Articles clipped from newspapers and brochures and much of the literature available from various government agencies, manufacturers, sport shows, and chambers of commerce can only be kept organized in file drawers. You don't need fancy full-suspension filing cabinets to house this material, although if you have one, all the better. The cardboard filing cabinets available from most office-supply outlets, some department stores, and such mail-order companies as Montgomery Ward are quite inexpensive and will do a fine job of storing your fishing material. Moreover, you can often find good, used metal filing cabinets at auctions where office equipment and furnishings are to be sold.

You should establish files for important lakes, reservoirs, and streams that are within your fishing radius. Then, as material is published by the state or in popular magazines and newspapers about these areas, you can file it for later reference. When the time comes to plan a trip to one of these spots, chances are you will have an abundance of literature that will aid you in your preliminary planning and in your fishing. You may have gathered maps, names, and addresses of guides and outfitters, locations of campgrounds and marinas, as well as articles on how to, where to, and when to fish those particular bodies of water for best results.

Publications from Government Agencies

You should certainly have on file all the available fishing literature that your home state provides. If you frequently fish neighboring states, publications from their state fish and game agencies should be in your files, too. And it is never too early to begin accumulating material on states you plan to travel to in the future.

If you travel extensively, you might even wish to set up files on all fifty states. My wife and I did this several years ago. For the price of fifty first-class postage stamps, fifty envelopes, and fifty copies of a letter requesting all available information on fishing, we filled a filing-cabinet drawer with useful literature—most of it geographically specialized, of course, but with a good bit that is excellent general reference material on fishing methods, species, tackle, and such. We have added to these files considerably since setting them up, and they are now three times their original size.

You will find that some states will just send you the usual public-relations flack; others will either send you useful books, maps, and scientific studies or will tell you how to order them. The state of Maine, for example, will send you a catalog of publications you can order. Dozens of them are on fish and fishing, fish culture, ecology, and other topics, and they range in price from free to 25¢ apiece.

Other states that offer excellent literature on fishing, camping, and other outdoor recreations are Alaska, Connecticut, Georgia, Illinois, Kansas, Maryland, Massachusetts, Michigan, Minnesota, Missouri, Nebraska, Nevada, North Carolina, Oklahoma, Oregon, Tennessee, Texas, Virginia, and Wisconsin. The states not mentioned will send you current fishing regulations and additional literature varying in levels of usefulness from very good to very poor.

You can also obtain literature on fishing from some branches of the U.S. Department of the Interior, and, in fact, this department has published a rather decent hardbound fishing book of 464 pages, entitled *Sport Fishing USA*. This anthology, containing articles by some of the biggest names in fishing, sells for $10 and is worth owning.

Label Your Gear

I am careful with my possessions, but even the most cautious outdoorsman loses something from time to time. Operating under the basic assumption that most of my fellow outdoorsmen are honest, I think I have a fair chance of having lost items returned if they are labeled. If they're not, I have no chance of getting them back.

I have used several methods for marking my outdoor gear with my name and address. I have etched items that can be etched and have used a wide assortment of sticky labels that aren't always sticky and, after a certain amount of wear, aren't always labels. A couple of years ago, though, I standardized my labeling with the purchase of a labelmaker—one of those plastic things that looks like a Star Trek phaser gun and uses rolls of plastic embossing tape for ammunition. This has proved to be one of the handiest tools I own, and the labels it makes are tough and waterproof. With it, I have labeled numerous items: fishing rods, tackle boxes (large and small), reels, photography gear, camp stoves, pack frames, coolers—you name it.

Since owning a labelmaker, I have put it to several other uses, too. For example, when I grew weary of rooting through countless

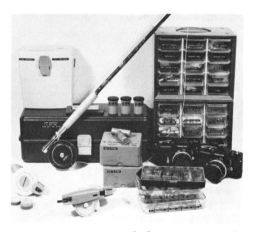

Any sportsman can find numerous uses for a labelmaker.

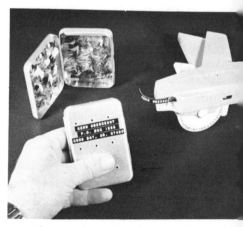

Items large and small can be identified with tough, waterproof labels.

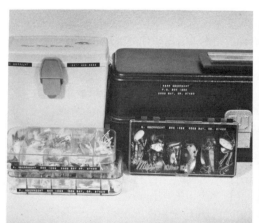

Another advantage is the versatility of the narrow embossing-tape strips that can be stuck to equipment of any shape or size.

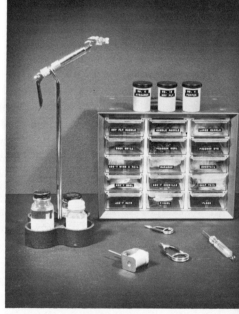

The labelmaker is a great timesaver when it is used to organize and systemize the fly tyer's bench.

look-alike jars and cans of nuts, bolts, washers, and all the other odds and ends so essential to any man's workshop, I spent a day sorting out all this paraphernalia and labeling each jar and can. Now, a quick glance at a row of labeled containers leads me to the one I need. On my fly-tying bench I have two small cabinets that house a wide array of materials. Instead of wasting time searching through the fifteen drawers in each cabinet, I can go instantly to the drawer containing what I need, since they are labeled Peacock Hearl, Duck Quill, Saddle Hackle, Tinsel, Chenille, or Floss.

Since I tie a wide variety of flies—from tiny nymphs and dry flies to salmon streamers, bass bugs, and poppers—I keep quite an assortment of hooks on hand. I have found that the plastic canisters that 35mm film comes in are ideal for keeping all of those various hooks organized and readily at hand. Embossed labels on these containers tell me what styles and sizes of hooks are inside.

Like many avid fishermen, my wife and I have several fly reels loaded with various kinds and sizes of lines, both sinking and floating. Each reel is labeled with the AFTMA line code—DT5F, WF7S, WF8F, etc.—that tells us what kind of line is on any particular reel. And just a number—4, 6, 10, 15, 20, or 30—on a spinning-reel spool tells us what pound-test line it carries.

Four identical fly boxes that I carry in my fishing-vest pockets are marked with my name and address. But they are also labeled Dry Flies, Wet Flies, Nymphs, and Streamers for quick identification. These labels are stuck to the tops of the fly boxes so they can be easily viewed while they are still in my vest pockets.

Many serious photographers like to carry two or three camera bodies or a camera with interchangeable film backs so they can use more than one kind of film at a time. When I reach into my crowded gadget bag, I find it convenient to have each camera body labeled with the kind of film it contains. Film canisters can be identified with embossed labels, too.

Another advantage to using these labels is their versatility. The narrow strips can accommodate just about any shape or size. On small or odd-shaped items, a single strip can be fitted into place. If there's not enough room for a name and address, a phone number will do. On expensive items the word "reward" is added insurance.

There are numerous other uses to which I have put the label-maker, and, surely, I will find others in the future. I'm sure that

Labels on camera bodies can indicate what kind of film is inside.

most sportsmen can find enough jobs for one to justify the small investment. With all the time-saving uses alone, a labelmaker can pay for itself in short order. And it's the cheapest form of insurance you'll ever buy.

Is Your Outdoor Gear Properly Insured?

Unless you keep close tabs on your belongings, have updated your homeowner's or renter's insurance within the past 12 months, and have added any recent purchases to your insurance policy, there's a good chance that your outdoor equipment is not adequately insured. Furthermore, if you have never specifically discussed all this gear with your insurance agent and had it itemized on your policy, it might not be covered at all. Or you may find that your gear is covered only while it is on your property.

A good bit of the gear used by outdoorsmen is considered by insurance companies to be target items for burglars and thieves. If such items have not been itemized on your policy, they might not be covered. Cameras are right at the top of the list, so be sure that your photography gear is adequately insured. You might be allowed a certain dollar value in coverage for camping and fishing gear. If the value of your gear exceeds that allowed by your policy, you could be required to declare that additional value and to pay a higher premium. But the increase is usually minimal.

As far as I'm concerned, anything less than all-risk coverage is useless for outdoor equipment. If I scuttle a boat and lose a tackle box with $200 worth of gear inside, if I drop a $150 camera lens overboard, if my vehicle or motel room gets ripped off, or if someone vandalizes my fishing camp, I want my insurance policy to cover it. And incidentally, if you think that your auto or recreational-vehicle insurance policy will cover fishing, camping, or photography equipment stolen from the vehicle, you are probably wrong. I have never heard of an auto policy that was as broad as that.

Most fishermen who have made a large investment in an expensive fishing boat, motor, and trailer are wise enough to realize that they ought to have such a rig insured. And if the boat is being fi-

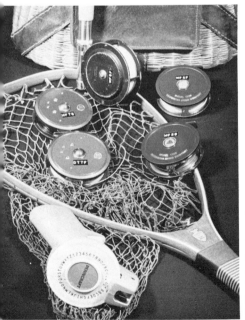

Labels readily identify the kinds of lines on reels.

Where space is insufficient for a complete address, a phone number will do. The word "reward" is added insurance.

nanced, insurance will be a condition of the contract with the bank or finance company. I daresay, though, that there are probably a lot of jon boats, canoes, and cartoppers around that aren't insured. Even if your investment is only a few hundred dollars, it makes sense to protect it with insurance. Furthermore, such a policy will only cost you a few dollars a year.

Some years ago I had a 12-foot aluminum jon boat that I bought on sale at Sears for $85. I never considered insuring it until a friend of mine who, over the years, had lost two similar boats to flood waters and one to thieves convinced me that insurance was smart. All-risk coverage cost me five dollars a year. When the boat was two years old some senseless creature put five .30-caliber holes in the hull. The heli-arc welding job cost me $30, which the insurance company paid within a week of notification. I sold the boat a few weeks later for $85. So two years of use, which included a lot of fishing, frog gigging, and duck hunting, cost me a mere $10—but without the insurace the tab would have been three times that.

The best advice I can give you is to spend some time with your insurance agent. Make sure your gear is adequately covered, off your property as well as on. Make a complete list of all your gear with accurate descriptions and serial numbers, and keep the list with other important papers and policies in a safe-deposit box.

The Fisherman's Log

The most valuable book in any fisherman's library is his own fishing log. In it, the angler will find the important data the he has compiled on the lakes and streams he frequents. After a couple of years of keeping an accurate and detailed account of every outing, the fisherman can apply the intelligence gathered to similar conditions in the future, and he will nearly always catch more fish as a result. Sometimes it will mean catching fish when nobody else is.

Case in point—the bass in my part of the country usually spawn in May and June. This is a handy bit of knowledge to have tucked away, but it is far too broad and general to be useful by itself. First, the bass aren't going to spawn for all of May and all of June, but rather for some time during that 61-day stretch. And there's that word "usually." There are always exceptions to the norm, because a fish's calendar is not a Gregorian matter of months and days. It is a natural matter of temperatures, water conditions, and chemistry.

My fishing log indicates that the best of the bass fishing in my favorite lake occurs during the four weeks prior to the spawning season, usually late April and early May, when the water level is high from the rainy season and spring runoff. At that time of the year, the high and roily waters cover much shoreline that will become dry land later. Weeds have not yet choked the shallows, and the bass are extremely active then. They move from deep to shallow waters and back many times during the day, gorging themselves on just about anything they can find—but mostly bluegills and crawfish.

With the lake water beginning to clear and recede and the temperature rising, the feeding slacks off. By the time the lake has dropped to its normal seasonal level, the bass have moved into the clear water of the weedy shallows to spawn. Fishing will still be good for a few more weeks, but not at the peak it reached during previous weeks.

This year it was a totally different picture. Our winter rainfall was less than half of normal. Weather was unseasonably warm and clear. The small, coastal mountain streams that feed the lake and that are normally high, muddy, and chilly in the spring were much lower and considerably clearer and warmer. The bass were on the spawning beds in April. And by the end of May, they were living according to their normal summer patterns and frequenting deeper waters farther offshore. Only the fishermen who were able to rely on previous experience and the reliable information in their fishing logs were able to reap the harvest of late March and early April.

The physical characteristics of a fisherman's log are a matter of the angler's choice. If you don't care to spend time designing your own, notebooks with printed log pages are available commercially from tackle shops and mail-order suppliers. But you can save a few bucks and perhaps come up with a better log by making your own. You will have to decide what sort of information you wish to include. You can determine this by looking at other logs and making use of the kind of information that applies to you and your kind of fishing.

My own fishing log is housed in a three-ring, loose-leaf binder. Inside I have two forms of my own design. One is my "Daily Aggregate Catch Report," one of which I complete for every day of every trip. The other is an "Individual Catch Report" that I use to record data only on large or unusual fish. When my notes run beyond the space I have allowed, I use loose-leaf paper to record the additional information.

Daily Aggregate Catch Report

Date: _____ Time: from _____ to _____ State: _____

General location: _____ Specific location: _____

_____ General weather: _____

Wind direction: _____ Wind velocity: _____ Temperature: _____

Barometer: _____ Humidity: _____ High tide: _____ Low tide: _____

Water condition: _____ Water clarity: _____ Depth: _____

Fishing depth: ___ Surface temperature: ___ Temperature at fishing depth: ___

Type of bottom: _____

Cover or structure: _____

Fishing methods: _____

Tackle used: _____

Baits used: _____

Best baits: _____

Species	Quantity	Size	Comments

Notes: _____

Individual Catch Report

Species: _____ Date: _____ Time: _____

Weight: _____ Length: _____ Girth: _____

Line: _____ Line test: _____ Other terminal tackle

and rigging: _____ Bait: _____

Weather condition: _____ Wind direction: _____

Wind velocity: _____ Barometer: _____ Humidity: _____ Temperature: _____

Water Condition: _____ Surface Temperature: _____

Temperature at fishing depth: _____ Water clarity: _____ Depth: _____

Fishing depth: _____ Type of bottom: _____ Cover or structure: _____

_____ Tide status: _____

Comments: _____

_____

_____

_____

_____

_____

_____

_____

_____

_____

Tag number: _____ Reference files: _____

_____

Photo reference files: _____

If you plan to make up your own log pages, type them neatly on clean, white, 8½-by-11-inch paper. Make sure the type on your typewriter is clean and that the ribbon is fresh; characters should be crisp and black. Then take these camera-ready forms to a local quick-print facility and have them offset printed in the quantity you desire. Remember that larger quantities will mean smaller per-page prices, so you might want to have several years' worth of pages printed up or join with a couple of fishing buddies to split the costs. If you have access to a photocopy machine where you can get copies for a good price, you might save money that way. But if you are having it done commercially, offset printing will be the cheaper method.

Naturally, a log such as the one I use is too big to lug around with me on the lake or stream. For one-day trips, it stays on a bookshelf until I return and enter data from the day's activities. On extended trips, I take it with me, but I leave it in camp or in the motel room or motor home while I'm out fishing. Instead, I carry a small pocket notebook to record anything that I don't trust my memory to retain. Of greatest importance is the recording of all data the same day. If you fear you might need memory joggers, by all means carry a notebook with you and take time to use it.

The value of any fishing log is cumulative. If you are just starting one, it will be of little or no value to you this year. But next year, you will be able to refer to it to examine your successes and failures and to plan your strategies accordingly. And your log will grow in value each year. The more fishing you do and the more explicit records you build up for future reference and study, the better fisherman you will become.

To give you an idea of the kind of information and organization you should incorporate into a fishing log, here are the two forms that I use. You will probably want to make some changes when you design your own, but basically, these pages include the most important data. These forms can be used for stream- or lake-fishing records. Since I live on the coast, I include tide data when it applies.

CHAPTER 15

Fishing Photography

The Best Cameras and Lenses for Fishermen

First, just as with fishing tackle, you should buy the best camera that you can reasonably afford. Secondly, you should use the kind of camera that is most comfortable to you. But for a number of reasons, to attain the highest degree of versatility, portability, simplicity, and picture quality, your camera should have an adjustable shutter and aperture (or electronic exposure with manual override capability) and should be of 35mm format. My personal preference, and the kind I would recommend for most purposes, is the 35mm single-lens reflex (SLR) with through-the-lens (TTL) metering.

The fixed-focus pocket cameras and the polaroid-type cameras are okay for snapshots and family-album prints, but if you are at all serious about taking good fishing photographs you need an adjustable camera. As for the formats larger than 35mm, most are too cumbersome and clumsy to be as useful for action photography as a 35mm camera is. Furthermore, the film is more expensive and capacities are smaller. I have used several cameras of larger format for outdoor photography, and while the larger negatives are pleasant to work with, the disadvantages far outweigh the advantages.

If you select a 35mm viewfinder-type camera (most compact models are viewfinders), you will be restricted to one lens, unless you buy something like a Leica or one of the old Nikon or Canon viewfinders. What I find most objectionable about these cameras, though, is that I'm looking through one lens and photographing with another. This can cause parallax problems in close-up work and can be bothersome when using filters and screens over the lens, especially when the light meter is separate from the lens.

Advantages of the compact viewfinder 35s are that they are lightweight and easy to handle. Most are equipped with semi-wide-angle lenses, too, which make them suitable for a wide range of fishing photography. When I'm wading a stream or walking the shoreline of a lake, I carry a little Olympus viewfinder camera and my wife carries another. That's when I want a lightweight camera and something I can tuck out of the way inside my fishing jacket.

For most of my fishing photography, though, I prefer my SLR cameras and their interchangeable lenses and accessories. What I like most about the SLR is that what you see is what you get. Since you view your subject through the same lens that takes the picture, there is no problem with parallax. And with a meter behind the lens, you need do no calculating and compensating when you put a filter or screen over the lens.

The lenses I use most with these cameras for fishing photography are the standard 50mm and wide-angle 35mm and 28mm. I usually carry a 200mm lens along when we're afloat to capture waterside wildlife on film. But the most useful of my lenses are the wide-angles with their wider fields of view and increased depth of field. To adequately handle photography from a 12-foot boat, a 28mm lens is a must. This focal length is also useful in larger boats, because it will catch the action in close while offering adequate depth of field.

By far, my most useful lens, and the one that has become my standard for most fishing photos, is the 35mm. This lens will focus close enough to handle perhaps 75 percent of my close-up photography. Yet it has a wide enough field of view to capture most of the action in boats of 14 feet and longer with good depth of field.

Any macro-focusing (close-focusing) lens is a handy item for fishing photos, as it allows for striking close-ups of fish, lures, and flies. But such lenses can be expensive. Instead, you might wish to carry close-up lenses that will screw into the front of one of your interchangeable lenses or extension rings that fit between the lens and camera and allow you to focus closer. A bellows will do the same job and is adjustable, but it is bulkier.

Perhaps the ultimate beauty of the SLR camera is that it is the basis for a system that can be gradually acquired. You can start modestly with one camera body and one lens and add to it as your needs demand or your budget allows. Don't overlook the advantages of zoom lenses when you begin building your SLR system. Zooms for years had the reputation of being inferior lenses. But many of the zoom lenses being manufactured today have excellent optical and mechanical components and offer the photographer far greater versatility than any lens with a fixed focal length. Some offer the added advantage of macro focusing. A photographer with a good wide-angle zoom and a telephoto zoom is equipped to handle just about any kind of photographic situation he is likely to encounter while fishing. Changing from one focal length to another takes only a fraction of a second.

More and more mechanical parts are being replaced with electronic components in 35mm SLR cameras these days. Cameras are becoming smaller, lighter, more foolproof, and easier to use. Photography has moved into every area of outdoor recreation. With the right equipment, photography can be a rewarding and enduring phase of all your fishing activities.

Keep Your Camera Ready

Do you keep your fly rod in a case between casts? Do you zip your spinning reel into a reel pouch as you leave one pool on your way to the next? Preposterous, you say, and I agree. Why is it, then, that so many amateur photographers keep their cameras encased at all times, removing the case only to snap a picture? The only reason I can think of is that the photographer wants to protect an expensive piece of equipment. That's a good idea, just as rifle cases, rod cases, and reel pouches are good ideas. But when you're out to get pictures, leave the case behind. It's an awkward, cumbersome nuisance that will only get in the way.

If you're worried about protecting the delicate lens, buy a clear glass, ultraviolet, or skylight filter that will screw into the lens and afford it plenty of protection. You can further guard the lens against damage by using a metal lens shade or keeping a lens cap in place when the camera is not in use. If you are concerned about inclement weather, carry a plastic bag in your pocket and seal your camera inside when it rains. It will give your gear better protection against rain than a case will.

Protect Your Photo Gear While Afloat

Those photographers who are reluctant to take their expensive cameras and lenses with them on fishing, canoeing, and boating trips for fear of dunking them in the drink usually miss a lot of opportunities for excellent photographs. One of the best ways to protect expensive photography gear while afloat, and to keep it readily at hand, is to house it in the tray of a large cooler with a locking lid.

Since these coolers are insulated and are air tight, they will protect equipment from the elements and will keep film cool. In the unlikely event of a capsizing, the cooler will even float.

Camera Overboard!

What should you do if you drop a camera or lens in the drink? Well, if you're in the middle of Lake Superior or the Ohio River when it happens, all you can do is curse a lot or just cry. But if the equipment is retrievable, the first thing to do is fetch it. The second thing to do, according to one camera repairman who should know, is freeze it. That's the advice one of my outdoor photography students got when he dropped a lens into a tide pool while taking pictures along the Oregon coast.

In a single day, water can rust a lot of expensive parts in a camera or lens. Freezing halts this corrosive action. So get the drenched gear into a freezer as soon as possible. After it has been there for a day and is frozen throughout, wrap it in several layers of newspaper and return it to the freezer, working quickly to keep it from thawing. Then contact a repairman and ask him to call you when he can see to the needed repairs. When you take the camera or lens in for repairs, pack it in a small cooler with dry ice to make sure it remains frozen until repairs will be made.

Film Is Cheap—Shoot Lots of It

Of all your photographic expenses, film will be the cheapest. Oddly enough, the more you shoot, the less you will waste in the long run, provided you are systematically exposing it and not thoughtlessly burning up frame after frame.

There are any number of reasons for a photograph to turn out dull, uninteresting, or technically poor in quality. Camera angle, aperture setting, shutter speed, time of day, and lighting conditions are just a few of the things that can work for or against you. Human elements must be considered, too. You must think before you shoot. You must determine whether the subject warrants a picture, and you must pay attention to all the details within your field of view.

If you go to the trouble of identifying a suitable subject and setting up the kind of picture you think will best depict that subject and then only expose one frame, you are gambling against high odds. When you later examine the resulting print or slide, you may find that the depth of field was too shallow or too deep, that the shutter speed wasn't right, that the camera angle could have been better, or that it was underexposed, overexposed, or whatever. In short, you won't be satisfied with the shot and will consider it wasted. If you shoot most of your pictures in this fashion, most will be wasted. You will chance onto a lucky shot from time to time, but you will be wasting much film in-between.

One way to remedy this problem is to examine your subject thoroughly. Study it from different angles and varying distances. Experiment with the depth of field. If you can't visualize what the finished product will look like, shoot it several ways. Chances are, one of those exposures will be precisely what you wanted. The others should be discarded, but they will not necessarily be wasted shots. By studying them in comparison to the successful photograph, you can determine what you did wrong and what you did right. Eventually, you will learn what it takes to make a striking photograph and will be able to visualize the finished photograph as you look through your viewfinder. That's when you will be able to set up a pleasing shot before you snap the shutter.

Even then, you still must contend with lighting problems. Regardless of what your light meter says, lighting conditions can be misleading. So it is always a good idea to bracket your exposures—that is, take the first shot according to your light meter reading. Then close your aperture down by one f-stop and expose another frame. The third frame of the sequence should be exposed with the aperture opened one f-stop above your meter reading. If depth of field is critical to the success of a photograph, and you do not wish to change the aperture setting, use different shutter speeds to bracket your exposures.

When you bracket, you will end up with one photograph exposed the way your light meter dictated; another will have been exposed with half the light, and the third with twice the light. You will find that this technique most often eliminates disappointing underexposures and overexposures, because one of the three will be just right.

If you have wondered why professional and serious amateur photographers are able to get all those outstanding photographs, it's because they realize that film is cheap. They don't hesitate to take as many shots of a subject as they need to guarantee that what they're after will be recorded on film.

Protect Your Film from the Elements

Before and after use, there is no better primary protection for 35mm film than the canisters that the cartridges are packed in. These waterproof and dustproof containers provide adequate protection from the elements. Other films that are not packed in canisters, such as 120- and 220-roll film, should be kept in their sealed packaging until they are loaded into the camera. After a roll is finished, it can be sealed in a small, plastic sandwich bag to protect it from moisture and dust.

Whenever possible, film should be kept cool. So it's a good idea to keep your film—unused and used alike—in a cooler or ice chest when you're out fishing. Seal the rolls in plastic bags for added protection inside the cooler.

Label Your Film

Before I go afield or afloat with my photography gear, I remove all of the paper and packaging from my film. This cuts down on clut-

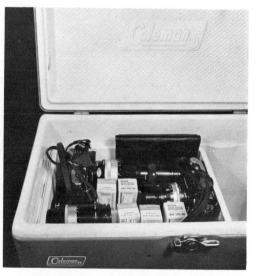

You can give your photography equipment and film maximum protection, and keep it readily at hand while afloat, if you store it in a cooler.

Make more room in your gadget bag by discarding film boxes and accompanying data sheets. Stick self-adhesive labels to the lids of the film with abbreviations that tell what kind of film is inside.

ter in my gadget bag, allows me to reload cameras without fumbling with film boxes and data sheets, and eliminates the problem of finding somewhere to discard all this trash—which invariably ends up stuffed in my pockets or scattered throughout my gadget bag. I stick small, pressure-sensitive, self-adhesive labels on the lids of the film canisters and identify them with an abbreviation that tells me what kind of film is inside. When I return an exposed roll of film to its container, I simply mark an X across the label. That way, I am able to distinguish, at a glance, between used and unused film.

Faster Film Can Improve Your Fishing Photographs

Fishing photography is often a matter of fast action, which calls for a fast shutter speed to freeze the motion of the subject. Early morning and late evening hours, when light levels are low, are often the times when fishing action is best. But fast action and low light levels require fast films—those which require less light, either in amount (function of the aperture) or duration (function of the shutter) of exposure.

Too many photographers saddle themselves with slow films and, consequently, are unable to get those great fishing photos. Their prints and slides come back from the processing lab as dismal under-exposures or as "fuzziograms" that result from too slow shutter speeds. These problems can be eliminated by using a faster film or by rating your current film at a higher exposure index (ASA).

In the U.S., the speed of film is determined by its American Standards Association (ASA) rating. The higher the ASA number, the faster the film. Although a film with an ASA of 25 will produce extremely fine grain and sharply detailed photographs if properly exposed, such a slow film is usually inadequate for fast action and low light levels. Films such as Kodak High Speed Ektachrome (ASA 160) are much better suited to the demands of high-speed or low-light photography.

For extremely adverse lighting conditions, even faster films are necessary. Most professional photographers will "push" or "boost" High Speed Ektachrome for this sort of work. That means the film is rated at ASA 400 and the light meter is set accordingly. Photo processors will charge extra for push processing. If Kodak pre-paid mailers are used for film development, a processing pusher for High Speed Ektachrome (Special Processing Envelope ESP-1) must be purchased and mailed with the film and the pre-paid mailer.

Not all color films can be pushed, so you should read the data sheets enclosed with films before attempting to change the recommended ASA rating. Also, if you use a local processing lab, be sure to check with them before pushing the film you are using. Most black-and-white films can be pushed, either with longer development or by using special developers formulated for high speed. Kodak Plus-X film (ASA 125), for example, can be rated from ASA 200 to ASA 640, depending on the type of developer being used. Kodak Tri-X (ASA 400) can be rated at ASA 800, 1200 or even higher. But, again, you will have to check with your processing lab to make sure they are equipped to develop pushed black-and-white film.

So if you have been using slow films and have been dissatisfied with your fast-action and low-light photographs, try switching to faster films or pushing for even more speed. You will be pleased with the results.

Pouches for Gadgets

There are many gadgets, small accessories, and other odds and ends that can clutter up a gadget bag. And it always seems that the gadget you need the most is the one you can't find—or the one that has worked its way to the most inaccessible part of your gadget bag.

You can eliminate the clutter problem and organize all of these accessories by keeping them in pouches that are easy to locate in your gadget bag. If you can't find suitable pouches at your photo shop, stop by a smoke shop or the tobacco counter of a department

Minimize clutter in your gadget bag by storing small gadgets in zippered tobacco pouches.

store and buy one or several zippered tobacco pouches. They will house all your little gadgets and will make them easier to find amidst all your other gear. When you're packing light, one tobacco pouch will hold a lot of photographic essentials and can slip into a pocket of your jacket.

Crop–Don't Chop

One reason for any photograph to be exciting is creative cropping with the camera. A good photographer knows to move in on his subject so that less important details are made subordinate to the subject and unimportant details are cropped out entirely. In cropping any photograph, though, the photographer must be careful not to chop details off inadvertently.

The most obvious kind of chop is the decapitation, and we all have seen classic examples. There's old Pete and that lunker largemouth he caught. When his partner took the picture, he was careful to see that the fish was prominently displayed in the photograph. But when the shutter snapped, it may as well have been a guillotine. Poor old Pete's head was lopped off at the top of the frame. And the bottom fourth of the picture is probably unnecessary foreground that does nothing for the photograph. The photographer only needed to pay attention to what he was doing and to tilt the camera slightly upward to picture Pete's pate.

It is perfectly acceptable to selectively remove portions of the anatomy when cropping any photograph, but there is a right way to do it. For example, it is fine to crop a photograph of your fishing partner by removing everything from the chest down. The result is a head and shoulders bust shot. But if you inadvertently chop him off at the knees or ankles, the result is ludicrous. The same holds true for photographing a fish. You might end up with an extremely effective photograph by moving in close and photographing the head only—that is, cropping out everything from the gill covers back. But a fish with only its tail chopped off looks silly.

Fish, People, Action, Scenery

There is much more to any fishing trip than hoisting up a big fish or a stringer of fish for others to admire. Consequently, if any collection of prints or slides from a fishing trip is going to be interesting,

When the action is close to the boat, shoot lots of pictures, and keep snapping the shutter as the angler lifts his catch aboard. (Photo by Pat Oberrecht.)

it must show more. Consider all the elements that combine to make any trip a fulfilling outdoor experience. Include pictures of the strikingly scenic aspects of the area where you fished. Get pictures of your camp, but make sure the camp is orderly and attractive looking. And get plenty of shots with people doing things.

A photograph of your camp can be vastly improved if it shows someone preparing a fish dinner, cleaning fish, or working on tackle. A scenic shot is much more pleasing if it includes a fisherman or two working a lake or stream. Be sure to get shots of native wildlife. They need not be trophy moose, deer, or elk to be interesting and to add something to your collection of photographs. Ducks, hawks, red-winged blackbirds, squirrels, racoons, beavers, otters, and any other wildlife that share your piece of the outdoors help to increase the variety and excitement of your trip and the photographs that record the experience. Don't overlook the native flora as well. Trees and flowers can be used to improve many kinds of pictures or can be used as the primary subjects.

Variety is the key, so vary your subjects and your techniques. Everything from broad panoramas to intricately detailed close-ups can be used to effectively record an adventure. Get an assortment of wide-angle and telephoto shots, people photos, wildlife, camp scenes, and plenty of fishing action shots.

Photographs Can Be Inexpensive Trophies

The problem with most pictures of dead fish is that they look like most pictures of dead fish. That is to say, they are too often dull, uninteresting clichés. Also, while there are no degrees of deadness, there are degrees of ripeness; the longer a fish has been dead, the less photogenic it becomes.

Well-executed and carefully composed photographs of freshly caught fish can be timeless portrayals and evocative reminders of the experience as well as strikingly handsome trophies for the den wall. Such trophies are far cheaper than any taxidermist's work, and you can, so to speak, have your fish and eat it, too. Photography has the added advantage of allowing the fisherman to collect a trophy photograph before releasing his catch unharmed.

Unposed action shots make some of the finest trophy photos, so it pays to keep the camera ready when a fish nears the boat or the net. Shoot plenty of film when the action is in close, and keep right on shooting as the angler lifts his catch from the water. The fish will be wet and lively then, and the angler will be concentrating on landing it, not on getting his picture taken. If you are photographing one or several fish that you plan to keep, the sooner you can photograph them the better. Colors and markings will often begin fading soon after the fish is caught.

Natural backgrounds are best for set-up shots, but find something that will be sufficiently contrasting. Large boulders or fallen logs are often good for this purpose, but try to get some foliage into the picture. Brightly colored wild flowers and green, leafy plants are especially good. In the fall of the year, leaves in their autumnal colors can add warmth to the picture.

Many anglers who go to all the trouble of setting up a shot often overlook one of the most important things of all: A freshly caught fish should be wet. So make sure yours is wet when you take a picture. Droplets of water often add a freshness to such a photo. Achieve this effect by flicking water onto the fish with your fingertips. A technique I have used with extremely pleasing results is to gently spray foliage and flowers with a plant atomizer which gives them a dew-laden appearance. Then a liberal moistening of the fish makes it look fresh from the water.

In any photograph, some size reference is helpful. Wicker creels, wooden-handled landing nets, and rods and reels are items favored by many fishing photographers. But they should not be thoughtlessly plunked into the setting. Arrange them carefully, balancing the photograph with the other elements. And don't use so many props that you overwhelm the subject. You need not have entire objects in the picture, either. Certainly, you won't be able to get a whole rod into it, unless you are photographing a mighty long fish, and even then it might not be desirable. Use just enough of a creel, landing net, or rod to allow it to be identifiable.

In a season, you can fill a den wall with trophy photographs at a fraction of what you would pay to have the fish mounted.

Better Prints from Slides

Photographers who use slide film and wish to have prints made from their slides are often disappointed with the results. Prints made from slides are frequently distorted in color rendition, are too contrasty, and exhibit loss of detail, especially in shadow areas.

When setting up a photograph of fish, make sure the fish are freshly caught. Find a suitable background, and put a size reference in the photo—such as a landing net, creel, rod, or reel.

Since most of my photography is for use in magazines, books, photography courses, and slide lectures, the color film I use is the transparency (slide) type. There are times, however, when I want to have a print made from a slide. But first, I have a color internegative made. From this, superior quality prints can be processed. My color lab charges me $2.00 to make a 2-by-3-inch internegative from a 35mm slide. I generally have 8-by-10-inch or 11-by-14-inch prints made from these negatives with remarkable retention of detail and perfect color rendition. On several occasions, I have had 16-by-20-inch enlargments made with surprisingly satisfactory results.

Next time you want to turn a favorite slide into a picture to hang on the wall, ask your local photo dealer about having an internegative made first. Kodak will make internegatives from slides and will make the enlargements from the negatives if you wish. One of the best companies offering complete color services, and the one I have been dealing with for years, is Meisel Photochrome Corporation. They have full-service labs in Dallas, Atlanta, Kansas City, and Seattle. You can send for their latest price list by writing MPC and ECONO-Color, P.O. Box 6067, Dallas, Texas 75281.

CHAPTER 16

Mixed Stringer

How to "Land" a Fish

When fishing from a gently sloping bank, gravel bar, or beach, the best way to land a fish—especially a large one—is to do exactly that: Land him. Don't use a net or a gaff. Simply guide the played-out fish toward you, keeping your rod tip high and the line taut. Essentially, the fish will land himself. Since he can't swim backwards, every move he makes will put him farther up on shore. Once the fish is high and dry, keep your rod tip up and reel yourself down to him.

Tips on Netting Fish

Since fish will often spook and run when they see a landing net moving toward them, some fishermen have reasoned that the best way to net a fish is from behind. But since it only takes a slight turn of the head for a fish to see a net moving up from the rear, the fish will usually spook and retreat. And it doesn't take much effort, even for a fish that's pretty well spent, to outrun the swipe of the net. Even if you see it done in fishing films by people who should know better, never net a fish from the rear.

First, make sure the fish is entirely played out before you attempt to net him. If you are wading a stream, keep your rod arm high and behind you. Tension on the line should cause the fish's head to come slightly out of the water. With your other hand, slip the net into the water at an angle before the fish is too near. Then simply guide the fish over the opening of the net, and scoop him up smoothly but swiftly.

If you are fishing from a boat, remember to play the fish out until he offers little resistance. Normally, you can keep from spooking the fish if your net is in the water well before he is netted. As in stream fishing, you just lead the spent fish over the partially submerged net, head first. If the water is rough enough to cause your boat to pitch and roll, however, leave the net out of the water until the moment the fish is ready to be netted. Speed is of utmost importance then, because waves and wind can pull the boat and net away from the fish, or vice versa. I have had waves wash fish around the side of the net when I wasn't fast enough, causing hooks to get hung up on the outside of the net. In such cases, the fish almost always flips quickly off the tangled hook and gets away.

Keep Your Net to Yourself

Even the best fishermen lose fish occasionally because of mistakes made with a landing net. These losses are always frustrating, but when someone else decides to give you a "helpful" assist with a net and doesn't know what he's doing, a loss can be infuriating. I learned the hard way that many fishermen don't know how to net a fish. On one occasion, I lost a big walleye when some stranger gave me his unwanted assistance by trying to net a wild fish that I had hooked close to shore only moments before.

On another occasion, the guy thought he knew how to handle a net; and indeed he did net my fish for me—too well, in fact. I was having no problems with the small chinook salmon. Since I had worked the fish downstream to where I could slide him up onto the beach with no difficulty, I tried to tell this character who came running with the net that I really didn't need any help. He wouldn't hear of it. Swoosh, up came the net from behind the fish, and the guy stood there grinning, figuring, I suppose, that he had done me a great favor. I didn't bother to tell him that by coming up on the fish from behind, he could have caused me to lose the fish. I just thanked him as if I meant it. Then I spent the next five minutes getting fish and hooks out of a tangled mess of net. When I plan to release a fish unharmed, I want to get him back into the water as soon as possible—and I don't want to waste valuable time untangling a net to do so.

Another time, I was easing a huge channel cat toward a sloping bank, with the intention of landing him without a net. Before I knew it, some character was flailing around, knee deep in the Big Muddy, trying to scoop up my fish with his net. To this day, I'm not sure what happened to that fish. In the brief foray, I just saw arms, legs, a misguided landing net, a lot of splashing around, and a big forked tail waving good-bye. My line went slack, and I went home.

Most of the time I prefer to land my own fish, unassisted. When

Always lead a played-out fish toward the landing net head first. (Photo by Pat Oberrecht.)

I need help, I ask for it. On the other hand, I'm always willing to give a fellow fisherman a hand, but only when I'm asked. If I see that an angler seems to be having problems, I will offer to assist— but, after all, he knows best. More often than not, I have found that seasoned anglers respond with a friendly "no thanks." It's good manners to keep your net to yourself and to offer your assistance verbally before giving it physically.

How to Keep Fish Alive on Stringers

Many fishermen seem to have trouble keeping fish alive on stringers. One reason for this is that they crowd too many fish on the stringer. Another reason is that they keep the stringer too close to shore or too near the surface where water temperatures are often too high.

I usually use a chain stringer, but it is too short to get the strung fish into deeper, cooler water by itself. When I'm fishing from a boat, I attach a length of rope to it that is secured to my boat. After stringing a fish, I can lower him to deep water where he will stay cool and quite lively.

When I'm fishing from shore, for catfish, for example, I attach a long rope stringer to my chain stringer. Then I look for a spot where the shoreline water is deepest to shove the pointed end of the rope stringer into the bank. When I string a fish, there is sufficient length to this stringer combination to allow the fish to reach the deeper, cooler waters that will keep him alive and healthy. Berkley and Co. makes an excellent 9-foot Steelon stringer that is perfect for attaching to a chain stringer to give it that added length.

Another mistake I have seen fishermen make is stringing fish through the gills. This causes the fish to hemorrhage and die within minutes. Always string a fish through the lower lip or jaw. This is easy with most fish, since the point on the clip of a chain stringer can be poked through the thin membrane behind the tougher cartilage of the lip or bone of the jaw. On larger fish, especially catfish, you might have to use the point of a knife to cut a slit in the membrane through which the stringer can fit.

Lunker Stringers

When you catch a really big fish, don't trust a store-bought stringer to hold it. I lost a big chinook when he managed to bend open the ring of a rope stringer and free himself. Another time, I lost a fine sockeye salmon when he pulled hard enough to open the clip on a chain stringer.

Use a length of ¼-inch or ⅜-inch nylon rope to string a lunker. Cut a slit in the fish's mandibular membrane large enough to accommodate the rope; then carefully tie a secure slip knot or improved clinch knot and slide the knot down to the jaw.

Be sure the other end of the rope is tied to something heavy or stationary. Once a big fish has rested, he will have unbelievable strength. When a big chinook regained his strength and was in the process of dragging my canoe and outboard into the river, I would have had to swim for my square-stern canoe had it not been for the alerting sound of an aluminum hull scraping over gravel. I got to it in time, but I quickly found a fallen tree to which the rope stringer could be tied.

How to Release Large Fish Unharmed

You have heard the old cliché, "the bigger they come, the harder they fall." Keep it in mind when you wish to release the fish you catch. A small bass, trout, or panfish seems to recuperate instantly after being caught and released, but a big fish often requires some assistance from the angler while it regains its strength. Always allow a fish sufficient time to rest up before turning it loose, and make sure it is able to swim off effortlessly. If not, it will probably go belly up and die.

Grasp the fish gently but firmly with your hands beneath it. Suspend it in the water, and watch to make sure it is taking water through its mouth and expelling it through its gills. If you are fishing in a stream, point the fish upstream, as the current will help move oxygenated water through its gills. In a lake or pond, you can slowly move the fish through the water.

If, after a reasonable time, the fish hasn't attempted to swim off, hold the fish upright near the front of the abdomen with one hand. Slide the other hand toward the tail and grasp the fish gently by the caudal peduncle, then slowly move the tail back and forth in a swimming motion. This will usually help to revive the fish and send it on its way.

The larger the fish and the longer it took to subdue it, the more care and attention you will have to give to reviving it. I once spent more than an hour fighting a 42-pound male king salmon. He was so worn out when I released him that I had to spend a full ten minutes with him as he regained his energy. It is important to spend as much time as necessary to assure that the lunker you release will live to give the same thrills to another angler.

How to Weigh a Fish Without a Scale

The best way to keep track of how much your fish weigh is to carry a small scale in your fishing vest or tackle box. If you are going after lunkers, carry a scale with a larger capacity. If you are out without a scale, though, you can get a pretty close estimate of the fish's weight by measuring its length and girth and applying a simple formula.

For slender-bodied fish, such as trout and pike, the formula is length times girth squared, divided by 900. For stockier fish, such as bass, divide by 800. For example, if you catch a bass that's 23-inches long and 16-inches around, your calculations would go like this: 16 times 16 equals 256; 23 times 256 equals 5,888; 5,888 divided by 800 equals 7.36, or about 7 pounds 6 ounces.

Trap Out Those Bluegills

My brother Phil and I used to spend a lot of time fishing farm ponds in Ohio. One of our favorite ponds belonged to a retired couple who secured permission for us to fish their neighbor's pond as well. The neighbor's pond, however, was overcrowded with stunted bluegills.

When we asked the old gentleman why the bluegills in his pond were so much fatter and healthier than those in his neighbor's pond, he told us it was a simple matter of pond management. Each spring, he set fish traps in his pond; between spring and fall, he trapped out several thousand small bluegills. The bass in the pond took their share of bluegills, too. The result was a population of bluegills that, kept under control, were able to gorge themselves on the abundant food supply in the fertile pond without severe competition.

If you want to improve the fishing in your favorite farm ponds, ask the owners for permission to trap out excess bluegills to keep them from overpopulating and becoming stunted.

Promote Bluegill Contests

No matter where they exist, prolific bluegills have the tendency to overpopulate, and it doesn't take long for a lake or reservoir to become full of stunted fish. If your favorite lake has bluegills in it, nothing can do more to improve the fishing than to promote bluegill contests. Such contests not only remove quantities of bluegills and help to reduce the competition for available food, but they also take some of the pressure off the predator species by diverting fishermen's interests.

If you belong to a rod and gun club, the promotion of bluegill contests is an excellent club project. You can also solicit the assistance of other sportsmen's and conservation organizations in your area. Seek the help of the local chamber of commerce, and get local tackle shops, marinas, and department stores to donate prizes.

You can offer prizes for the largest and smallest bluegill caught and for the most bluegills taken by an individual and by any team of two. You can add to the prize list by including special categories for youngsters and senior citizens. A rewarding addition to any such contest is a special category for mentally retarded or physically handicapped anglers. The best bluegill contest will last for a weekend and will culminate in a bluegill fish fry for all contestants. Get members of local sportsmen's clubs to volunteer for the cleaning and cooking chores.

Although bluegill populations can stand up against constant contest pressures and fishing will be improved as a result, the logistics of setting up contests prohibit great frequency. The more contests you can conduct, within reason, the better, but you probably can't expect maximum turnout for contests held more often than monthly during the fishing season. Start out with an annual contest, and increase the frequency until participation dictates a leveling off. When you hold regular contests, you can increase incentive and participation by offering end-of-season grand prizes in all categories. A point system can aid you in determining grand-prize winners.

An anglers' banquet at the end of the season is not only a good way to honor the champions and have a lot of fun, but can be an excellent opportunity for fund-raising activities that will help finance future contests. Even if you can only organize one contest a year, you will do much to improve local bluegill fishing by introducing more people to the joy of fishing for bluegills and the enjoyment of dining on them.

Be a Quick-Change Artist

The ability to switch from one lure to another offers the angler a versatility that can add fish to the stringer. As I have said before, carrying along extra rods and reels, each rigged with a different type of lure suited to different habitats and techniques, allows the fisherman to cover more water; he can cast to weeds and snags and still be able to quickly switch lures for open-water or surface fishing.

Lure snaps allow the one-rod fisherman similar versatility and the ability to change lures quickly.

But there's another reason for being prepared to change lures in seconds. When you get into fish and are hooking up on nearly every cast, your action usually lasts only until the fish become wary of your offerings. By quickly switching to another lure, you can often revive the frantic fishing you were experiencing before the fish got used to your offerings.

Such techniques are not limited to schooling fish, though. Sometimes an individual fish will make a half-hearted pass at a lure and miss it. Subsequent casts to the same spot with the same lure might elicit a similarly listless response from the fish or no response at all. If you can quickly switch to another lure, the new offering will coax the fish into a savage strike more often than not.

To illustrate, several years ago, I was casting a Hula Popper along a shoreline for bass and had put several fair fish on my stringer. As my partner sculled the boat within casting range of a pocket in a floating bog, I laid the lure right up next to the sprouting vegetation and began a slow, popping retrieve. Suddenly, there was a bulge beneath the lure. I struck and missed. My next cast into the same spot brought a similar response, but no connection. In all, I made five casts to the same spot and had five almost playful rises and five misses. Finally, I unsnapped my lure and replaced the yellow Hula Popper with a red-and-white jointed Jitterbug. I quickly cast to the pocket in the bog and began a fast, gurgling retrieve. Before the lure had traveled 10 feet, a fat and scrappy pickerel leaped out of the water and smashed the Jitterbug on the way down, as if he hadn't eaten in weeks. The ability to change lures quickly added another fish to my stringer and got me a handshake for persistence from my partner.

How to Start a Feeding Spree

When you have been working a stream for a while with little or no success, there's a last-resort trick that will sometimes start feeding frenzy. Move to the head of a pool, wade into the ripples, and start turning rocks over. Nymphs and larvae living beneath the rocks will be dislodged and washed into the pool by the current. Sometimes this will trigger a feeding spree. If you are prepared to drift nymph patterns to the feeding fish, the action can be great.

Tailwaters beneath dams provide some of the finest fishing to be found anywhere.

Dam Good Fishing

Dams have destroyed some of our finest streams and have totally altered fishing conditions throughout the U.S. There's not much we can do about the dams already built, but we can take advantage of some of the fine fishing that exists below them. There are few streams of any size in the U.S. that haven't been dammed somewhere at some time. On many of our smaller streams, old mill dams exist; on major water courses, huge dams have been erected for hydroelectric power, flood control, navigation, or recreation.

Despite the destruction of habitat caused by many of our dams, some excellent fishing is to be found in their tailwaters. A dam of any size is an obstruction to upstream migrations of all kinds of fish, from suckers to salmon. So the pools beneath dams are often full of fish on their way upstream. Water flowing over small dams on small streams often creates pools where highly oxygenated waters attract fish. Furthermore, the pools beneath dams are frequently deep and cool and offer comfortable havens to fish in warmer months.

The type of fishing to be found in the tailraces of a large dam depends upon how the water is discharged. If the water comes from the upper portion of the reservoir behind the dam, the waters below will be warm in the summer months and will consequently produce a warm-water fishery for such species as smallmouth bass, white bass, sauger, crappie, catfish, carp, suckers, fresh-water drum, and the like. If the discharge water is taken from the cold depths of the reservoir, the tailwaters will be cold for several miles downstream. Often some fine trout fishing is to be found in such cold tailraces.

You should know about all the dams in your locale and should find out what kind of fishing is available. Many tailwaters offer seasonal peaks for some species; you will want to know about these. When you travel, search out the tailraces. They will sometimes provide better fishing than the reservoirs, especially in summer.

In some places the fishing is tricky and sometimes dangerous. A guide can be a big help then. If no guides are available, talk to local anglers and tackle-shop proprietors to find out about any special techniques or potential dangers. Be sure to request such information when you write to fish and game departments, too.

When you plan to fish beneath a large hydroelectric dam, it is important to find out what time of day the turbines will be running at peak level. Water levels and turbulence can change drastically then, often scattering the fish and creating potential perils for the unknowing angler. If you don't know the discharge schedule, stick to early morning and weekend fishing. As electricity demand is less then, turbines won't be so much of a problem.

In some places, though, the running of turbines creates some great fishing. Huge catfish, usually blues in most areas, congregate in the tailraces to feed on hunks of fish that get slashed to pieces as they go through the turbines.

Much research has been conducted since the early 1950s by various state fish and game agencies and the U.S. Bureau of Sport Fisheries and Wildlife on the management of tailwaters and on the design and operation of dams for optimum sport-fishing oportunities. No matter where you live or travel to in search of fish, don't overlook the dams and the excellent fishing below them.

Rainy-Weather Fishing

I have spent considerable time fishing in torrential downpours, but heavy rainfall will usually keep me at home. If given the choice between a drizzly day and one of clear skies and sunshine, however, I will always opt for the former. In both lakes and streams, I have experienced more consistently good fishing on reasonably rainy days than on sunny ones.

My favorite kind of fishing day is one that shows no stars in the sky in the predawn hours and that remains heavily overcast all day. The sun never shows—or if so, only briefly from time to time—and the rain gently falls, on and off, for the entire day. I always feel better about the fishing on such days, and perhaps I work a bit harder at it as a result. Although that might partially account for the greater success, it's not the whole reason.

When the bass aren't bothered by the penetration of bright sunlight, they feed more actively and are always easier to find. They spend more time in shallower water where cover is more visible and fishing is more fun. I have made my best catches of crappies and white bass on rainy days, too. The walleye fishing is always better when dark clouds keep the daylight dim. And the predominantly nocturnal catfish is always more active on cloudy, rainy days than he is on clear ones.

Besides the reduced light penetration, something else works in the fisherman's favor when it rains. Raindrops striking the surface of the water make it extremely difficult for a fish to see an angler, and, therefore, easier for you to approach fish that might spook on a clearer day with no rain. After a long dry spell, a good rain will often trigger a frantic feeding spree, especially during the summer doldrums that put fish down. At such times, there are particularly productive places I look for on lakes and streams. Creeks that feed large reservoirs or lakes will rise fast in a summer downpour, and as the rain-swollen streams dump into the lake, they bring with them much food. Fish will gather at the mouths of these streams to take advantage of the free lunch.

The same thing happens on streams, and the spots to look for are where small tributaries empty into the main stream. If the rainfall has been substantial, though, streams can get high and muddy in short order. That's a time to be using natural or prepared baits for the best results. Often, the fishing will be good for several days after a good rain. So don't let the inclement weather keep you from fishing. You might well discover that the fishing is best then. Get yourself a good rain suit and take advantage of the rainy-weather fishing.

Moonlight Fishing

For some kinds of night fishing, the ring of light cast by a bright lantern is of no consequence. Some fish, such as crappies, are even attracted to the light. But when fishing at night for bass, you should use as little light as you can get by with; lantern light can put bass down. For this reason, I prefer to fish on nights when the moon is bright and full, or nearly so.

When I'm going after bass at night, I fish only waters that are fa-

When the moon is full or nearly so, you can be sure that it's a good time to fish for bass. (Photo by Pat Oberrecht.)

miliar to me—coves and shorelines that I have fished during the daytime where I know the fish's haunts. I like to be on the water an hour or so before nightfall so my eyes will gradually and fully adjust to the low light levels. In the bright moonlight, I am able to fish without artificial light. By knowing well the waters where I fish, I can stealthily stalk my quarry.

I like to use spinner baits at night, because they are nearly weedless and are noisy lures that bass can home in on. I also use noisy surface lures, big poppers, and shallow-running lures with built-in rattles, such as the pot-bellied alphabet lures. Although I have read that black is the best color for lures used at night, I have found that one color seems to be as good as another on moonlit nights. However, I avoid the transparent and translucent lures and stick to solid colors and color combinations. It is most important that the lures make plenty of commotion in the water.

Autumn Is Ultralight Time

In most parts of the country, some of the best fishing to be had is in the fall of the year. Fish that may have been sluggish in the heat of summer begin feeding actively again as waters turn cooler. And fishing pressure is drastically reduced then. Most of the time, though, waters are low and clear. These conditions call for a cautious approach. That's when ultralight spinning tackle is in its element. Small, light lures can be cast with ease on light lines, creating a minimum of disturbance; and the light lines are less likely to be detected by the fish.

Improve Your Fishing Success Rate

If you confine yourself to one kind of fishing, you miss out on the fun of catching other species. And you will probably catch fewer fish than the angler who seeks out other species, especially during seasonal peaks.

If you know your region of the country well and are aware of seasonal habits and migrations of fish you can plan to fish accordingly. For example, instead of beating the water to a froth in the early spring when bass are still sluggish, go after other species that are easier to catch then. Suckers, for instance, migrate upstream in late winter and early spring and can provide much action then. And at that time of the year, their flesh is firm and sweet, if a bit bony.

As soon as water temperatures reach 50° in the spring, bullheads and perch get the spawning urge and can be taken in shallow shoreline waters in great numbers. Later in the spring, you can take advantage of fine spring fishing for such species as crappies, white bass, and walleyes. During the dog days, don't put your gear away. Go for catfish at night. In some waters during hot weather, you can cast to the shallow-water cover in the early morning and late evening, then move out for deep-water trolling the rest of the day. This enables you to catch several different species in one day of fishing.

You need to develop a plan if you are going to succeed. The first step is to list the various species of fish that are found in your region of the country. Find as many waters as you can that harbor any one kind of fish. Then learn as much as you can about the habits and habitats of all your local species. You will find that some species inhabit the same waters as others, and you will discover that fishing-peak periods will sometimes overlap, especially during the spring months. But best of all, you are going to discover that by broadening your scope, you will be able to cash in on most of these hot fishing periods and will spend more time catching fish.

Peak fishing for some species in some areas may be as brief as two weeks. But if you spend your time fishing the peaks and working for numerous species, instead of concentrating on one or two kinds of fish, you will vastly improve your fishing success rate.

Pool Your Resources

No matter where you live in the U.S., conditions will be varied enough to require a fleet of different types of boats in order to take advantage of all the available fishing opportunities. If, for example, you live in the Great Lakes region, or near one of our larger impoundments—such as Santee-Cooper—you could very well utilize a sport cruiser or open offshore fisherman as well as smaller craft for smaller waters. Or you might be able to put a bass boat to good use for your lake and reservoir fishing and use a canoe or jon boat for float trips.

Perhaps you can't even financially justify the purchase of one boat, let alone several. By sharing costs with one or two of your fishing partners, the financial burden for any individual is markedly reduced. You can own one boat or several for a fraction of what it would cost you if you made the purchase alone. For an investment of $2,000 you can be fishing from a comfortable, efficient, high-performance $6,000 bass boat if you have two partners to join you in the venture. A $300 canoe will cost you but $100, and your share of a $150 cartopper or jon boat is a mere $50. Furthermore, maintenance, repair chores, and expenses can be reduced similarly.

And it doesn't stop with boats. A fishing cabin on a favorite lake might only be a dream, but it could become a reality if you and your fishing partners share the costs and the labors. The cost and expenses of a motor home or camper can be shared, too. In fact, any major investment is easier to handle if you have a couple of good friends to share it with.

Aside from the major purchases, there are other ways to pool your resources and save money in the long run. You can start a fund to which each of you contribute a set amount at regular intervals—say, $10 a month. Times three, that's $30 a month or $360 a year, and that's enough to finance a week-long fishing trip or several trips of shorter duration for the three of you. Just draw from the fund as required. You can also use such a fund to purchase tackle in large quantities, and you can usually save money by buying in bulk. For example, you can buy your hooks, sinkers, swivels, and other terminal tackle in packages of 100 or more. Lures by the dozen are always cheaper than those bought individually. Line purchased on bulk spools costs less, too.

You can even save more money by getting together with your partners to make much of your tackle, such as spinners, spoons, spinner baits, jigs, flies, crank baits, plastic worms, and sinkers. You can purchase your supplies, components, molds, and tools in large quantities, and then hold tackle-making sessions once a week, twice a month, or however often you wish. There are many advantages to pooling your resources, and I'm sure you can think of some that I haven't mentioned. You not only share the costs, but also the fun and friendship as well.

Lease a Lake

There are many lakes, ponds, and streams throughout the country that go unfished because the landowner simply doesn't want strangers traipsing over his property. Perhaps he has had a bad experience in the past—a broken-down fence, litter left behind, a gate left open for cattle to escape—that has soured him on all fishermen. If you know of a particularly fine pond or lake that you would like to fish regularly and have been unable to convince the landowner of your respect for his property, there's a good way to secure fishing rights. Offer to lease the pond, lake, or stream bank from him on a yearly basis.

In the case of a small stock pond or access to a stream that flows through the property, a token payment of a few dollars a month should be enough. But for recreational rights to a larger lake, you might have to pay considerably more—perhaps several hundred to a thousand dollars or more a year. The investment could be well worth it, and if it is shared by several fishing partners, any individual's contribution can be reduced considerably. After a trial year, if all parties involved in the lease are satisfied, you should negotiate something of longer range. You might also consider sharing in the management and the stocking of the pond or lake if necessary.

How to Discard Old Monofilament

Probably the greatest boon to fishing since the fish hook was the development of monofilament line. But carelessly discarded monofilament is one of the greatest detriments to our waterways and to the wildlife that inhabits them and their shores.

When you have to trim back the frayed end of your line, put the old monofilament in your pocket, and discard it properly later. If you have to change lines, make sure your old line is not left on the banks of a lake or stream. And when your lure gets tangled up in a length of line left or lost by another fisherman, make every effort to retrieve all of the old mono and to keep it with the rest of the line you plan to discard.

There is only one way to adequately dispose of old monofilament: Burn it. Whether you are at home or on a fishing trip, never put old mono into a trash receptical. Eventually, it will find its way to an open dump or sanitary-landfill operation where crows, ravens, sea gulls, and other scavengers can become entangled in it. And even worse, birds can carry it off to other areas where it will do even more harm.

Wrap the old line into a fairly tight wad. In your fishing camp, you can toss it into the campfire where it will melt into a harmless glob. When the campfire is put out, you can retrieve what's left of the melted mono and discard it with other trash. At home, you can burn it in a fireplace. Or you can punch several ventilation holes in the side of a large coffee can, put a tightly wadded sheet of newspaper in the can with the line, and set the paper on fire.

Appendices

APPENDIX A

Tackle Suppliers and Manufacturers

The following is a partial listing of fishing-tackle suppliers and manufacturers that should prove helpful when you need to write for catalogs and other information. There are virtually hundreds of tackle manufacturers, distributors, and mail-order suppliers throughout the U.S. Some of the major companies are included in this appendix. Beneath each address, in parentheses, you will find the types of tackle in which each company specializes.

Action Lures
P.O. Box 10529
Jackson, MS 30209
(lures)

Aladdin Laboratories, Inc.
620 S. 8th St.
Minneapolis, MN 55404
(reels, fly boxes)

Al's Goldfish Lure Co.
P.O. Box 13
Indian Orchard, MA 01151
(lures, terminal tackle)

Andy's Flytying
P.O. Box 30018—Station B
Calgary, Alberta, Canada T2M 4N7
(fly materials)

Aquasonic Lures, Inc.
P.O. Box 118
Cibolo, TX 78108
(lures)

Arnold Tackle Corp.
100 Commercial Ave.
Paw Paw, MI 49079
(ice-fishing tackle)

Bass Attacker
Box 557
Florissant, MO 63033
(rods, rod components)

Bead Chain Tackle Co.
Bridgeport, CT 06605
(lures, terminal tackle)

Berkley & Co.
Spirit Lake, IA 51360
(rods, reels, line, etc.)

Bill's Wholesale Bait
41 Grapevine Rd.
Levittown, PA 19057
(lures, accessories)

Bomber Bait Co.
P.O. Box 1058
Gainesville, TX 76240
(lures)

Browning
Rt. #1
Morgan, UT 84050
(rods, reels, rod blanks)

Burke Fishing Lures
1969 S. Airport Rd.
Traverse City, MI 49684
(lures)

Capitol Plastics Of Ohio, Inc.
333 Van Camp Rd.
Bowling Green, OH 43402
(rod cases)

Cisco Kid Tackle, Inc.
2630 N.W. First Ave.
Boca Raton, FL 33432
(lures)

Dale Clemens Custom Tackle
Rt. #2, Box 850-A
Wescosville, PA 18106
(rod components & materials)

Cortland Line Co.
P.O. Box 1362
Cortland, NY 13045
(line)

Creative Sports Enterprises
2333 Boulevard Circle
Walnut Creek, CA 94595
(fly materials & tools)

Creek Chub Baits
Garrett, IN 46738
(lures)

Creme Lure Co.
P.O. Box 87
Tyler, TX 75710
(lures)

J. Lee Cuddy Associates, Inc.
145 N.E. 79th St.
Miami, FL 33138
(rod components & materials)

Daiwa
P.O. Box 2287
Gardena, CA 90247
(rods, reels)

Jack Dickerson's, Inc.
Lake of the Ozarks
Camdenton, MO 65020
(rods, reels, lures, terminal
tackle, accessories)

Dickey Tackle Co.
Land O' Lakes, WI 54540
(ice-fishing tackle)

Doll Tackle, Inc.
P.O. Box 2206
Hot Springs, AR 71901
(lures)

Earlybird Co.
P.O. Box 1485
Boise, ID 83701
(prepared baits, worm bedding,
bait containers)

Lou J. Eppinger Mfg. Co.
6340 Schaefer Hwy.
Dearborn, MI 48126
(Dardevle lures)

Factory Distributors
500 S. 7th St.
Ft. Smith, AR 72901
(Rabble Rouser lures)

Featherweight Products
3454-58 Ocean View Blvd.
Glendale, CA 91208
(rod components)

Fenwick
14799 Chestnut St.
Westminster, CA 92683
(rods, rod components, lures,
terminal tackle)

Fly Fisherman's Bookcase & Tackle
Serv.
3890 Steward Rd.
Eugene, OR 97402
(rods, reels, tackle, accessories,
fly materials, tools)

Gander Mountain, Inc.
Box 248
Wilmot, WI 53192
(rods, reels, lures, tackle,
accessories, supplies)

Gapen's World Of Fishin', Inc.
Hwy. 10
Big Lake, MN 55309
(lures, terminal tackle)

The Garcia Corp.
329 Alfred Ave.
Teaneck, NJ 07666
(rods, reels, line, lures)

Gudebrod Bros. Silk Co., Inc.
12 S. 12th St.
Philadelphia, PA 19107
(lines, winding threads)

James Heddon's Sons
Dowagiac, MI 49047
(rods, reels, lures)

Hefner Plastics, Inc.
P.O. Box 638
Troup, TX 75789
(tackle boxes)

Jet-Aer Corp.
100 Sixth Ave
Paterson, NJ 07524
(G-96 products & tackle)

Lindy-Little Joe
Box 27
Isle, MN 56342
(lures, terminal tackle, accessories)

Louis Johnson Co.
Box 21
Amsterdam, MO 64723
(lures)

Lazy Ike Corp.
P.O. Box 1177
Fort Dodge, IA 50501
(lures, prepared baits)

Limit Mfg. Corp.
Box 369
Richardson, TX 75080
(rod components, lure components,
materials, supplies)

Lisk-Fly Mfg. Co.
P.O. Box 5126
Greensboro, NC 27403
(lures)

Magic Worm Bedding Co., Inc.
P.O. Box 38
Amherst Junction, WI 54407
(worm bedding, worm food, worm
containers)

Mann's Bait Co.
P.O. Box 604
Eufaula, AL 36027
(lures)

Martin Reel Co.
P.O. Drawer 8
Mohawk, NY 13407
(rods, reels)

Martin Tackle & Mfg. Co.
512 Minor Ave. North
Seattle, WA 98109
(lures, terminal tackle)

Mildrum Mfg. Co.
East Berlin, CT 06023
(rod mountings)

O. Mustad & Son (U.S.A.), Inc.
P.O. Box 838
Auburn, NY 13021
(hooks)

Netcraft Co.
3102 Sylvania Ave.
Toledo, OH 43613
(rods, reels, lures, nets, terminal
tackle, components, materials, kits,
tools)

Normark Corp.
1710 E. 78th St.
Minneapolis, MN 55423
(Rapala lures, fillet knives, fillet
boards, skinning boards, rods)

Nylon Net Co.
P.O. Box 592
Memphis, TN 38101
(seines, nets, terminal tackle)

Orvis
10 River Rd.
Manchester, VT 05254
(rods, reels, lures, flies, waders,
clothes, accessories, supplces, tools)

Padre Island Co.
P.O. Box 5310
San Antonio, TX 78201
(PICO lures)

Plano Molding Co.
Plano, IL 60545
(tackle boxes)

Plas/Steel Products, Inc.
Walkerton, IN 46574
(telescopic poles)

Quick Corporation of America
P.O. Box 938
Costa Mesa, CA 92627
(rods, reels)

Hank Roberts
P.O. Box 308
Boulder, CO 80302
(flies, kits, fishing attire)

Ryobi America Corp.
1555 Carmen Dr.
Elk Grove Village, IL 60007
(reels)

Shakespeare
P.O. Box 246
Columbia, SC 29202
(rods, reels, line)

Sheldon's, Inc.
P.O. Box 508
Antigo, WI 54409
(Mepps lures)

South Bend Tackle Co., Inc.
P.O. Box 6249
Syracuse, NY 13217
(rods, reels)

Storm Mfg. Co.
P.O. Box 265
Norman, OK 73069
(lures)

Strader Tackle, Inc.
P.O. Box 708
Havana, FL 32333
(lures)

Trimarc Corp.
High Point Plaza
Hillside, IL 60162
(telescopic rods)

Anton Udwary, Jr.
1432-B Dover Rd.
Spartanburg, SC 29301
(cane fly rods, fly reels)

UMCO Corp.
P.O. Box 608
Watertown, MN 55388
(tackle boxes)

Uncle Josh Bait Co.
P.O. Box 130
Ft. Atkinson, WI 53538
(pork-rind baits, lures)

Uniroyal Clothing Division
17 N.E. Fourth St.
Washington, IN 47501
(Royal Red Ball rainwear)

Uniroyal Footwear Division
58 Maple St.
Naugatuck, CT 06770
(Royal Red Ball boots & waders)

Val-Craft, Inc.
67 North Worcester St.
Chartley, MA 02712
(Valentine fly reels)

Varmac Mfg. Co., Inc.
4201 Redwood Ave.
Los Angeles, CA 90066
(rod components)

Vlchek Plastics Co.
P.O. Box 97
Middlefield, OH 44062
(tackle boxes, bait buckets)

Weber Tackle Co.
1039 Ellis St.
Stevens Point, WI 54481
(lures, flies, kits, terminal tackle)

Wille Products Co.
P.O. Box 532
Brookfield, WI 53005
(tackle boxes)

Woodstream Corp.
Lititz, PA 17543
(tackle boxes, bait buckets,
bait containers)

Wright & McGill Co.
P.O. Box 16011
Denver, CO 80216
(Eagle Claw rods, reels, hooks,
terminal tackle)

Zak Tackle Mfg. Co.
235 South 59th St.
Tacoma, WA 98408
(lures, terminal tackle, accessories)

Zebco
P.O. Box 270
Tulsa, OK 74101
(rods, reels)

APPENDIX B

State Agencies

This list of addresses should be of help to all anglers planning a fishing trip or vacation to any of the fifty states.

ALABAMA

Dept. of Conservation & Natural
    Resources
64 N. Union St.
Montgomery. AL 36104

Bureau of Publicity & Information
Room 116, State Capitol
Montgomery, AL 36104

ALASKA

Dept. of Fish & Game
Subport Bldg.
Juneau, AK 99801

Dept. of Natural Resources
Division of Parks
Pouch M
Juneau, AK 99801

Travel Division
Dept. of Economic Development
Pouch E
Juneau, AK 99801

ARIZONA

Game & Fish Dept.
2222 W. Greenway
Phoenix, AZ 85023

Outdoor Recreation Coordinating
    Committee
4422 N. 19th Ave.
Phoenix, AZ 85015

ARKANSAS

Game & Fish Commission
Game & Fish Commission Building
Little Rock, AR 72201

Dept. of Parks & Tourism
149 State Capitol
Little Rock, AR 72201

CALIFORNIA

Dept. of Fish & Game
1416 Ninth St.
Sacramento, CA 95814

Dept. of Parks & Recreation
Same address as above

Office of Tourism
926 J Building, Room 812
Sacramento, CA 95814

COLORADO

Game & Fish Dept.
6060 Broadway
Denver, CO 80216

Div. of Parks & Outdoor Recreation
1845 Sherman
Denver, CO 80203

Colorado Publicity Dept.
600 State Services Bldg.
Denver, CO 80203

CONNECTICUT

Dept. of Environmental Protection
State Office Bldg.
165 Capitol Ave.
Hartford, CT 06115

Development Commission
State Office Building
Hartford, CT 06115

DELAWARE

Div. of Fish & Wildlife
The Edward Tatnall Bldg.
Legislative Ave. & Wm. Penn St.
Dover, DE 19901

Div. of Parks & Recreation
The Edward Tatnall Bldg.
Same address as above

Bureau of Travel Development
State of Delaware
45 The Green
Dover, DE 19901

FLORIDA

Game & Fresh Water Fish Commission
620 S. Meridian
Tallahassee, FL 32304

Div. of Recreation & Parks
Crown Bldg.
202 Blount St.
Tallahassee, FL 32304

Florida Development Commission
107 W. Gaines
Tallahassee, FL 32304

GEORGIA

Game & Fish Division
270 Washington St., S.W.
Atlanta, GA 30334

Dept. of Industry & Trade
Tourist Division
100 State Capitol
Atlanta, GA 30334

HAWAII

Div. of Fish & Game
1179 Punchbowl St.
Honolulu, HI 96813

Div. of State Parks
P.O. Box 621
Honolulu, HI 96809

Hawaii Visitors Bureau
400 N. Michigan Ave.
Chicago, IL 60611

IDAHO

Fish & Game Dept.
600 S. Walnut
Box 25
Boise, ID 83707

Dept. of Parks & Recreation
Statehouse
Boise, ID 83720

Dept. of Commerce & Development
Room 108
State Capitol Bldg.
Boise, ID 83720

ILLINOIS

Dept. of Conservation
602 State Office Bldg.
Springfield, IL 62706

Nature Preserves Commission
819 N. Main
Rockford, IL 61103

Dept. of Business & Economic
    Development
Div. of Tourism
222 South College
Springfield, IL 62706

Chicago Convention & Tourism Bureau
332 S. Michigan Ave.
Chicago, IL 60604

INDIANA

Div. of Fish & Wildlife
608 State Office Bldg.
Indianapolis, IN 46204

Div. of State Parks
Same address as above

Div. of Nature Preserves
Same address as above

Div. of Outdoor Recreation
Same address as above

Tourist Division
Indiana Dept. of Commerce
334 State House
Indianapolis, IN 46204

IOWA

State Conservation Commission
State Office Bldg.
300 4th St.
Des Moines, IA 50319

Iowa Development Commission
Tourism & Travel Div.
250 Jewett Bldg.
Des Moines, IA 50309

KANSAS

Forestry, Fish & Game Commission
Box 1028
Pratt, KS 67124

State Park & Resources Authority
801 Harrison
Topeka, KS 66612

Dept. of Economic Development
State Office Bldg.
Topeka, KS 66612

KENTUCKY

Dept. of Fish & Wildlife Resources
Capitol Plaza Tower
Frankfort, KY 40601

Dept. of Parks
Capitol Plaza Bldg.—10th Floor
Frankfort, KY 40601

Dept. of Public Information
New Capitol Annex
Frankfort, KY 40601

LOUISIANA

Wildlife & Fisheries Commission
400 Royal St.
New Orleans, LA 70130

State Parks & Recreation Commission
P.O. Drawer 1111
Baton Rouge, LA 70821

Tourist Development Commission
Box 44291
Baton Rouge, LA 70804

MAINE

Dept. of Inland Fisheries & Game
State Office Bldg.
284 State St.
Augusta, ME 04330

Bureau of Parks & Recreation
State Office Bldg.
Augusta, ME 04430

Dept. of Economic Development
State Office Bldg.
Augusta, ME 04330

MARYLAND

Dept. of Natural Resources
Tawes State Office Bldg.
Annapolis, MD 21401

Dept. of Economic Development
State Office Bldg.
Annapolis, MD 21402

MASSACHUSETTS

Div. of Fisheries & Game
100 Cambridge St.
Boston, MA 02202

Div. of Forests & Parks
Leverett Salton Stall Bldg.
100 Cambridge St.
Boston, MA 02202

Dept. of Commerce & Development
100 Cambridge St.
Boston, MA 02202

MICHIGAN

Dept. of Natural Resources
Steven T. Mason Bldg.
515 W. Michigan Ave.
Lansing, MI 48926

Michigan Tourist Council
Steven T. Mason Bldg.
515 W. Michigan Ave.
Lansing, MI 48926

Upper Michigan Tourist Assn.
P.O. Box 400
Iron Mountain, MI 48901

West Michigan Tourist Assn.
136 Fulton, East
Grand Rapids, MI 49502

East Michigan Tourist Assn.
Log Office, Box 5
Bay City, MI 48706

Southeast Michigan Tourist Assn.
1404 Broderick Tower
Detroit, MI 48226

MINNESOTA

Div. of Fish & Wildlife
301 Centennial Bldg.
658 Cedar St.
St. Paul, MN 55155

Div. of Parks & Recreation
301 Centennial Bldg.
658 Cedar St.
St. Paul, MN 55155

Vacation Information Center
State Capitol
St. Paul, MN 55101

MISSISSIPPI

Game & Fish Commission
Robert E. Lee Office Bldg.
239 N. Lamar St.
Jackson, MS 39205

Mississippi Park Commission
717 Robert E. Lee Office Bldg.
Jackson, MS 39201

Travel Dept.
Miss. Agricultural & Industrial Board
1504 State Office Bldg.
Jackson, MS 39201

MISSOURI

Dept. of Conservation
P.O. Box 180
Jefferson City, MO 65101

Div. of Parks & Recreation
Jefferson Bldg., Room 1204
Jefferson City, MO 65101

Missouri Tourism Commission
Box 1055
Jefferson City, MO 65101

MONTANA

Fish & Game Dept.
Fisheries Div.
Helena, MT 59601

Advertising Dept.
Montana Highway Commission
204 Laboratory Bldg., MRC
Helena, MT 59601

NEBRASKA

Game & Parks Commission
2200 N. 33rd St.
P.O. Box 30370
Lincoln, NE 68503

NEVADA

Dept. of Fish & Game
Box 10678
Reno, NV 89510

Dept. of Conservation & Nat. Res.
Nye Bldg.
201 S. Fall St.
Carson City, NV 89701

Dept. of Economic Development
Carson City, NV 89701

NEW HAMPSHIRE

Fish & Game Dept.
34 Bridge St.
Concord, NH 03301

Dept. of Economic Development
318 State House Annex
Concord, NH 03301

NEW JERSEY

Div. of Fish, Game & Shellfisheries
Lab Labor & Industry Bldg.
Box 1390
Trenton, NJ 08625

Promotion Section
Dept. of Conservation & Econ. Dev.
Box 1889
Trenton, NJ 08625

NEW MEXICO

Dept. of Game & Fish
State Capitol
Santa Fe, NM 87501

State Parks & Recreation Commission
P.O. Box 1147
Santa Fe, NM 87501

Tourist Div.
Dept. of Development
State Capitol
Santa Fe, NM 87501

NEW YORK

Div. of Fish & Wildlife
50 Wolf Rd.
Albany, NY 12201

State Office of Parks & Recreation
Empire State Plaza
Albany, NY 12238

Dept. of Commerce
Travel Bureau
112 State St.
Albany, NY 12207

New York Convention & Visitors
  Bureau
90 E. 42nd St.
New York, NY 10017

NORTH CAROLINA

Wildlife Resources Commission
Albemarle Bldg.
325 N. Salisbury St.
Raleigh, NC 27611

Dept. of Natural & Economic Resources
P.O. Box 27687
Raleigh, NC 27611

NORTH DAKOTA

State Game & Fish Dept.
2121 Lovett Ave.
Bismarck, ND 58501

State Outdoor Recreation Agency
900 East Blvd.
Bismarck, ND 58501

State Park Service
R.D. #2, Box 139
Mandan, ND 58554

State Travel Dept.
Capitol Bldg.
Bismark, ND 58501

OHIO

Div. of Wildlife
Fountain Square
Columbus, OH 43224

Div. of Parks & Recreation
Same address as above

Dept. of Economic & Community Dev.
Box 1001
Columbus, OH 43216

OKLAHOMA

Dept. of Wildlife Conservation
1801 N. Lincoln
P.O. Box 53465
Oklahoma City, OK 73105

Tourism & Recreation Dept.
500 Will Rogers Memorial Bldg.
Oklahoma City, OK 73105

OREGON

Dept. of Fish & Wildlife
Box 3503
Portland, OR 97208

Travel Information Div.
State Highway Dept.
101 State Highway Bldg.
Salem, OR 97310

PENNSYLVANIA

Fish Commission
P.O. Box 1673
Harrisburg, PA 17120

Travel Development Bureau
Dept. of Commerce
South Office Bldg.
Harrisburg, PA 17120

RHODE ISLAND

Div. of Fish & Wildlife
83 Park St.
Providence, RI 02903

Div. of Parks & Recreation
Same address as above

Rhode Island Development Council
49 Hayes St.
Providence, RI 02908

SOUTH CAROLINA

Wildlife & Marine Resources Dept.
Dutch Plaza, Bldg. D
Box 167
Columbia, SC 29202

Dept. of Parks, Recreation & Tourism
Edgar A. Brown Bldg., Box 113
1205 Pendleton St.
Columbia, SC 29201

SOUTH DAKOTA

Dept. of Game, Fish & Parks
State Office Bldg.
Pierre, SD 57501

Publicity Div.
Dept. of Highways
Pierre, SD 57501

TENNESSEE

Tennessee Wildlife Resources Agency
P.O. Box 40747
Ellington Agricultural Center
Nashville, TN 37204

Div. of State Parks
2611 W. End Ave
Nashville, TN 37203

Div. of Tourism Promotion
Same address as above

TEXAS

Parks & Wildlife Dept.
John H. Reagan Bldg.
Austin, TX 78701

Tourist Development Agency
Box TT
Capitol Station
Austin, TX 78711

Highway Dept.
Travel & Information Div.
Austin, TX 78701

UTAH

Div. of Wildlife Resources
1596 W. North Temple
Salt Lake City, UT 84116

Div. of Parks & Recreation
Same address as above

Tourist & Publicity Council
Council Hall
State Capitol
Salt Lake City, UT 84114

VERMONT

Fish & Game Dept.
Montpelier, VT 05602

Dept. of Forests & Parks
Same address as above

Publicity Division
Vermont Development Dept.
Montpelier, VT 05602

VIRGINIA

Commission of Game & Inland
    Fisheries
4010 W. Broad St.
Box 11104
Richmond, VA 23230

Commission of Outdoor Recreation
8th St. Office Bldg.
803 E. Broad St.
Richmond, VA 23219

Div. of Parks
1100 State Office Bldg.
Richmond, VA 23219

Dept. of Conservation & Development
Commonwealth of Virginia
Richmond, VA 23219

WASHINGTON

Dept. of Fisheries
115 General Admin. Bldg.
Olympia, WA 98504

State Parks & Recreation Commission
P.O. Box 1128
Olympia, WA 98504

Tourist Promotion Div.
Dept. of Commerce & Economic
    Development
General Admin. Bldg.
Olympia, WA 98501

WEST VIRGINIA

Dept. of Natural Resources
1800 Washington St., East
Charleston, WV 25305

Travel Development Div.
Dept. of Commerce
Capitol Bldg.
Charleston, WV 25305

WISCONSIN

Dept. of Natural Resources
Box 450
Madison, WI 53701

Wisconsin Conservation Dept.
Vacation & Travel Service
Box 450
Madison, WI 53701

State of Wisconsin
Vacation & Travel Service
205 N. Michigan Ave.
Chicago, IL 60601

WYOMING

Game & Fish Dept.
5400 Bishop Blvd.
Cheyenne, WY 82001

Recreation Commission
Cheyenne, WY 82002

Wyoming Travel Commission
2320 Capitol Ave
Cheyenne, WY 82001

APPENDIX C

Federal Agencies and Regional Offices

For general information and lists of maps and publications available from the U.S. Fish and Wildlife Service, U.S. Forest Service, National Park Service, and Bureau of Land Management, you can address inquiries to the U.S. Department of the Interior, Washington, D.C. 20240. Topographical maps are available from two offices of the U.S. Geological Survey. For maps east of the Mississippi River write: U.S. Geological Survey Service, Department of the Interior, Washington, D.C. 20240. For maps west of the Mississippi River write: U.S. Geological Survey, Federal Center, Denver, CO 80200. Other brochures and maps of interest to fishermen and campers are available from the following regional offices.

U.S. FOREST SERVICE
NATIONAL FOREST
REGIONAL OFFICES

Northern Region U.S.F.S.
Federal Building
Missoula, MT 59801

Rocky Mountain Region U.S.F.S.
Denver Federal Center
Building 85
Denver, CO 80225

Southwestern Region U.S.F.S.
Federal Building
Albuquerque, NM 87101

Intermountain Region U.S.F.S.
Forest Service Building
Ogden, UT 84403

California Region U.S.F.S.
630 Sansome St.
San Francisco, CA 94111

Pacific Northwest Region U.S.F.S.
P.O. Box 3263
Portland, OR 97212

Eastern Region U.S.F.S.
6816 Market St.
Upper Darby, PA 19082

Southern Region U.S.F.S.
50 Seventh St., N.E.
Atlanta, GA 30323

North Central Region U.S.F.S.
710 N. 6th St.
Milwaukee, WI 53203

Alaska Region U.S.F.S.
Fifth St. Office Bldg.
Juneau, AK 99801

NATIONAL PARK SERVICE
NATIONAL PARK
REGIONAL OFFICES

Southeast Regional Office N.P.S.
Federal Building
Box 10008
Richmond, VA 23240

Midwest Regional Office N.P.S.
1709 Jackson St.
Omaha, NE 68102

Southwest Regional Office N.P.S.
Box 728
Santa Fe, NM 87501

Western Regional Office N.P.S.
450 Golden Gate Ave.
San Francisco, CA 94105

Northeast Regional Office N.P.S.
143 S. Third St.
Philadelphia, PA 19106

Northwest Regional Office N.P.S.
1424 Fourth Ave.
Seattle, WA 98101

APPENDIX D

Fishing Schools

American Institute of
Bass Fishing
Box 2324
Hot Springs National Park,
AR 71901

Fenwick Fishing Schools
Box 729
Westminster, CA 92683

Garcia Fishing Schools
American Sportsman's Clubs
650 S. Lipan St.
Denver, CO 80223

H.L. Leonard Co.
25 Cottage St.
Midland Park, NJ 07432

McClane's Fishing Schools
% Burke Fishing Lures
1969 Airport Rd
Traverse City, MI 49684

Montana School of Fly Fishing
P.O. Box 6
Nye, MT 59061

Orvis Fly Fishing Schools
The Orvis Co.
Manchester, VT 05254

The Snug Co.
P.O. Box 598
Sun Valley, ID 83353

Doug Swisher Fly Fishing Schools
Box 9037
Spirit Lake, IA 51360

APPENDIX E

Manufacturers of Boats, Motors, and Accessories

If you are shopping for a fishing boat, outboard motor, or accessories for your boat
or canoe, the following companies should be able to provide information and literature.

AMF Crestliner
609 N.E. 13th Ave.
Little Falls, MN 56435
(aluminum & fiberglass boats)

Alladin Laboratories, Inc.
620 S. 8th St.
Minneapolis, MN 55404
(drink holders for boats)

Allied Sports Co.
P.O. Box 251
Eufaula, AL 36027
(depth-sounder fish finders)

Alumacraft Boat Co.
315 W. St. Julien St.
St. Peter, MN 56082
(aluminum boats & canoes)

American Honda Motor Corp.
100 W. Alondra Blvd.
Gardena, CA 90247
(outboard motors)

Aquabug International, Inc.
100 Merrick Rd.
Rockville Centre, NY 11570
(outboard motors)

Bayliner Marine Corp.
P.O. Box 24467
Seattle, WA 98134
(fiberglass boats)

Beckson Mfg., Inc.
P.O. Box 3336
Bridgeport, CT 06605
(hand-operated pumps)

Big Jon, Inc.
14393 Peninsula Dr.
Traverse City, MI 49684
(downriggers)

Blue Hole Canoe Co.
P.O. Box 51
Sunbright, TN 37872
(canoes)

Bonair Boats, Inc.
15501 W. 109th St.
Lenexa, KS 66219
(inflatable boats)

Bremer Mfg. Co., Inc.
Rt. #2, Box 100
Elkhart Lake, WI 53020
(accessories)

Chrysler Corp.
Marine Products Operation
P.O. Box 2641
Detroit, MI 48231
(boats & motors)

Clinton Engines Corp.
Maquoketa, IA 52060
(outboard motors)

Dutton-Lainson Co.
Hastings, NE 68901
(trailer components)

Evinrude
P.O. Box 663
Milwaukee, WI 53201
(outboard & electric trolling motors)

Fish Hawk Electronics
4220 Waller Dr. (Ridgefield)
Crystal Lake, IL 60014
(electronic fishing instruments)

Glen-L
9152 Rosecrans
Bellflower, CA 90706
(boat plans & kits)

Grumman Boats
Marathon, NY 13803
(aluminum boats & canoes)

Holsclaw Bros., Inc.
P.O. Box 4128
Evansville, IN 47711
(trailers)

Imtra Corp.
151 Mistic Ave.
Medford, MA 02155
(Avon inflatables)

Ray Jefferson
Main & Cotton Sts.
Philadelphia, PA 19127
(electronic fishing instruments)

Johnson Outboards
200 Sea-Horse Dr.
Waukegan, IL 60085
(outboard & trolling motors)

Lowrance Electronics Mfg. Corp.
12000 E. Skelly Dr.
Tulsa, OK 74128
(electronic fishing instruments)

Lund American, Inc.
New York Mills, MN 56567
(aluminum & fiberglass boats)

Mariner Outboards
Division of Brunswick Corp.
Fond Du Lac, WI 54935
(outboard motors)

Master Lock Co.
2600 N. 32nd St.
Milwaukee, WI 53210
(boat, motor & trailer locks)

Mercury Marine
1939 Pioneer Rd.
Fond Du Lac, WI 54935
(outboard & sterndrive engines)

Mirro Marine Division
Oconto, WI 54153
(aluminum & fiberglass boats)

Old Town Canoe Co.
35 Middle St.
Old Town, ME 04468
(multilaminate, fiberglass & wood
    canoes)

Penquin Industries, Inc.
P.O. Box 97
Parkesburg, PA 19365
(accessories)

Polar Kraft Mfg. Co.
P.O. Drawer 708
Olive Branch, MS 38654
(aluminum boats)

Sawyer Canoe Co.
234 S. State St.
Oscoda, MI 48750
(fiberglass canoes)

Tempo Products Co.
6200 Cochran Rd.
Cleveland, OH 44139
(accessories)

Ter Mar, Inc.
2300 8th St.
S.W. Lehigh Acres, FL 83396
(outboard motors)

Trailex
120 Industrial Park Dr.
Canfield, OH 44406
(trailers)

Wood Mfg. Co.
P.O. Box 262
Flippin, AR 72634
(fiberglass bass boats)

Selected Bibliography

Brooks, Joe. *Trout Fishing.* New York: Outdoor Life/Harper & Row, 1972.

Clemens, Dale P. *Fiberglass Rod Making.* New York: Winchester Press, 1974.

Flick, Art, editor. *Art Flick's Master Fly-Tying Guide.* New York: Crown Publishers, Inc., 1972.

Gresham, Grits. *Complete Book of Bass Fishing.* New York: Outdoor Life/Harper & Row, 1967.

Hellekson, Terry. *Popular Fly Patterns.* Salt Lake City: Peregrine Smith, Inc., 1976.

Livingston, A.D. *Fly-Rodding For Bass.* Philadelphia & New York: J.B. Lippincott Co., 1976.

McClane, A.J., editor. *McClane's New Standard Fishing Encyclopedia and International Angling Guide.* New York: Holt, Rinehart & Winston, 1965.

Marinaro, Vincent C. *A Modern Dry-Fly Code.* New York: Crown Publishers, Inc., 1970.

Ovington, Ray. *Tactics on Trout.* New York: Crown Publishers, Inc., 1974.

Rice, Philip F. *America's Favorite Fishing.* New York: Outdoor Life/Harper & Row, 1964.

Schwiebert, Ernest. *Matching the Hatch.* New York: The Macmillan Co., 1962.

————. *Nymphs.* New York: Winchester Press, 1973.

Swisher, Doug, and Richards, Carl. *Fly Fishing Strategy.* New York: Crown Publishers, Inc., 1975.

Walker, Michael, editor. *Sport Fishing USA.* Washington, D.C.: U.S. Government Printing Office, 1971.

Weiss, John. *Advanced Bass Fishing.* New York: E.P. Dutton & Co., Inc., 1976.

INDEX

(boldface numbers refer to illustrations)